Public Theology and Ethics of Life-World: Biopolitical Formation

Paul S. Chung

Public Theology and Ethics of Life-World: Biopolitical Formation

First Edition: 2023

ISBN: 9781524318437
ISBN eBook: 9781524328382

© of the text:
   Paul S. Chung

© Layout, design and production of this edition: 2023 EBL

All rights reserved. No part of this publication may be reproduced, distributed, or transmitted in any form or by any means, including photocopying, recording, or other electronic or mechanical methods, without the prior written permission of the Publisher.

Celebrating my granddaughter, Elliana Yuna Chae (March 20, 2022).

Table of Contents

Acknowledgement 9

Introduction 11

Chapter 1. Public Ethics, Life-World, and Human Body 27
    1. Ethical Theology in the Public Sphere 28
    2. Theology and Social Scientific Approach 44
    3. Discourse Ethics, Biopolitics, and Human Body 56

Chapter 2. Public Ethics, Interpretation, and Responsibility . 67
    1. Responsible Self 68
    2. Responsible Self and the Other 87
    3. H. R. Niebuhr: Sin and Salvation 94

Chapter 3. Colonialism, Hegel's Dialectics, and Empire 107
    1. Postcolonial Hegel: Recognition and Struggle 108
    2. Christian Public Theology and Hegel 131
    3. Biopolitical Formation: Colonial Racism and Sovereignty ... 139
    4. Global Racism, Negative Dialectics, and Dictatorship 152

Chapter 4. Prophetic Public Theology: Political and
Emancipatory 171
    1. Political Theology and Public Theology 172
    2. Class Struggle, Politics of Eschatology, and Civil State 193
    3. Liberation Theology and Postcolonial Significance 206
    4. Public Theology and Critical Epistemology 217

Chapter 5. Biopolitical Sociology: Late Capitalism and
Global Empire 245
   1. Capitalist Revolution: Scientific Technology and Ecology 246
   2. Biopolitical Sociology: State Apparatuses and Capital
   Accumulation 260
   3. Eurocentric Position: World System and Structure of
   Imperialism 273
   4. Globalization, Neocolonial Condition, and Biopolitical
   Sociology 282
   5. A Biopolitical State, Racism, and Theology............................300

Chapter 6. Public Ethics, Biopolitics, and Biomedical Justice 309
   1. Theological Deliberation of Biomedical Field 310
   2. Biomedical Science and Ethical Interpretation 317
   3. Biopolitical Time, Human Dignity, and Practical
   Solidarity 329
   4. Theological Construction, Evolution, and Biomedical
   Science 331

Conclusion 347
Afterword: Genealogy of Jeju 4.3 Massacre and Biopolitics 359
   Jeju 4.3 Event as Effective History 362
Epilogue.. 379
Bibliography 381
   Journal 396
   Internet Resources 397
About the author 401
Index 403

Acknowledgement

Public theology focuses on social, cultural, and institutional spheres as their distinguished regimes located in civil society stratified in a hierarchical manner. It acknowledges that the latter is embedded within the neocolonial reality between the metropolis and periphery. In this combined regime public theology takes into account the postcolonial condition.

As a rule, theology is conceptualized at an epistemological level in dealing with the relationship between faith and God through the Scripture and human experience, as concerned with God, humanity, and the world in terms of 'faith seeking understanding.'

In distinction from faith-epistemology, however, I undertake public theology specifically at a moral, practical level in the sense of ethical theology, which seeks to explicate the ways human life is embedded within life-world, or givenness of life in diverse social fields stratified and embedded within postcolonial reality (ethnicity, race, immigration problem, sexuality, other culture, religious pluralism, and public health).

Actualizing the meaning of the Gospel in its reconciliation with the world, public theology serves for the church to be faithful to responsibility, shalom, and solidarity with those on the margins. This epistemic stance incorporates the postcolonial problematic of the subaltern into an ethical framework and practical performance of life-scripts or documents through socio-biographical narrative and struggle against the reality of impersonal forces.

I appreciate Prof. Ted Peters at the Graduate Theological Union, Berkeley, who reviewed Chapter six and helped to improve on its limitations through valuable comments. I extend my gratitude to Peter Watters, who clarified my argument and position in sharpening my writing style. Finally, I extend my gratitude to all the team at EBL for helping bring the two books of *Public Theology and Civil Society* as well as *Public Theology and Ethics of Life-World* to light.

Easter 2022
Paul S. Chung
Hercules, CA

Introduction

Basically, what mediates public theology with ethics is a skill of interpretation and discourse clarification. This doublet becomes central in undertaking appropriate evaluation of meaningful moral action and deliberate judgment upon the external reality and event. It scrutinizes the extent to which human knowledge and moral action would be embedded with life-world and social location, as exposed to the network of power structures and ideological legitimacy.

In Hannah Arendt's articulation, the public sphere is a social environment in which a human being could be cultivated, and human activities can be classified into three realms: labor, work, and action. In enumeration of the human activities by looking at labor-work-action, she maintains that action occupies the highest position, as it relates to the political sphere of human life; this estimation is obvious in pre-Platonic opinion of Greek polis life.

For ancient Greeks a life of contemplation (*vita contemplativa*) is of highest order because its superiority is placed over the political way of life of the citizen in the polis. However, active life (*vita activa*) can be seen to be more crucial in Christian command of love of one's neighbor.[1]

Christian active life of love is featured in faith and moral commandment, while contrasting with Aristotle's teleological reasoning of ethics for good life, as imbued with life of contemplation. For Aristotle the activity of intellect, which

---

[1] *The Portable Hannah Arendt,* ed. Peter Baehr, 168-9.

would be the most divine element in us, will be contemplative–superior in worth and aiming at no end beyond itself.[2]

On the contrary, I take up the Christian tradition of *vita activa* to configure Christian public theology and ethical practice of life-world. In the triadic explanation of labor-work-action, I relocate such connection within diverse spheres of civil society by including mutual recognition in struggle against the reality of impersonal forces.

Life-World and Power Mechanism

I utilize Hegel's phenomenology of the master and servitude to refine such themes as struggle, labor, desire, critical discourse, and universal recognition in a reified order of things in civil society. His dialectical theory of the whole helps to comprehend the multiple realities of social formation in terms of social cultural and economic process through rationalization, calculation, specialization, and bureaucratization. This social mechanism perpetuates itself into stratifying and estranging social formation along with legal system. This refers to "the phenomenon of reification" in the universal, technological sense.[3]

A critical theory of social stratification remains crucial in elaborating public theology and its ethical practice by involving diverse fields in civil society (family, culture, religion, education, social institutions, occupation, human rights movement, ecological network, and public health). These are exposed and vulnerable to power mechanisms (political technology of governance, bureaucracy, economic system of injustice and ideology of mass media and its commercializing type of

---

[2] "Nicomachean Ethics," BK X. Ch. 7. In *A New Aristotle Reader*, ed. Ackrill, 470.

[3] Lukacs, *History and Class Consciousness*, 83.

social discourse); it is bound up with the neocolonial reality of structural violence under global Empire.

This complex reality, both internal and external, challenges me to construct public theology and ethics of life-world in taking issue with problems of public sphere. I attempt to differentiate a conception of civil society from the bourgeois–economic society. The latter is driven by self-interest and laissez faire by pursuing economic gain and profit in the midst of competition and survival of the fittest.

I draw attention to other broader realms of civil society than power/competition-driven mechanism. These are closely related to the ideal of life-world in contrast to the power mechanism imbued with the phenomenon of impersonal forces. Thus, I define the notion of life-world as the reservoir of meaning and intelligibility (history as effect, cultural tradition, morality, religion, literary world, and language). It also becomes the source of immanent critique in examining regimes of what could be distorted and falsified in the course of history and society contrary to the authenticity of the life-world.

At a hermeneutical level, life-world constitutes the universal horizon in dialogical encounter with the reader who interacts with the world of literary text and understands it by way of language; it is influential in inscribing the experience of textual horizon into life-script underlying the reader's identity, biography, and cultural authenticity. The horizon of life-world within the literary text critically correlates and is semantically fused with the intentionality or reflection of the reader. Such synthesis of horizons is constituted and exposed procedurally as a historically effected event; it is involved in the semantic circle and its surplus meaning in linguistic experience.[4]

---

[4] Gadamer, *Truth and Method*, 2nd rev. 300.

Truth events appear to be a meaningful step-by-step in the procedure of adumbration in the phenomenological thick description of the subject matter of reconciliation and life-world in dealing with the basic structures of life. Such exposition is made at micro-analytical clarification in dealing with diverse social fields and discourses. The skill of interpretation is not excluded from promoting ethical practice of life-script in resistance against political, economic governance of life, race, and body.

Narrative type of discourse is based on a schema of life-script underwriting one's identity and cultural authenticity, which contrasts with a political type of social discourse. It is fair to say that we require social scientific clarification of discourse in terms of cultural validity, meaning, moral formation, and power; these factors are examined in micro-analytical description of diverse types of representation (artistic, literary, religious, ethical, and intelligible).

Such description of multiple discourse cuts across limitations of Foucault's assumption of knowledge/power, which appears to be exaggerated in Edward Said's generality of Orientalist discourse of representation; it is caught up in power reductionism and artificial invention of binary opposition. Dialectical diversity and difference must be recognized at the sociological level in its micro-analytical explanation of multiple realities in social, cultural, and political interaction.

At the sociological level, life-world is established as social regime of knowledge-system (episteme), in which any epistemic position is bound up with social discourse, institutional norm, personality, moral integrity, cultural validity, and education. In this social community, or civil society, an individual becomes a citizen as a political, moral subject in the democratic sense of identity, participation, and universal recognition among equals.

The political society is rationalized and differentiated into State, its ideological apparatuses, and their bureaucratic administration. Likewise, economic society is organized, managed, and specialized according to the rational division of labor, the capitalist system of competition and profit. A logic of capital and market is allied with regime of mass media, while financing, controlling, and commercializing its social discourse and system of communication. Although language and cultural tradition hold a transcendental status as constitutive for the life-world, its realm together with human consciousness is threatened to be violated and internally colonized through inner dynamics of power system.[5]

Natural world is mathematically measured, exploited, and reified in scientific technology and mastery over the ecological network of nature. To the extent that social mechanisms are driven and differentiated by way of political power and market, their technology of governance makes the life-world recede into areas of culture, religion, morality, personality, family, and education.

Public Ethics and Biopolitics

Insofar as public theology is framed in social ethical frame (identity, authenticity, and life-script), I qualify it in terms of ethical theology imbued with life-world. Ethics as an intellectual discipline seeks to establish moral rationality in terms of the highest good or the common good (such as duty, virtue, utility, responsibility, recognition or justice). Ethics in comparative study of religion and culture is concerned with comparative moral reasoning by interaction with such moral values in different, cross-cultural contexts at large.

---

[5] Habermas, *The Theory of Communicative Action* 2: 333.

In the current study of public theology and ethics of life-world, however, I bring different types of ethics in theology, philosophy, and sociology together for contemporary relevancy and postcolonial problems. Public theology in this deliberation can be constructed in taking on the three basic elements of the ethical reality of life (the given-ness of life, the giving of life, and reflection on life).[6]

The three basic structures of life characterize life-world as meta-ethical principle, in which I take on a moral deliberation of the dominated life (labor-work-activity) in society and culture. An ethical consideration of life-world finds it conspicuous to appropriate sociological clarification of political technology of human bodily life, which can be explored in the discussion of race, sexuality, gender, medicine, and public health.

Remarkable in this discussion is a micro-analytical device in examining economic organization of human bodies through discipline, surveillance, and utility. Biopower as a form of power over the body, according to Foucault, regulates social life and commands over the entire of life of the population in production and reproduction of life.[7]

The human bodily dimension has come to be a major object to power mechanisms. Thus political control, economic utility, and scientific technology of discipline seek to increase productivity and effective competition for commodity and profit.

Politico-scientific technology of the human body remains crucial in facilitating moral reflection of human life in relation to the COVID-19 pandemic. Biopolitical problems can be scrutinized in treating a genealogy of mass media and regulation of social distancing; it consolidates citizens into the process of subjectivation under the power of the State. This refers to the

---

[6] Rendtorff, *Ethics* I: v-vii.
[7] Foucault, *The History of Sexuality* 1: 139-41.

process of subjugating a citizen body into political governance and scientific administration. Human freedom and dignity are seriously restrained in the name of public safety, as propagated by mass media. Government authority brings populations under political control by managing public health in regulation of their public life en masse. We are made subjects in the political technology of subjectivation within a society.

Given this, I seek to scrutinize the COVID-19 pandemic as a major regime, which changes considerably the structural formation, determines public health, and allocates distributive justice of biomedical resources in an unfair and hierarchical manner. The three basic structures of life are embedded with and regulated by the political technology and management. There occurs inequality and underprivileged relation in access to biomedical wealth in society as well as in international relation between the metropolis, semi-periphery, and periphery on the globe.

Cosmopolitan principle ought to be an ethical criterion in upholding the transnational collaboration for global health policy and distributive justice, because life of the human being occupies the normative concern and moral standard, which cut across neo-liberal capitalism and international order. This ethical stance indicates how important we should understand a global connection of biomedical problem to be and interpret its distributive justice according to responsibility, appropriateness, and fair treatment.

At this point, H. R. Niebuhr deserves attention, because he conceptualizes Christian moral philosophy in its distinctive manner in terms of interpretation of what is going on in the world. In his ethics of responsible self, interpretation remains crucial owing to his reflection of the fitting rationality into a total interaction as response. This moral theory refers to a type of human being-as-the-responder, focusing on the prior question of "What is going on?" prior to the moral question ("What shall I do?").[8]

It articulates an importance of interpretation at the metaethical level in dealing with moral questions. However, Niebuhr tends to sidestep in his moral philosophy a regime of life-script and its ethical narrative of socio-biography, which is rooted in lifeworld. I relocate Niebuhr's responsible ethics within the realm of life-world to address its ethical dimension in the discussion of three basic structures of life.

Genealogy, Body Politics, and Empire

Faith seeks understanding in an ethical reality of life, in other words, faith seeks moral understanding through the way we interpret human life, society, and culture in the interest of the living and liberating word of God. Such interpretation brings public theology to be allied with a hermeneutical reading of the Scripture for ethical orientation.

Such an exegetical position relates ethical deliberation of diversity and complexity of human life in taking on the contemporary reality of postcolonial society. I explore postcolonial theory by reemploying a sociological study of rationalization, division of labor, domination, and religious ethics (Weber and Durkheim). A critical, dialectical theory is furthered in treating the postcolonial reading of struggle, social discourse, and recognition in Hegel. His phenomenology can be advanced in reference to the interplay between power and knowledge and global sovereignty of Empire.

In this multivariate framework, I utilize the political technology of the human body and race in order to critically

---

[8] H. R. Niebuhr, *The Responsible Self*, 63.

reinterpret its insight into the historical problem of colonialism, racism, and death politics. The genealogical explanation of the historical reality of colonialism is taken as an empirical point of departure, which underlines a social scientific approach to Eurocentric discourse and postcolonial condition beset by the pathology of the neocolonial mechanism.

At the postmodern level, Michael Hardt and Antonio Negri elaborate Foucault's theory of biopolitics in order to formulate the significance of global sovereignty of the Empire and its world economic system. It refers to the new global form of sovereignty, which is called Empire.[9] Empire has no territorial center of power, works by decentering the apparatus of rule and manages hybrid identities. The First World is found in the Third, and vice versa in the imperial global system through "differentiation, homogenization, deterritorialization, and reterritorialization."[10]

This epistemic stance defines what the postcolonial condition is established at the level of correlation between domestic society and Empire. The power mechanism stratifies, dominates, and violates the three basic structures of human life, together with the problem of ecological sustainability. Embodied life is bound up with complexities, diversities, and ambiguities of life questions. Life questions are thickly described in terms of discourse, clarification of power relations and at micro-analytical description of multiple realities stratified in society and culture.

In a similar manner, I engage in critically refining Foucault's genealogy of discourse and power relations in examining cultural justice of gender and sexuality. Gender and sexuality are organized and established in society in terms of political control over human body, sex, and gender differential. Discourse about gender and sexuality is undertaken by professionals, bureaucrats,

---

[9] Hardt and Negri, *Empire*, xii.
[10] Ibid., xiii.

and religious leaders. Its discursive formation is disseminated as a power dynamic to the point of becoming the normal discourse (hegemony) through the support of the State, social institutions, judiciary legitimacy, and bureaucratic administration. Such procedure elicits a new form of sexual racism, which can be seen in fascism, apartheid, and the lynching tree.

At this point, I wield genealogy of body politics for the ethical deliberation of the bodily dimension of human life, sexuality, and racial justice. Ethics of life-world takes issue with, at the micro-analytical level, a representing type of social discourse and its normalizing technology, which is entangled with pathologies of power. In dealing with the relation between public health care and human rights, biomedical treatment becomes central in moral deliberation, because it is a basic part of human dignity.[11]

Biopolitics indicate a significant regime to complement Hegel's phenomenology of the master and the slave, which finds its actuality in the genealogical discussion of European discourse ("Scramble for Africa" in the 19th century) and its colonial racism. The duplet of biopolitical racism and civilizing mission continues to become historical burden for public theology in an African context to overcome on the one hand. On the other hand, it seeks to galvanize a decolonizing interpretation of the Scripture for cultural authenticity, universal recognition among equals, ecological stewardship, and servant hearted leadership. Here, public health and biomedical justice appear to characterize African public theology in highlighting the basic human rights and dignity against the pathology of power entangled in global sovereignty of Empire.[12]

A project of public theology acquires its significance for the Global South, because it embodies theological discourse and

---

[11] Farmer, *Pathologies of Power*, 239.
[12] *African Public Theology*, Sunday B. Agang et al.

power relations within the broader spectrum of decolonization and multiple realities in society and culture toward politics of recognition and difference. It relocates an idea of God's mission in the prolepsis of reconciliation and *theologia crucis*, while refining it to strengthen one's faith identity, cultural authenticity, moral integrity, and ethical practice of life-script in a concrete and universal manner.

In sociological clarification of discourse and power interplay, it is plausible to articulate religious construction of reality in examining the extent to which religious discourse is bound to an elective affinity with material interests in agency. In fact, religious agents are involved in socially distributing and managing their status and economic monopoly accorded with power relations.

This epistemic approach includes political regime of governance (surveillance, discipline, and bureaucratic administration in ideological state apparatuses). The underlying premise here is that social formation is shifted from disciplinary society toward the society of control. A control extends throughout human consciousness, the entirety of social relations, and bodies of population.[13]

However, a postmodern theory of global sovereignty can be met with criticism, which comes from the global system of capitalism. It is driven in the libertarian principle of free trade, yet with privilege and monopoly centered in the metropolis over the semi-periphery and the periphery. Neocolonial reality can be seen in its structural violence and power mechanisms, which work throughout nation-states in the metropolis. Their inter-state rivalry, competition, and hegemony in alliance are built into infrastructure of the neocolonial power. They threaten global sovereignty of Empire in post-national codification. This international reality becomes obvious and even dangerous in the

---

[13] Hardt and Negri, *Empire*, 27.

Russian invasion of Ukraine, in which a new Cold War appears to be possible between the metropolis and the periphery between global powers.

To clarify the world economy system, I draw attention to Helmut Gollwitzer's thesis of capitalist revolution. I take him as a prophetic type of public theologian, who provides a keen insight into the neocolonial type of imperialism. His theological position of peace movement finds an actuality in a critical discussion of warfare and military politics in late capitalism.

In the discussion of social stratification and global capitalism, I focus on the Gospel about the kingdom of God and its prolepsis of reconciliation which entails the source of the immanent critique and turnaround from the previous wrong steps. In the elaboration of *theologia crucis* as seen for the margins and from them, I underwrite ethics of life-world against phenomenon of impersonal forces woven in the structural violence. Gospel becomes universal in its concrete manifestation of reparative justice and solidarity for the politics of universal recognition and difference in postcolonial civil society.

Subject Matter, Scope, and Argument

In fact, public theology premises ethical subject matter of reconciliation upon *theologia crucis* and prolepsis of God's reign by constructing these themes in a fresh and reliable manner with reference to basic structures of life. The interpretive skill focuses on clarifying a doublet of discourse-power in advancing Christian public theology and ethical practice of life-world toward postcolonial society of recognition.

Given this, ethics is defined as a moral deliberation in intersubjective relations engaged in interpreting life-questions, the external event, and respect of other individualities. Ethical reflection is bound up with meaningful action according to practical reasoning and prudence, which guide one's involvement with responsibility, communication, recognition, and solidarity. This epistemic stance is evaluated and renewed in the feedback of justifications, assessments, or modifications of what has been done in accordance with the effect of external facts, while bringing forth more appropriate actions and evaluations.

In treating a project of public theology and ethics of life-world, Chapter one is a study of mapping the relation between public theology, life-world, and ethical deliberation. I bring to the agenda of ethical theology (Rendtorff and Troeltsch) in interrogation with diverse theological ethics (in the tradition of Barth, Bonhoeffer, and Lehmann) in regard to theocentric ethics (H.R. Niebuhr and Gustafson). I further discuss biopolitical theory to advance the ethical dimension of human body in terms of sexuality, gender, and biomedical science.

Chapter two is a study of H. R. Niebuhr's Christian moral philosophy of response and interpretation. I critically complement a hermeneutical clarification of his moral theory in terms of ethics of life-world. I compare H. R. Niebuhr's ethics of responsibility with Emmanuel Levinas' ethics of the responsibility. In this comparative study I seek to critically renew a theocentric principle of responsibility by deepening it from the standpoint of the significant Other in its own life-script. This ethical position characterizes the significant Other in the Global South in terms of God's love and justice.

Chapter three seeks to develop public theology in terms of postcolonial epistemology by featuring a social scientific study of colonialism and racism in the past as well in the present. Historical heritage is not simply called good, because it is tainted with violence, the colonial atrocity of racism, and the European Christian character of capital accumulation.

I draw attention to postcolonial reading of Hegel, by featuring him as an intellectual Caliban. Furthermore, I undertake sociological interpretation in taking on a liberating role of discourse and life-world in approach to religion and absolute knowledge in Hegel's system. It casts public morals and civil society upon his dialectics of recognition and struggle in terms of anamnesis and reparative justice. I seek to synthesize Hegel's dialectical theory of struggle and recognition with biopolitical technology in colonial racism and death politics, as seen in the African apocalypse (Joseph Conrad's *Heart of Darkness*) and African American experience. Finally, I conceptualize an integrative approach to State and civil society in postcolonial context in terms of recognition, participation, and reparative justice. Excursus deals with legacy of Bartholomew de Las Casas, who can be featured as the prophetic voice in the postcolonial discussion.

Chapter four is a study of constructing prophetic public theology in interrogation with Helmut Gollwitzer, who is rooted in the tradition of religious socialism and the Barthian movement of Confessing Church. A critical, constructive analysis of liberation theology can be performed through the angle of critical theory and social scientific inquiry. Such critique can be made to bring the vitality and challenge of liberation theology for helping the public theology to heed the reality of the life questions embedded in underside of civil society in the West. Then, I further discuss several issues such as State, bureaucracy, democracy, role of ideology, and public health for the significance of public theology.

In Chapter five I incorporate the theory of global capitalism in a post-Eurocentric frame of reference, in which I scrutinize Helmut Gollwitzer's theory of capitalist revolution with social scientific theory of late capitalism and Empire. It is significant to incorporate a biopolitical, sociological articulation into the discussion of relation between capitalism and religion. A post-Eurocentric position can be made in reinterpreting Gollwitzer's theology in taking on structural theory of imperialism, military politics, and sociology of war.

It is important to conceptualize biopolitical sociology in terms of elective affinity in the discussion of discourse and its formation in correlation with material interests, ideological legitimacy, and power relations. Through the lens of biopolitical sociology, I seek to feature public theology in dealing with problem of global capitalism and its neocolonial condition beset by international divisions of labor, exploitation, infiltration, and racism, while complementing several social scientists regarding the problematics that Gollwitzer tends to sidestep.

Chapter six involves biopolitical theory and biomedical morality, which are important components of shaping public theology in taking on theology of nature and gene-ethics. I take into account several diverse issues for public theology and ethics of life-world and human dignity (such as the stem cell debate, the human genome project, germ-line intervention, human cloning, artificial gametes, and sexuality). I involve reinterpreting the biblical symbol of creation, original sin, image of God, freedom, and responsibility in dialogue with theory of evolution and genetic science. The biomedical realm in theology of nature indicates one of the greatest assets, which features the ethical significance of public theology for Christianity in the Global South.

The epilogue is a reflection of the discussion of public theology and ethics of life-world in which I look at their critical synthesis in relevance for civil society as well as for postcolonial reflection of global Empire. I synthesize public theology of reconciliation and *theologia crucis* with a phenomenological study of labor, struggle, liberating social discourse, and recognition. Here, I characterize public theology as philosophical theology in a social scientific framework, in which its ethical theology of life-world is highlighted in terms of interpretation, discourse clarification, and genealogy of biopolitics.

The afterword is written with my personal memory and life-script, while developing social scientific approach to the Jeju 4.3 event (1947-49) in the context of decolonization and civilian movement. It is a postcolonial genealogy of effective history and biopolitics in a comparative framework in which I deal with American colonial power in The Philippines and South Korea (1945-50). I dedicate the afterward to respecting my family-related victims in the Jeju violence.

Chapter 1.

Public Ethics, Life-World, and Human Body

Life is given. A phenomenological deliberation of ethical significance of life as givenness becomes an undercurrent in developing public theology in terms of ethical theology. In dealing with givenness of life for the ethical standpoint, I seek to employ a social scientific approach to public theology and ethics within the framework of life-world.

For this ethical direction, it is necessary to construe a position of discourse ethics which considers religious ideas, material interests, and power relations upon human life and ethical attitude. A mode of interpretation regards what is going on in public spheres and civil society, as well as in global relation in the postcolonial context. Human life is given and embodied, thus public ethics is concerned with the way it interprets the bodily dimension of human life, which is regulated and controlled by biopolitical governance.

Accordingly, this chapter discusses public theology in terms of ethical theology in reviewing several important ethicists and theologians. Further debate continues to deal with Christian moral philosophy and social typology, in which I focus on the significance of Emile Durkheim's public morality in reference to Max Weber and phenomenology of life-world. The theory of life-world remains decisive in communicative–discourse ethics underwriting deliberate democracy and public moral vision in civil society.

Given this, public theology is positioned in discourse ethics in reference to emancipation and postcolonial relevance. Thus, historical effect, language hierarchy, and the social condition are analyzed in their relation between social discourse and power relations. This ethical stance takes into account the postcolonial epistemology, in which public theology scrutinizes the extent to which biopolitical control of the human body reifies human life as givenness.

1. Ethical Theology in the Public Sphere

Ethics has to do with taking on life questions as givenness in terms of interpretation and responsibility. This basic statement of givenness of life characterizes ethics as an intensified form of the human experience of reality. Ethics is comprehended as a way of life, involving the ethical meaning of the life reality in the pursuit of the good and the right. Ethics refers to the theory of explicating the conduct of human life, in which it draws attention to concrete life situations, ethical questions, and moral inquiry.[1]

If ethics deals with the reality of human life and its inquiry of life questions about the good and the right, ethical theology has a share in moral theory with regard to philosophy (moral philosophy) and sociology in its treatment of the moral significance of social life. Philosophical ethics, also known as moral philosophy, is confined not merely to the concept of good or bad; it also undertakes to investigate the values and guidelines

---

[1] Rendtorff, *Ethics* I: 3.

in its assessment of their norm and validity with respect to the right or wrong in light of a universal principle or common good.

What strikes in this interdisciplinary relationship is to qualify the term 'ethical theology' within the whole theoretical structure of Christian public theology in reference to philosophy of moral theory, sociological inquiry, and political theology.

In the articulation of public theology and ethical deliberation, a hermeneutical reflection is sought between the deontology and the teleology for justice and recognition, which can be elaborated in sociological and scientific approach to life-world. Herein, ethical hermeneutics seeks to bring together the history as effect as well as social location, which is embedded in a structure of discourse, material interests, and power relations underlying a political mechanism of hegemony and privilege in the postcolonial context.

Public Theology and Ethics in Correlation

Public theology comprehends basic moral problems. Their social and ethical significance can be elaborated on when dealing with the realities of life in an interdisciplinary collaboration. It has the task to undertake an exegetical work of the Scripture in which it draws attention to the relation between an indicative and an imperative. Such correlation is seen as providing the formal structure of the ethical dimension of the Torah as well as New Testament ethics. In the treatment of God's relation with humanity in the social historical realm, the indicative of divine promise becomes the imperative of the divine command.

Public theology is concerned with developing the ethical exegesis of the Torah covenant and the Gospel in social location, and it focuses upon its public significance and contextual development in the first Christian generation with respect to the subsequent historical development (our public, global reality included).

In a like manner, Paul Lehmann finds it substantial to incorporate biblical hermeneutics into Christian ethics. He calls attention to the principle of the Scripture: The internal witness of the Holy Spirit in connection with the Scripture as the Word of God.[2] He comprehends Deuteronomy as an interpretation of Israel's faith and recaptures the true spirit and meaning of God's covenant on Sinai. It interprets obligation and responsibility in a covenant context and becomes the basis of reform through prophetic protest against social injustice and violence. In Jesus' confrontation with the Pharisees Jesus utilizes the prophet Isaiah in interpreting the fifth commandment against the tradition of the elders in the Pharisees' teaching (Mark 7:6-13).[3]

Lehmann derives his idea of koinonia ethics from Paul's passages of the fellowship between the believer and Jesus Christ, in which the nature of the Church is defined as the body of Christ. The Church as the body of Christ is the fellowship (koinonia), which is the fellowship-creating reality of Christ's presence in the world.[4] Involved in doing the will of God, Lehmann focuses upon the koinonia context and character of Christian ethics to give moral significance to seeking and doing God's will.[5] Here, interpretation plays a major role in developing the koinonia ethics in reference to God's activity in society and world. What matters is a priority in reflection of what God is doing in the social situation, and then ethical questions and concerns arise in accordance with the will of God.[6]

---

[2] Lehmann, *Ethics in a Christian Context*, 30.
[3] Ibid., 79.
[4] Ibid., 49.
[5] Ibid., 80.
[6] Ibid., 131.

Acknowledging the interpretive horizon of the koinonia ethics, however, I am more concerned with analysis of the significance of interpretation in a social scientific manner by learning from other academic disciplines. Public theology is involved in public affairs of society and seeks the common good of the whole of society through open discourse and democratic procedure; it takes part in justice and promotes solidarity with those disadvantaged by, and victims of, the diverse public fields. It has in view the moral values of the social ethos and different cultures, which should acquire general relevance in the social life. In this epistemological procedure, public theology can establish the common good in the light of God's kingdom.

In the construction of public theology, the primary task is to introduce a social scientific method into the ethical discourse in considering complexities, diversities, and ambiguities of life questions in culture and society. An ethical reasoning becomes a significant component of public theology in taking on social scientific inquiry into relation between religious ideas and material interests in the public sphere. The latter is stratified in diverse fields (politics, economics, social institutions, culture, education, and religion) in terms of rationalization, specialization, and differentiation; the society is built upon the dominant system of knowledge, ideological function, and power relations.

Public Ethics and the Givenness of Life

Public ethics is constructed in terms of hermeneutical reflection by interpreting the givenness of life in social location and history of life-world, which continues to influence and shape human ethical attitude. Ethical reflection takes place in the context of the life history within which the conduct of life is embedded with intersubjective significance. We are living in community and in relationship with others. This perspective searches for narratives of life in its orientation to the moral conduct of life and attains its contextual character. The experience of the reality of life becomes primary and crucial for public theology and ethical reflection in correlation.

Accordingly, Bonhoeffer articulates the basic ethical situation in the following manner. "The question of good always finds us already in a situation which can no longer be reversed: we are alive...We are not asking what is good in itself; but we are asking what, on the assumption that life is given, is good for us as living men...The question of good is posed and is decided...in the midst of our living relationships with men, things, institutions and powers, in other words in the midst of our historical existence. The question of good cannot now be separated from the question of life, the question of history."[7]

We are bound to life, and under the presupposition of the givenness of life we ask what is good for us. And we inquire about good by looking deeply into life in the midst of our historical existence. To be good is to live, because "I am the life" (John 14:6). No question about life can be comprehended without this 'I am,' but only in relation to Jesus Christ whose life comes to us entirely from without, outside us. God has accepted the humanity and is reconciled with it. God "in the form of the poorest of our brothers" is God become man.[8]

Bonhoeffer conceptualizes the ethical and the Christian as a unifying theme. The ethical refers to a definite structure of human society and sociological relations in which all the ethical discourse does not take place in the abstract, but in a concrete

---

[7] Bonhoeffer, *Ethics*, 211.
[8] Ibid., 218.

context in the givenness of life. This socially constructed principle is linked with particular persons, times, and places.[9]

In a general phenomenology of the ethical we are surrounded with the givenness of life, and the ethical is restricted at any particular time and place by tradition and society. Christian ethics cannot be a book of moral prepositions or a work of reference, which embodies a life on moral principle or its ideal type.[10]

The ethicist is concerned with sharing him/herself in the whole fullness of life within the obligations of 'shall' and 'should.' God's commandment as divine speech to the concrete person is also concerned with the sharing of God's oikonomia in the life of Israel by comprising the ethical. Christian ethics keeps in view the positive contents of divine commandment for human life as well as the freedom of the person. It contrasts with a moralist system of casuistry.[11]

In the question of the good and the right under the givenness of life, it is significant for public theology to overcome two alternatives, namely, normative ethics or situation ethics. The normative ethics is concerned with accentuating the basic criteria of ethics through a general normative standard of conduct. The basis of ethics is constituted by timeless norms and laws of conduct prior to life. However, situation ethics calls attention to the specific demands in each concrete situation. The individual nature of each action is directed against an understanding of norms, if they are hostile to life and enforced the fixed statement regardless of the situation.

An ethical phenomenology of givenness of life brings up biblical commandment at the level of life situation in which self-reflection of agent has its own freedom and decision in

---

[9] Ibid., 267-8.
[10] Ibid., 265.
[11] Ibid., 280.

interpreting what is good and right for life in the concrete context. It entails a contextual character without disregarding the life-world influencing an ethical subject.

Contextual Ethics and God's Politics

Contextual ethics of God's politics can be undertaken in regard to 'what God is doing in the world.' God's action is seen in terms of the contextual character of the activity of God in Christ and the faith community. This perspective embraces the Christian life in the church as well as in the world. Lehmann concurs with Barth: "a wide reading of contemporary secular literature—especially of newspapers!—is therefore recommended to any one desirous of understanding the Epistle to the Romans."[12]

Accordingly, Lehmann focuses on a systematic reflection on the ethical nature of Christianity and a reflective analysis of faith and the behavior of the believer. 'How to live by the faith' comes into view rather than establishing how to prescribe the way Christians ought to behave. As he states, "*Christian ethics, as a theological discipline, is the reflection upon the question, and its answer: What am I, as a believer in Jesus Christ and as a member of his church, to do?* To undertake the reflection upon and analysis of this question and its answer—This is Christian ethics."[13]

In this definition of a Christian ethics, I observe that revelation, faith, and the Church are at the center of underlying the Christian ethics rather than morality itself. In its orientation to revelation, Christian ethics aims at maturity of faith, which produces morality.[14] Mature life of faith, which is based in faith community, fellowship, and integrity, refers to bodily growth

---

[12] Lehmann, *Ethics in a Christian Context*, 74. See Barth, *Epistle to the Romans*, 425.
[13] Ibid., 25.
[14] Ibid., 54.

toward maturity. This aspect characterizes the ethics in terms of koinonia, such that the koinonia of the church is the fellowship with reality of Christ's presence, who is also working in the world. It is conspicuous to clarify relations and function with concrete and contextual character rather than establish moral principles and precepts.[15]

The question, 'what God is doing in the world', can be answered by an interpretation of the activity of God in terms of politics and ethics, in which Lehmann takes on Aristotle. For Aristotle, ethics is a branch of politics as the science of the highest or supreme good. Politics is a theory of the political community, the city-state (the polis), which is the ideal form of human civil association. The human being is by nature a political animal. Ethics as the science of the good is a branch of politics, while politics is the science of the highest good.

Lehmann seeks to mediate Aristotle's political ethics with God's politics in the world. This perspective comes to terms with God's covenantal relation with Israel and the Church in the social, political sense. "In short, the God of the Church," Lehmann holds, "*is* the God of politics!"[16] I find it substantial to expand and elaborate Lehmann's position in a philosophical and sociological manner. Human life is actively involved in the society or world into which we are born. The intersection between life, ethics, and political being becomes obvious in Aristotle's idea of human beings as political animals.

The political correlates with the social by distinguishing human life (nurture, cultivation, and culture) from biological life (nature). Human capacity for political organization or city-state is differentiated from private life made up of household (oikos)

---

[15] Ibid., 49. 124.
[16] Ibid., 82.

and family. Only in the city-state do we acquire political life through action (praxis) and speech underlying the body politic.

More than Aristotle, according to Hannah Arendt, "However, while certainly only the foundation of the city-state enabled men to spend their whole lives in the political realm, in action and speech, the conviction that these two human capacities belonged together and are the highest of all seems to have preceded the *polis* and was already present in pre-Socratic thought."[17]

In Greek self-understanding, to be political means to live in a *polis,* in the sense that everything was to be decided through words and persuasion in contrast to force and violence. In Aristotle's definition of a human being as "a living being capable of speech," he does not define a human being in general nor according to human highest capacity (*logos,* speech or reason). Rather it is "*nous,* the capacity of contemplation, whose chief characteristic is that its content cannot be rendered in speech."[18]

At this point, I sense that there is a need to take into account the aspect of communication as a critical renewal of Aristotle's notion of speech and contemplation. Communication in an intersubjective context comes to terms with interpretation, which facilitates reinvigorating the koinonia ethics in a contextual, political manner. If Christian ethics is a critical reflection of what is to be done as a Christian, he/she is already in the political and social cultural realm. His/her reflection of the 'ought' cannot avoid the way the external situation can be interpreted in an intersubjective manner through dialogue and responsibility.

Insofar as the givenness of life itself constitutes the norm for all special situations, this indicates the content and method of ethical reflection which involves the liberating word of God; this goes beyond Aristotle's teleological moral reasoning and entails a

---

[17] *The Portable Hannah Arendt,* 183.
[18] Ibid., 184.

validity of categorical imperative in taking on the significance of God's politics and rights in the public sphere. Given this, Ernst Troeltsch deserves attention, because he affirms the sociological condition of Christian ethics in dealing with society and culture, which runs counter to ethical absolutism.

Protestant Principle and Descriptive Method

Ernst Troeltsch makes a great contribution to shaping and accentuating the contextual character of social ethics. He develops his systematic, religious exposition of the Protestant Principle in which the Scripture and the history of Christianity acquire full significance. His Protestant principle takes into account the contemporary forms of religious experience. The message of Jesus is to be considered as the one that sets forth a personal religious-moral life and spirit. It has little to do with "a set of unassailable dogmatic propositions."[19]

Troeltsch's approach to Jesus' personality is driven in terms of the modern historical-critical inquiry which sees the personality and work of Jesus in correlation with the prophets and their faith in God and ethics. Jesus also is made the object of the apostolic faith in opposition to Jewish law. The Gospel of Jesus within the framework of the entire biblical connection implies as the source of immanent critique the original and seminal form of the Christian life.

Troeltsch advances the sociological character of Christian ethics by analyzing its validity and norm in the Scripture, the Gospel of Jesus, and the apostles' writings with respect to the early and medieval history of Christianity, the Reformation, and the post-Reformation trends. He appropriates modern

---

[19] Troeltsch, *The Christian Faith*, 25.

religious life and thought by blending and unifying modern influence upon religious life with personal religious experience. The contemporary religious experience is accepted as the genuine decisive source and authority, along with the Gospel of Jesus as the original and seminal form of the Christian life or principle. Thus, the Gospel of Jesus is not defined as "the sole source and norm of belief."[20] But it is reinterpreted as the original and seminal source in interaction with different times and places in the historical course and context.

Troeltsch conceptualizes his Protestant principle and sociological study in his historical, critical analysis of relativism and differences of Christian ethical teachings. His social ethics and historical criticism contrasts with Aristotle's teleological reasoning with ahistorical implication. In fact, Troelstch's historical sociological method remains crucial in shaping his public theology as ethical theology in a constructive, contextual manner.

Troeltsch considers ethics to be the apex of theology, because it seeks to embrace a comprehensive horizon of history, society and culture to shape the future afresh in engagement with the present reality. Because there is no absolute religious ethic from heaven, it is plausible to undertake a constant wrestling with the present life and challenge. As the apex of theology, ethics has the task in analyzing theological norms and clarifying belief systems and arguments for a new synthesis in the discussion of a moral, individual commitment and social, ethical standpoint.[21] Troeltsch adopts a descriptive method in elaborating the concept of God, which is in contrast to the deductive method. In the latter, the concept of God is comprehended as an objectively

---

[20] Ibid., 25. 27.
[21] For details Chung, *Critical Theory and Political Theology*, 277-85.

established fact by deducing everything from it (beginning with creation, covenant, and redemption).

Rather, his descriptive method underlays his systematic, public theology in dealing with the givenness of life in history and society. The point is to appropriate God's impact on us and to analyze our thoughts about God in social historical development and background. It explicates "the preconditions and contents of the Christian consciousness of faith" in its "living, practical-theoretical orientation to God, the world, [and] humanity."[22]

His historical descriptive approach implies method of correlation between Christianity and other religions within the universal framework of history-of-religions. The descriptive ethics can be seen in his involvement with life in public sphere, employing sociological investigation of interaction of Christian churches with society, culture, and history.

Theocentric Ethics

Troeltsch finds his significance in Gustafson who presents theocentric ethics. His theocentric stance does not necessarily mean that the world should be taken from God's standpoint, because the human being is not capable of adopting God's eternal or transcendental standpoint.[23] His epistemological stance lies in asserting that God is not an object like phenomena which are subject to scientific investigation. This situation makes the language of theology into analogical or perhaps metaphorical at best.[24]

Together with the use of metaphors and similes, narrative and story are supported by the Scripture and grip the reader. Events

---

[22] Troeltsch, *The Christian Faith*, 111-12.
[23] Gustafson, *Ethics* I: 3.
[24] Ibid., 33.

in the Scripture are portrayed in parables or narrative accounts, and these genres are not reduced to dogmatic assertions or philosophical arguments. Biography and autobiography play a significant role in helping to know and understand ourselves. Stories, narratives, metaphors, similes, and other aesthetic presentations of life have meaningful powers and religious importance in the interpretation of the significance of events in life.[25] Gustafson's theocentric ethics is of narrative character in dealing with biblical scripture. It is moved within H. R. Niebuhr's notion of radical monotheism and responsibility. "All life has the character of responsiveness, I maintain."[26]

For Gustafson an ideal type is seen in accepting accountability for developing aspects of a tradition in terms of selection, retrieval, and recombination. Retrieval is selective in theology, and theological ethical development emerges through selected themes and is reformulated in some distinguished manner. Various theological themes, doctrines, and principles are recombined as a result of this procedure for the reinterpretation and construction. Selection is undertaken in "the processes of recombination, reinterpretation, and innovation."[27]

This perspective requires a radical shift in thinking and attitude, and it contradicts the general and traditional direction of moral philosophy. "All traditional ethics is anthropocentric."[28] Of special significance is that God is the measure of all things in contrast to the human-centered strand. Unlike Troeltsch, however, Gustafson tends to undermine the historical dynamism of ethical development in human involvement with history, society, and culture. A sociological analysis of ethical

---

[25] Ibid., 29-30.
[26] Ibid., 150.
[27] Ibid., 143, 142, 154.
[28] Ibid., 73; footnote 116.

difference in historical development is not valued for Gustafson in connection with historical critical understanding of religious ethics in the universal framework of history-of-religions.

Gustafson maintains that Barth contains a theocentric ethics, but the human experience of dependence is undermined in his rejection of natural knowledge of God. His problem with Barth is found not at the ethical level, but at the theological epistemology. In Gustafson's basic statement: "a Deity who does many different things, is addressed in many different ways, and is manifest in many different events and places."[29]

Barth and Special Ethics

Barth's theological ethics, which is grounded in God's self-communication in Jesus Christ, cannot be adequately comprehended apart from his reflection of God's speech act. God's speech act does not disavow divine freedom and sovereignty in speaking in many different ways. Barth conceptualizes special ethics in the context of the creation. The task of the special ethics integrates the action of God and its goodness with active human being and its goodness. The latter can be seen only from the standpoint of the true and active God and divine goodness.

Barth's objective ethics is basically of deontic character against the natural law tradition. What is to be conformed is God's command to be heard and obeyed in concrete time and place rather than following a universal moral principle. For Barth the ethical event occurs as it is revealed in the Word of God, in which God's creature as the covenant partner is addressed in concrete spheres and context instead of in a vacuum. Barth's special ethics

---

[29] Gustafson, *Ethics* II: 35.

is of interpretive and contextual profile, thus "ethics still have to leave the final judgment to God."[30]

Barth grounds the task of theological ethics in comprehending the Word of God as the command of God. "There is none good but one, that is, God" (Mk 10:18). God is the source of all goodness and human action is good (sanctification) as he/she hears and obeys the Word and command of God. He bases general ethics on the divine action, decision, and judgment, whereas his special ethics focuses upon human action under the command of God. Human activity is always concrete, and the sphere of its conduct is varied, and its conditions and possibilities are determined according to time, space, society, and history.

Barth's special ethics does not agree with the way of casuistry, a casuistic ethics. Three reasons are mentioned against the ethic of casuistry. (1) Moralist attempt to set him/herself on God's throne in terms of distinguishing good and evil; "a violation of the divine mystery in the ethical event."[31] (2) Here, the command of God is assumed as a universal rule, in other words, an empty form. The command of the living God is given in concrete fullness and instilled with definite content rather than universally and formally fixed; (3) casuistic ethics destructs the Christian freedom.[32]

Bonhoeffer finds significance in Barth's ethical orientation. "An ethic cannot be a work of reference for moral action which is guaranteed to be unexceptionable, and the ethicist cannot be the competent critic and judge of every human activity....and the ethicist cannot be the embodiment or ideal type of a life which is, on principal, moral."[33]

---

[30] Barth, *Church Dogmatics* (CD) III/4: 31.
[31] CD III/4: 11.
[32] Ibid., 12.
[33] Ibid., 10.

When the ethical event occurs according to the word of God, there are definite spheres and relationships, in other words, orders or ordinances in which such an encounter transpires. These are not misunderstood as laws, prescriptions, and imperatives, but they are understood only as the general form of the ethical event in contrast to a casuistic grasp.[34]

Barth's special ethics has a strong political implication, in which interpretation plays an important part in his special ethics of reconciliation in coping with the reality of impersonal forces in diverse social spheres.[35] Barth's critique of modern phenomena of lordless, impersonal forces remains crucial in featuring his special ethics of reconciliation as public ethics. Barth's agential position steers a middle course between Scylla of divine orders of creation (a *lex naturae* inscribed upon the human heart) and Charybdis of relativism. However, the ethical event as the decisive factor would not be our understanding, our interpretation, and our application. Freedom of obedience comes first, then interpretation and application become meaningful in witnessing to this special commending here and now.[36]

In Barth's unilateral position centered on obedience and interpretation, he is inclined to sidestep significance of the hermeneutical process of understanding in listening and reading the word of God in social location; in other words, obedience (with listening heart) is a part of hermeneutical process, which includes social condition of human life.

When I conceptualize public theology in its ethical frame of reference, Barth's ethics of reconciliation and his theology of speech act remains an undercurrent in the discussion of diversity of public spheres embedded within the reality of impersonal

---

[34] Ibid., 30.
[35] Barth, *Christian Life*, 220-21.
[36] CD III/4: 14. 23.

forces. However, his overemphasis on human obedience in correspondence to God's action appears to be self-assertive, having a lack of conceptual clarity in a sociological, hermeneutical manner. One's life is given in history, culture, and society, which is a basis of understanding the word of God in approximate procedure. Human obedience, a part of listening heart and discipleship, can be developed in the social scientific analysis of human life, whose givenness is already influenced and moved in the horizon of life-world.

2. Theology and Social Scientific Approach

In our discussion of public theology as ethical theology, I articulate public ethics from the standpoint of givenness of life in taking on the reality of social stratification and human life. A phenomenological reflection of life as given is of descriptive and interpretive character in social scientific manner, which is concerned with ethical issue for public moral, common good, and justice.

For the task of the relation between theology and sociological type, I call attention to H. R. Niebuhr. He is sociologically informed, conceptualizing a type of radical monotheism, henotheism, and polytheism, which is considerably indebted to Emile Durkheim's sociology of religion. H.R. Niebuhr sets out to analyze his henotheistic type of faith, an example of which can be seen in national flags as sacred objects to be respected with holy fear. The documents of national history become sacred books in the sense of civil religion.[37]

---

[37] H. R. Niebuhr, *Radical Monotheism and Western Culture*, 52.

As radical monotheism has emerged through the disenchantment of the world, it has progressed and differentiated into the political, the scientific, the economic, and the aesthetic spheres. In this process of rationalization H.R. Niebuhr discerns that many tendencies would occur toward polytheism and especially a henotheistic type of social faith.[38] Social faith is disguised as monotheism in its mixture. This reality of impersonal force can be seen, for instance, in early Protestantism or in Puritan New England, in which the conflict appeared between church sovereignty, popular sovereignty, and its democracy.[39]

Niebuhr's henotheistic type of social faith is considerably indebted to Durkheim's position, in which "the idea of society" is defined as "the soul of religion."[40] What is decisive in Durkheim is to affirm that religious forces are moral powers. Moral collectivity underwriting a moral being impacts on other moral beings. "Their authority is but one aspect of the moral influence that society exerts on its members…religion was able to be the womb in which the principal seeds of human civilization have developed."[41]

This perspective facilitates public theology in involving the diverse spheres of life in a comprehensive and maximalist spectrum in order to initiate its ethical stance of public intellectuals for common good, freedom, deliberate democracy, and solidarity. Public theology comes to terms with sociological theory of religious construction of reality, while coping with religious nationalism or a negative form of civil religion in its quasi-religious forces.

---

[38] Ibid., 31. 39.
[39] Ibid., 72.
[40] Ibid., 26.
[41] Durkheim, *The Elementary Forms of Religious Life*, 224-5.

According to Durkheim, "there is something eternal in religion which is destined to survive all the particular symbols in which religious thought has successively enveloped itself...What essential difference is there between an assembly of Christians celebrating the principal dates of the life of Christ, or of Jews remembering the exodus from Egypt or the promulgation of the Decalogue, and a reunion of citizens commemorating the promulgation of a new moral or legal system or some great event in the national life?"[42]

A concept of civil religion is born from such dynamic process. If God is the symbol of society or cultural unity, each society justifies its own interest and purpose by creating God according to its own image and symbolism. Thus, public theology has a task to scrutinize ways civil religion would be morally influential in shaping civil society (for example, the human rights movement, or critiques of slavery or nationalism).

On the other hand, public theology holds in check the detrimental effect of religion allied with nationalism, collective egotism, or colonialism, which is in need of immanent critique from religious sources. Various religious systems may have very different historical causes and reasons for emergence, whereas all of them may serve the common function of drawing people together in devotion to religious symbols and rites.

Given this, Robert Bellah articulates the eschatological hope of American civil religion in reference to a world civil religion.[43] However, I do not concur with a notion of world civil religion in the sense of a democratic and republican religion. Unlike Bellah, I focus on a concept of public theology as a way of understanding religious construction of social, cultural reality, in which civil

---

[42] Ibid., 200-1.
[43] Bellah, "Civil Religion in America," in *Beyond Belief*, 180. 186.

religion is critically investigated according to democratic ideals, social justice, and solidarity.

Religion, Public Moral, and Life-World

I reemploy Durkheim's sociological method for a theory of life-world, because Durkheim helps to cut through limitations of an evolutionary view of religion through his study of the totem principle and collective representations. There is no discrimination of religion or culture by way of differentiation of one lower, primitive religion from higher, civilized religion. All religions are true and unique after their own fashion, and their basis is in the real, which is applied to all social forms of existence and morality.

Religion is no longer a private affair, but the ground of society. Religious experience is made in society, because "they are rich in social elements."[44] For Durkheim religion can be a form of life-world shaping moral consciousness and social bond. "If religion gave birth to all that is essential in society, that is so because the idea of society is the soul of religion."[45] The soul of religion, or religious ideas are bound up to the idea of society by shaping its organization and collective representations in the socially established knowledge system (episteme). Religion acts as a mechanism underlying and justifying the moral norms and values within a particular society and culture. Indeed, the primary function of the religion is to act upon the moral life of the individual in society, and the individual has learnt social life to form ideals.

This sociological view of religion finds its pivot in Christian public theology and in its comparative study of other religions,

---

[44] Durkheim, *The Elementary Forms of Religious Life*, 9.
[45] Ibid., 421.

which strive to promote moral collaboration, common good, interreligious justice, and peace. Religion is public because it has a meaningful whole in shaping and determining social formation and human life (existence, consciousness, and collective representations). The hallmark of moral authority is invested in religion, and moral consciousness and human conscience are with the aid of religious symbols.[46]

However, a pathological consequence in social cultural development would occur in a mechanical, coercive transition imposed or coerced from outside. It is fair to distinguish a morality-enhancing type of religious practice (solidarity effect) from its pathological type (disgrace effect) in dealing with the relation between religious discourse, economic rationalization, and cultural formation.

This position disputes with Hebert Spencer's social Darwinism, which is disconnected from the real by neglecting the moral character of human life in society.[47] Durkheim provides an eminent insight to overcome Spencer's social Darwinism, in which individuals were free to compete for survival. Only the fittest survived prevails in the natural order of things. The struggle for existence and the survival of the fittest are ridden in naturally directional, progressive development in justifying colonialism and slavery. Applicable to the races, the inherent inferior is made unfit for full citizenship and should submit itself to the discipline and guidance of the inherently superior.[48]

On the contrary, Durkheim maintains that the so-called primitive religion served complex and parallel social functions with advanced societies. Society is called 'a thing in itself' or *sui generis*, because a study focuses on the unique forms of social

---

[46] Ibid., 211.
[47] Ibid., xx.
[48] McCarthy, *Race, Empire, and the Ideas of Human Development*, 77.

life, called social facts, without attaching the social Darwinian version.

Religion has a public moral in influencing human consciousness and shaping society, and there is no discrimination of each religious life-world. Religious force is conceived of as embodied in the emblem, and it is endowed with a kind of transcendence. It symbolizes the clan or nation, by becoming real only within and by them. Religions exist as an eminently social thing,[49] because human beings exist as social beings.

As religious categories are organized upon its morphology (its religious moral and social economic institutions), the religious individual is separated from the social. The social (the whole) can no longer be derived from the individual (the part). In differentiation from individual representations, "Society is a reality sui generis."[50]

Even in the Judeo-Christian context, God is not separated from the society. Social life is only possible, since religious life is inevitable. Social life is constituted in terms of its vast religious symbolism, as seen in the physical emblems and figurative representations.[51] Religion engenders all that is essential and substantial in society, thus Durkheim maintains that "the idea of society is the soul of religion."[52]

I conceptualize this sociological theory of public moral in terms of religious construction of social reality, which resonates with a theory of life-world in the sense of history, culture, and society; the latter influences and guides the individual life through

---

[49] Durkheim, *The Elementary Forms of Religious Life*, 9.
[50] Ibid., 15.
[51] Ibid., 223.
[52] Ibid., 421. Durkheim's notion of the apotheosis between the god and the society can be seen in his explanation of the totemic principle or god in terms of the symbol of both the god and the society in its equation. Ibid., 208.

political legitimacy, the economic system, judiciary organization, social discourse, institution, and education. Religion undertakes its construction of social reality and underlays public moral through collective representations, which condition individual consciousness, and practical, ethical lifestyle.

On the other hand, Weber holds, the prophetic ethics of conviction is combined with political ethics of responsibility. The honor of the political leader assumes an exclusive personal responsibility against the demagogue. His political ethics is expressed for the politicians in terms of "passion [in the sense of matter-of-factness], a feeling of responsibility, and a sense of proportion."[53] This position counters the deadly sin in the field of politics: lack of objectivity and irresponsibility.

Along with responsibility ethics, Weber articulates the significance of the absolute ethic of the gospel, "an acosmic ethic of ultimate ends," which rejects the insistence that "civil war is the only legitimate war."[54] The absolute ethic of the gospel (a prophetic form of conviction) as expressed in the Sermon on the Mount does not ask for consequences because of its value rationality. It is responsible for the believer in an ethic of ultimate ends to adopt "the flame of protesting against the injustice of social order."[55]

Ethical demand in the political leadership has to be elaborated in the sense of complementarity of responsibility and prophetic conviction. An ethic of ultimate ends is not identical to irresponsibility, nor is an ethic of responsibility identical to unprincipled opportunism. The supplementary

---

[53] "Politics as a Vocation," *From Max Weber*, 115.
[54] Ibid., 120. 124.
[55] Ibid., 121.

unison constitutes a genuine person who can have the calling for politics.[56]

Sociological explication of religion and culture facilitates public theology in engaging with problems of world Christianity, which are characterized by translation, inculturation, and politics of life-script in struggle for decolonization, racial justice, and recognition of cultural authenticity. Politics of recognition remains an undercurrent in the sociological study of religion and culture. Seen through the life-world, religion can be a source of moral binding and organic solidarity, in which religious ideas can function as the immanent critique in dealing with the detrimental consequences, which would be caused in the historical course.

Religious ideas or discourse cannot be fully comprehended only through human projection in society, but they occur and take shape in human religious experience with God, the Ultimate reality. Religious carriers find elective affinity with material interests, political legitimacy, and power relations in their course of life in a broader spectrum. Here, religious ethics plays a major role in guiding the process of rationalization and forming social organization and political constitution.

A critical theory of sociological articulation is concerned with mediating religious-functional symbolism (Durkheim) and sociological-generative analysis of rationalization and political legitimacy (Weber), featuring the significance of public ethics in terms of interpretation, discourse clarification, power relations, and world construal.

In the project of public ethics and religious construction of reality, it is of special significance to appreciate Husserl's theory of life-world. A phenomenological reflection begins with suspense (epoché) or problematization of the natural world by a return to or with recourse to the regime of meaningful world.

---

[56] Ibid., 127.

Phenomenon of life and its meaning (noema) appear in the mode of givenness through self-reflection (noesis), correlation, and continuity. The process of understanding and meaning horizon is operative in the intellectual stream, which is not fixed at all, rather it continually changes and moves dynamically in the ongoing flux through self-regard in its interaction with the meaningful source of the life-world.

Adumbrations occur in continuous multiplicities of meaning and in different manners; in other words, in different adumbrations of meaning.[57] Appearance of meaning and adumbration in mental process are in correlation by virtue of which a horizon of intentionalities is enhanced and widened along with the regime of a meaningful world.

This epistemological procedure is undertaken in problematization of what has been neglected and marginalized in natural attitudes. Horizons can be opened up, according to Husserl, only through a critical reflection of the life-world and human beings. It requires responsible critique and emancipation from what has been sedimented as prejudices and obscurities by way of tradition and culture.[58]

The fusion of horizons occurs in encounter between past and present through awakening recollection or self-reflection to form reality of vivid present. It is awakened through explication of the given horizon and the new horizons in a continuous manner.[59] A theory of life-world does not necessarily lead to sheer relativism, but recognizes cultural validity, identity, and moral norm in unique development of each different life-world in Europe, Asia, and Africa. Different types of life-world, in spite of all relativity,

---

[57] "The Basic Approach to Phenomenology," in *The Essential Husserl*, 71.
[58] "The Mathematization of Nature," ibid., 362.
[59] "The Noetic and Noematic Structure of Consciousness," ibid., 109.

have much in common through pursuing human dignity, common good, and justice within the world horizon.

If the goal of truth is established about the objects as unconditionally valid for all in different traditions and cultures,[60] the world horizon becomes an undercurrent in underwriting the public moral in a democratic pluralist society for dialogue, common good and social justice. This perspective helps public theology to develop a phenomenological reflection of life as givenness for an ethical project through critical attitude, interpretation, responsible critique, and emancipation. It integrates Troeltsch's descriptive method and its historical sociological significance into ethical deliberation of life as givenness in reference to God in the universal framework of history-of-religions.

Communicative Ethics and Civil Society

A theory of life-world finds its full expression in Habermas' theory of communicative rationality and civil society with a strong ethical component. Life-world is conceptualized in social differentiation from the two systems, in other words, the administrative state and the market economy.

Civil society emerges from the network of the personal life histories meshed with other life histories for sharing the moral wisdom, retaining internal relationship with the life-world. Externally, institutions of civil society form the organizational substratum of the general public of citizens, and its core comprises a network of associations. The network of rights of religion, speech, and association is a necessary condition for the

---

[60] "Elements of a Science of the Life-World," ibid., 373.

operation of civil society, which is in collaboration with political public sphere.[61]

For Habermas, the rationality is inherent in the practice of argumentation and the rationality is proper to the communicative practice of everyday life. It excludes the strategic use of coercion and violence in an emotional, institutional, cultural, and political manner. A theory of argumentation is driven by moral claims, critique, and truth, and it underlays the concept of communicative rationality.[62]

Habermas characterizes civil society in a different category from Hegel, who identifies it with bourgeoisie economic society. In the formation of the public sphere of civil society, Habermas holds, the press plays a significant role, since the nation state employed the press to disseminate information into creating a new public sphere for a stratum of people. People can form and develop critical opinion and judgment by using their public use of reason against the authorities.[63]

Habermas elaborates Weber's theory of rationalization in western society into a modern society by differentiating the life-world from the system (the administrative state and market economy). The life-world has come along with the development of modern society, and it has become differentiated and specialized into culture (cultural reproduction), society (social integration), and personality (socialization). The reality of system continues to invade and violate life-world (culture, society, and personality), even by fashioning and colonizing it according to its image. Habermas seeks to erect a democratic dam against the colonizing system of encroachment.

---

[61] Habermas, *Between Facts and Norms*, 367.
[62] Habermas, *The Theory of Communicative Action*, I: 17-8.
[63] Habermas, *The Structural Transformation of the Public Sphere*, 27.

What features Habermas' deliberative democracy is communicative reasoning, argumentation, and action in the intersubjective, everyday speech context. It underpins political formation of public moral-ethical opinion. The lawmaking process of the constitutional state should be open to participation of the nongovernmental, political public sphere within civil society. Civil society is connected with democratic, moral formation of public sphere in terms of the socially integrating dimension of solidarity and justice.

The public sphere implies a communication structure which is grounded in life-world as realized through the network of associations of civil society. It is a social phenomenon, which refers to a network for communicating information and opinions. The public sphere is reproduced through everyday communicative action and practice, as the life-world works in the same way. The public sphere is generated as the social space through communicative action.[64]

Communicative ethics is concerned with unveiling the systematically distorted side of communication, that is a critique of its ideological function. Democratic revolution can be best described as a project to carry forward in a permanent and quotidian manner, the framework of communicative practice, which challenges the reality of life-world colonized by the system.[65]

However, it is difficult to fully comply with Habermas' definition of civil society in terms of generating the public sphere. It is important to take into account a radical side of Rousseau's notion of civil society in terms of participatory democracy, general will, and solidarity with those economically weaker. Civil society in Rousseau's sense is not merely defined as a political

---

[64] Habermas, *Between Facts and Norms*, 360.
[65] Ibid., 470.

public sphere, but it is a foundational function for the body politics of state through general will and citizens' consent.

Thus, the State, or its political institutions, has to serve the common good of citizens. The economic and social power is best arranged for equality and solidarity as expressed by general will underlying legislature and judiciary legitimacy. Rousseau's political position allows the local direct co-determination of lifeworld (for example, through direct democracy in township). A control becomes feasible in restraining central power of government and market economy (international or national economy of unified management and controlled enterprise) through representative corporations.[66]

Civil society and citizens are differentiated from bourgeois society and bureaucrats, thus democratic government is established by act of each individual citizen's consent and common agreement, which includes significance of communicative rationality and action in the public sphere. Citizen as political subject cannot be imposed by the state through "any burden which is useless to the community."[67]

3. Discourse Ethics, Biopolitics, and Human Body

Discourse ethics can be featured in the context of conversation or communication rationality; it finds affinity with the hermeneutical theory of history of effect by taking on genealogical analysis of social influence upon language and its system of hierarchy. This perspective shapes and enriches a communicative character of responsible self through social scientific analysis of

---

[66] Fetscher, *Rousseaus politische Philosophie*, 18.
[67] Rousseau, *On the Social Contract*, 62.

religious discourse in its elective affinity with material interests, critique of ideological function, and power relations.

This sociological stance is met with the theological position of public ethics, which integrates Christian discourse of *parrhesia* (speaking the truth audaciously) in defense of the disadvantaged and the innocent victim.[68] Language is not simply a means of communication, but an instrument or a medium of power relations, which are invested in social conditions, rational organization, authority, and real-life questions. Such an example of communication becomes obvious in a colonial or postcolonial context. Utterances can produce effects through social discourse and representation. *"Authority comes to language from the outside."*[69]

Social discourse of representation is relevant to Edward Said's theory of Orientalism. A discourse of representation is fabricated in power relations, and it makes an epistemological distinction between the Orient and the Occident.[70] What matters in the relationship between Occident and Orient is a network between power, domination, and a complex hegemony. In Said's theory of Orientalism, it is important to decipher an ideological form of Western representation in portraying the Oriental societies and to advance a moral critique of such political hegemony. Linguistic type of representation is revealed in dealing with race, gender and sexuality. These realms cannot be properly comprehended without analyzing influence and strategy of biopower from outside upon human body and life.

Such discourse is a conjuncture which is produced and reproduced in a set of socially constituted dispositions (a linguistic habitus). Social habitus nested in the social structure

---

[68] Bonhoeffer, *Ethics*, 358-67.
[69] Bourdieu and Wacquant, *An Invitation to Reflexive Sociology*, 147.
[70] "Orientalism (1978)," in *The Edward Said Reader*, 69.

is expressed through the linguistic habitus, thus *"language is a technique of the body."*[71] Structures of discourse have political charge upon the social world, but it is not necessary to subscribe to Foucauldian genealogy anchored simply in power/knowledge assumptions.

Reflexivity in an epistemological sense, or self-refection for vivid present can be undertaken in a phenomenological frame of reference. It strives for "the systematic exploration of the unthought categories of thought, which delimit the thinkable and predetermine the thought."[72] The reflexive turn, or epistemic reflexivity is elaborated in anamnestic reasoning of what has been unthought and marginalized. Such inquiry seeks to reveal "the most profoundly buried structures of various social worlds"[73] and their mechanism in reproduction and transformation.

The objectivity of the first order is constituted by the distribution of material resources and means based on social division of labor (producing species of capital). The objectivity of the second order is undertaken in the form of systems of classification or representation; it functions as symbolic templates for the practical activities (conduct, thoughts, feelings, and judgments) on the part of social agents.[74]

There is a regime of moral rationality and political significance in sociological analysis of social division of labor and rationalization, because moral reasoning or meaningful action in hermeneutical regime is not merely reduced to ideology of superstructure or to power relations.[75] If the social discourse is a technique of the body through biopolitical governance, such sociological inquiry of human moral agency helps an

---

[71] Bourdieu and Wacquant, *An Invitation to Reflexive Sociology*, 149.
[72] Ibid., 40.
[73] Ibid., 7.
[74] Ibid.
[75] Ibid., 47. 49.

ethical deliberation of the human body in critique of masculine domination and symbolic violence. A social reality is projected in terms of a definite representation in dealing with race, gender, and sexuality.

Cultural Sexualization and Race

Cultures are internally diverse in social stratification in terms of status groups and class situation, which are affected by religious discourse, rationalization (social division of labor), social institutions, political legitimacy, and power relations. In access to diverse resources, there is an unequal order of things; it is necessary to unveil the aspect of symbolic domination and a structural type of violence as manifested in multiple forms of power differentials and masculine domination between social groups. Power relations in symbolic materialistic frameworks include mechanisms of violence—invisible and imperceptible even to the victims. This symbolic reality is operative in different social domains such as race, ethnic identity, gender, and sexual orientation.[76]

In effect, sexual identity is constituted in the social environment such as family, society, education, or religion, while exposed to political technology of body, race, and sexuality through the network of discourse-power. Cultural values and hierarchy of language influence the way economy and politics are arranged and managed, while the latter promote cultural ideals of the privileged.[77]

When people are organized into ranked groups, or social prestige or status in hierarchies, social inequality becomes crucial in access to resources and distribution of social and cultural

---

[76] Bourdieu, *Masculine Domination*, 2.
[77] West, *Race Matters*, 19.

capitals; the social structure constitutes the biological side of race in wider cultural characteristics underlying discrimination and injustice. Race or ethnicity correlates with social problems such as poverty, inequality, unemployment, violence, and imprisonment.

A shadow of racial ideology or a system of racism can be seen in the separation or segregation of individuals, families, and communities. More than Black-centrism, however, there is a combination between sexuality and the symbolism of blood, which are grounded in the regimes of power. Racism took shape in the type of political power in which the purity of the blood is protected, and the triumph of the race is ensured.[78]

Sexual racism is experienced in its discrimination in terms of interracial marriage and its judicial system. An act of discrimination is embedded with the occupational system, or positions of employment, in which privilege is organized in accordance with accepted gendered norms and heterosexual normativity. It refers to sexualization of racial gender norms, in which gender and race can be explicated according to heterosexual ways of normalization, underwriting a diverse reality of social cultural formation in this league.

Gender and Sexuality

Gender and sexuality are both grounded in the sexual body, and they are differently experienced at distinct societies and cultures. The authenticity of experience can be found in a different life-world, in which such experience is narrated as inscribed into personal identity and cultural authenticity through the prism of life-script. In the technology of sexual division of labor, I draw attention to the body as the site of power and domination through

---

[78] Foucault, *The History of Sexuality* 1: 149.

docility, surveillance, discipline, and control. The scientific discourse about sexuality plays a crucial role in producing hegemonic power in marginalizing other discourses about it. The discourse of marginalized groups is suppressed by rationalizing discourse, becoming sites of resistance. This characterizes a task of discourse clarification of personal identity and cultural authenticity, which becomes crucial in conceptualizing public theology and ethical practice of life-world against a structural violence of power mechanism.

In so doing, ethics of life-world relocates politics of recognition and cultural authenticity within mutual recognition of difference in its distinctive character. It is worth considering whether an Asian American needs recognition from the white culture when he/she expresses his/her identity, or sexual orientation, or cultural authenticity. "My identity is crucially constituted through concepts and practices made available to me by religion, society, school, and state, and mediated to varying degrees by the family."[79]

In fact, Asian-American identity and cultural authenticity are shaped, developed and reinforced in the Asian-American life-world, or life-script in resistance against power mechanism and its structural violence of impersonal forces. Ethics of life-world relocates an ideal type of authenticity within life-scripts in positive construction through narrative of one's social biography, resistance to assimilation, while developing creative interpretation of reservoir of life-world for positive retrieval of life-scripts. It implies politics of difference in its distinctive life-script which cuts across a paradox of antiracist racism, a path

---

[79] Appiah, "Multicultural Societies and Social Reproduction," Taylor, et al. *Multiculturalism*, 154.

to the abolition of differences of race toward assimilations and homogenization.[80]

A biblical narrative of anti-discrimination is rooted in the gospel of reconciliation with reference to God's solidarity in the life of the subjugated or Jesus's identification with the lowest of the low (*massa perditionis*: public sinner, tax collector, and the prostitute)

Biopolitics and Public Health

Foucault's concept of governmentality is central in his theory of biopolitics, which facilitates comprehending micro-processes of administration and control over the human body through local institutions and authorities. Driven by socio-political practices or technologies, human life is politically constructed, and his/her body is made docile through discipline, docility, and regulation. A biopolitical theory can be incorporated into the phenomenology of givenness of life, in which human body comes into ethical focus.

In all authentic ethical discourse, there is a concrete limitation, because it is undertaken only in a concrete context, dealing with social reality of givenness of life. This perspective evinces public theology as ethical theology by taking into account the aspect of embodiment in the social political context. We experience the world through our bodies that are inscribed, represented, embodied, and ranked within the reality of social stratification.

Embodiment and lived experience are integral components of shaping ethical attitude in phenomenological description of public health, sexuality, gender, and race. In fact, the human body is produced, cultivated, regulated, and disciplined to become docile in its subjection to the biopolitics of the State.

---

[80] Ibid., 162 footnote 12.

An ethical deliberation of givenness of life comes to terms with a meta-ethical analysis of biopolitical impact upon the human body. An ethical deliberation of the human body provides social critical reasoning in investigating the body of the poor and biomedical advance, while incorporating a prophetic dimension of solidarity and social justice into the biomedical sphere imbued with pathologies of power.[81]

Medicine is reified as commerce and its commodification is driven for gaining a profit in the medical industrial enterprise. This reality is seen in inequalities in distribution of health services and medical treatment in domestic as well as global contexts. Biopolitical strategy brings its way of governmentality in regulating and controlling the human body, especially inflicting the structure of oppression upon the body of the poor. Our being in-the-life-world is colonized by the dominance of the biopolitical technology, its social discourse, and bureaucratic domination.[82]

A postcolonial reality characterizes the aftermath of the previous colonial reality, a neo-colonial condition in a cosmopolitan context, weaving the latter into an indispensable part of social stratification in the metropolis. A racialized nationalism in the form of ethno-racism is embedded with immigration problems in debates. The public sphere is fraught with violent attacks on the immigration of people from the periphery to the metropolis, in which we see a politically stirred form of anti-immigration movement, or religious fundamentalism. Common sense discourse is racialized in many spheres of life, as being taken for granted.[83]

Structural violence and inequality is operative in neoliberal market forces. If medical care is a basic part of human rights, it is necessary to promote a public program of health and human

---

[81] Farmer, *Pathologies of Power*, 201.
[82] Turner, *The Body and Society*, 15.
[83] McCarthy, *Race, Empire, and the Idea of Human Development*, 9.

rights for everyone. A concept of pragmatic solidarity becomes crucial in the bioethical stance for pragmatic solidarity, which emphasizes a right of everyone "to share in scientific advancement and its benefits."[84] Church in the sense of the body of Christ characterizes its relationship with the gospel of embodiment, in which Jesus adopts a prophetic advocacy for those economically weaker, socially maltreated and culturally outcast. Embodiment at the heart of social life remains also crucial in theological understanding of body of Christ in the sense of assumption of 'human flesh' in sinful condition and the gospel of reconciliation. It buttresses the ethical solidarity with those on the margins or naked in the midst of biopolitical times and pandemic.

Conclusion

In the discussion of public theology, life-world, and ethics, I have dealt with the relation between public theology and ethical deliberation in dealing with diverse types of theological ethics. My major concern falls on ethical phenomenology of life-world and givenness of life, which is embodied in social stratification. It requires social scientific reasoning of public theology and interpretation of the ethical position in taking issue with a reality of colonizing encroachment upon life-world. Public ethics weigh in the place of the human body, which is classified into a structure of injustice and inequality through biopolitical strategy, its bureaucratic administration, and public medicine.

Public theology alerts the church in the Global North to heed the victims under institutionalized violence and imposed structure of hegemony upon the Third World. Its hermeneutics of liberation in scriptural frame of reference helps to acknowledge how the word of God should be heard and obeyed in a new

---

[84] Farmer, *Pathologies of Power*, 239.

and fresh manner in regard to the poor, the victim, the racially discriminated against, and the under-privileged in the West.

Meta-ethical reasoning of interpretation focuses on what is going on in diverse public spheres in light of the biblical symbol of the kingdom of God and reconciliation, which underwrites an anamnestic stance of *theologia crucis*, recognition of the other religions, and advocacy for the margins in democratic, pluralist society.

Public theology focuses on exegetical work of biblical narrative in which God provides the place through the creation by separating God's creation from "a formless void and darkness" (Gen. 1: 2). Theology of creation points to eschatological meaning of the kingdom of glory in the apocalypse of John, thus becoming theology of liberation.[85]

Longing for God's place is the important moment precipitating the utopia within the eschatological hope. "For in this tent we groan, longing to be clothed with our heavenly dwelling." (2 Cor. 5: 2) If eschatology teaches about hope, utopian longing awakes us for the God the provider of the indwelling place.[86] The Biblical thought of the dwelling place is characterized thoroughly in a social, historical sense. A praxis, which corresponds to God's new heaven and new earth, can be featured in utopian longing. "Build up, build up, prepare the way, remove every obstruction from my people's way" (Isa, 57:14).

Eschatology encourages public theology to strive for responsibility, social justice, common good, and emancipation for solidarity in critically examining symbolic domination and structural violence in access to political legitimacy, health care, economic inequality, education, and global sovereignty of the metropolis upon the peripheral in postcolonial context.

---

[85] Marquardt, *Eia, warn wir da – eine theologische Utopie*, 318.
[86] Ibid., 22-3.

Chapter 2.

Public Ethics, Interpretation, and Responsibility

We interact with each other and influence the lives of others in daily life, involving and sharing in the life of the world. Structuring one's life as a life for others gives ethical significance in the service of good through the ordinances of life.[1] This chapter is a study of public ethics, interpretation, and responsibility, which is a specific basis for Christian public theology in relation to God as well as fellow people. Public theology requires a task of interpretation, which plays a major role in understanding human response and responsibility in a social historical context.

In this regard, I take H. R. Niebuhr as the classic example of public ethics. He contributes to the ethics of responsibility at a meta-ethical level in terms of human response in accordance with interpretation. I am concerned with his responsible ethics, while renewing some limitations of his Christian moral philosophy in comparison with Emmanuel Levinas' ethical philosophy. A biblical idea of reconciliation within Christian eschatology helps to cut through limitations of ethical passivity in Niebuhr's Christian moral philosophy. Finally, a phenomenological inquiry of theology and ethics can be configured and undertaken in discussion with the Other in the postcolonial context.

---

[1] Rentorff, *Ethics* I: 51-2.

1. Responsible Self

A construction of public ethics is engaged in meta-ethical epistemology and methodical inquiry in taking on moral semantics, moral ontology, and moral epistemology. The question of the meaning of moral terms or judgments refers to moral semantics, in which the words 'good' or 'bad' and 'right' or 'wrong' is to be evaluated in accordance to its meaning and its value. The question of the nature of moral judgments refers to moral ontology, which deals with moral judgments according to universal-normative criterion or cultural-relative or subjective-emotive one.

The question centers around how we know whether something is right or wrong and whether moral judgments can be supported or defended; this implies moral epistemology. These questions are distinguished yet internally connected by shaping each question and direction in terms of semantics, ontology, and epistemology.[2]

Duty and responsibility are mediated through the givenness of life and take on an ethical quality, because the basis of ethics is not constituted by timeless norms and laws of conduct. Ethical inquiry seeks to clarify the life situation by being involved in that situation and interpretation of the external events in a fitting, rational manner.

It is H. Richard Niebuhr that makes a major contribution to ethics of responsibility in terms of exploring human response in a moral sense. His standpoint is based on a theistic moral philosophy, taking human existence as the starting point in relation to God. Paul's statement in front of Areopagus informs Niebuhr's moral reasoning of human responsibility in the light of theistic moral philosophy. "For 'In him we live and move and

---

[2] Garner and Rosen, *Moral Philosophy*, 215.

have our being'; as even some of your own poets have said, 'For we too are his offspring'" (Acts 17: 22).

An inquiry is undertaken regarding human moral life in general rather than dealing with the Christian life as such. Nonetheless, his theistic moral philosophy entails an endeavor to understand human life from a Christian point of view in terms of sin and salvation in Jesus Christ.[3] Niebuhr's stance is formulated very aptly: "All life has the character of responsiveness, I maintain."[4] We do respond by interpretation, in which interpretation of actions has diversity and difference in our response to external actions or events upon us. Moral epistemology is sought in the way how to respond to external event according to interpretation of it in a rational, fitting manner.

Within the framework of response and interpretation, Niebuhr explicates several types of ethics in terms of meaning of responsibility or moral semantics. The meaning of responsibility is seen in the statement that "the great God has treated us as responsible beings."[5] The term responsible being has become common only in the nineteenth and twentieth centuries, and it is relatively late arrival in comparison with virtue, duty, good or moral.[6]

A Human Being-the-Maker

With the symbol of responsibility in mind, Niebuhr sees the double purpose of ethics in an ancient Greek commandment: *Gnothi seauton* (Know thyself) in terms of obedience and seeking guidance for our activity. For this double task of ethics, Niebuhr first introduces a type of teleology in description of a

---

[3] H. R. Niebuhr, *The Responsible Self*, 44-5.
[4] Ibid., 46.
[5] Ibid., 47.
[6] Ibid.

human being as the maker or the fashioner. A human being as an artificer constructs things according to an idea and on behalf of an end. He cites Aristotle in this regard: "Every art and every inquiry and similarly every action and pursuit, is thought to aim at some good."[7]

Aristotle makes his philosophical influence on the theological development of Thomas Aquinas. Human beings are rational moral agents, thus one's moral will expresses one's rational character. A habit is ingrained in us through upbringing, education, and our choices, and it becomes a disposition of the moral will, which decides and acts. In cultivating appetite or habit under control of reason, it expresses virtue, which refers to habit or disposition of the will toward a good end. It fulfills our potential telos, becoming the means to the ultimate end of happiness. It implies moral ontology in terms of cultivation of virtue. The four cardinal virtues (prudence, justice, temperance, and fortitude) are located in the ends of human existence, which are universally valid to rational persons.

Niebuhr credits the Thomist position into a type of synthesis between ethics of the gospel and ethics of culture (Aristotle), while placing Christ above culture. All nature conceptualized by reason is purposive in character, which is known as creation of God. For Thomas, a Christian Aristotelian, the human intellect or reason may attain God as its end, while the ultimate happiness is freely bestowed upon the believer by God.

A rule for social life must be found by reason, which is bound to natural law rather than found in the gospels. The natural law is based on the ethical law, which shares in the mind of God. Therefore, "culture is the work of God-given reason in God-given nature."[8]

---

[7] Cited in ibid., 49.
[8] H. R. Niebuhr, *Christ and Culture*, 135.

The divine law through prophets and revelation is partly coincident with the natural law, whereas partly transcending it. In the synthesis between reason and revelation there is the basis of right which is rooted in the given, created culture of human being and the world. The type of synthesis facilitates intelligent collaboration between Christians with non-Christians in the world of culture, by distinguishing Christian faith over the culture.

However, in Niebuhr's account, the Thomist type of synthesis or moral epistemology has a lack of historical understanding, in which all human achievement is relative, temporal, and passing. It is also in readiness to institutionalize Christ and the gospel in a heretical manner. This synthesis type is exposed to radical attack by the action of a free Lord for obedience to the divine commandment, thus it is subject to conversion, replacement, and usurpation.[9] The effort in synthesis between Christ and culture "tends, perhaps inevitably, to the absolutizing of what is relative, the reduction of the infinite to a finite form, and the materialization of the dynamic."[10]

According to Thomas Aquinas, all actions are caused by the power of the will, which acts in relation to its object. But for Aquinas, "the object of the will is some end in the shape of good. Therefore, all human actions must be for an end."[11]

Given the action for an end, Niebuhr typologies "man-the-maker" who acts for an end. Purposiveness comes to terms with humanity. In acting with a purpose or telos, it is important to inquire into the fitness of the steps in procedure toward the desired goal.

---

[9] Ibid., 147.
[10] Ibid., 145.
[11] Cited in H. R. Niebuhr, *The Responsible Self*, 49.

Education, science, or legislation can be classified in a teleological manner with respect to telos. The freedom of a human being appears in this context to be the necessity of self-determination by final causes, and his/her practical reason relates to fitting materials with the purpose. Aristotle might have in mind means as a fitting response, which constitutes virtue. For him, "to feel fear, confidence, appetite, anger, and pity 'at the right times, with reference to the right objects, towards the right people, with the right motive and in the right way is what is intermediate and best.'"[12]

Furthermore, Niebuhr classifies Stoic ethics as primarily teleological, concerned with law. What is remarkable is the Stoics' concept of the world immanence of natural law (the general divine law of nature), on which all ordinances of positive law are based and accordingly the state and society develop. Since all true law is understood to reflect the universal reason of God, civil law and the law of peoples should be judged in accordance with the universal natural law.

A cosmos is described to be grounded in the mind of God, and human beings are understood as a reflection of this same rationality despite their corruption. All are, by nature, rational beings, thus fundamentally equal. Based on this reason, human beings are rational beings in essence and can be self-disciplined in the face of the accidents, life experience, and adversity.[13]

However, the Stoic rationality is differentiated from the biblical narrative in which God's rationality is often not congruent with what humans find rational (for example, the book of Job, and even the Christ narrative of passion).

Based on the divine universal law, however, the Stoics hold the character of divine providence and religious feeling, which has

---

[12] Cited in ibid., 57.
[13] Wogman, *Christian Ethics*, 20.

developed into personal fellowship with God. But they tend to downgrade the will of God or world renewal through a coming kingdom of God in opposition to the world and sin, thus affinity between God and human being turns into human affinity with the nature. In the Stoic ideal a teleological character in the hope for future would be connected with intensive cultivation and moral knowledge, which was fostered in the aristocratic spirit of ruling class; it has the ethical response and reform of the existing social order.

In fact, equality in the basic moral reality can be seen in range from the slave Epictetus, the writer Seneca, the orator Cicero, and finally to the Roman emperor Marcus Aurelius. Despite the theistic character of stoicism, it is suggested that pantheist elements continue to resurge.[14]

It deals with the ethics of suffering through *apatheia* to be free of the suffering; it has responses with no passion, yet with reason. This reason in the Stoic context refers to the interpretative power in understanding the rationale in moral action of the self. This skill of interpretation enables the moral self to respond rationally and freely from the influence of passion with emphasis on the virtue. A clear, distinct interpretation of all events sees these as intelligible, rational events. The idea of response is guided by the rational interpretation of the events, beings and the moral subject's reaction to these. The clear, intelligible interpretation plays a major role in substituting self-centered, emotion-arousing interpretations of what is happening to the moral subject. The human freedom from the passions, or from the tyranny of events has to do with freedom, which is to be gained through correct interpretation, changing responses of the self to the events.[15]

---

[14] Troeltsch, *The Social Teaching of the Christian Churches*, I: 66-8.
[15] H. R. Niebuhr, *The Responsible Self*, 58.

Interpretation and Responsibility

Niebuhr calls attention to the issue of suffering which tends to be undermined in moral theory or theological ethics. Human response to the suffering can be shaped by the interpretations of what he/she suffers. In response to suffering, people define themselves, taking on character and developing their ethos. It implies learning from suffering in terms of interpretation.

My response, which is the first element in the theory of responsibility, is a function of my interpretation of what is happening to me as well as the external actions or events upon me. An ethics of response does not begin with telos nor moral law, but with the question of the moral self in response-relations to the events.

Interpretation, which is the second element in the theory of responsibility, has to do with the question of what is going on, taking into responsibility in a fitting manner. This question at the meta-ethical level precedes the ought question (what shall I do?). The ethics cannot be brought properly within the teleological type ("man-the-maker") or the deontological type ("man-the-citizen"). Teleology deals with the question of what my goal or telos is concerning moral ontology underlying moral semantics. It concerns the highest good which subordinates the right into the good. The right in moral judgment is sought in the good.

Against this, deontology in the sense of Kant seeks to answer the moral inquiry in light of the right by asking what the first moral law is in my life. Duty or right is placed over the good or telos of virtue. The moral meaning or its semantics is sought in doing the right in the sense of deontology against the teleology.

In the deontology the moral self is associated with other selves in obedience to the laws or in respect for them. A human being as self-legislator lives as a moral self, first of all, in the presence of law, not other selves. The self exists in relation to other selves under the universally valid moral law in the form of a commandment, a demand, and requirement.[16] "Man-the-citizen" is no less than a human being the-self-legislator.

In distinction from deontology and teleology, Niebuhr takes the fitting action in response to become decisive in his ethics of responsibility. He allocates the fitness into a total interaction as response, which is conducive to the good and the right. It is one of the major contributions that Niebuhr has done in terms of moral epistemology in which interpretation precedes the good and the right.

A meta-ethical reasoning of interpretation gives a new impulse to public theology by facilitating the latter in engaging with diverse reality of public spheres in social stratification. Interpretation is involved in shaping and undergirding the fitting action. What is crucial in the idea of responsibility is response to external actions or events upon us through the interpretation in an appropriate manner. Human response becomes moral action, when interpreted with meaningful action in terms of the fittingness underlying the meaningful action. It is of subjective, emotive character in response.

The large patterns of interpretation influence or determine my response to action upon me. This refers to a type of a human being-the-responder or the interpreter, who includes the rational mind as well as feelings and intuitions. Responsive action is undertaken in accordance with interpretation of external factors and events, and in our responsibility we attempt to answer the question ("what shall I do?") by raising the prior question: "what is going on?" Then we interpret this question to answer the moral

---

[16] Ibid., 71.

question with accountability (the third element in the theory of responsibility).[17]

Here, I sense that Niebuhr employs the practical ends-means in asking about the purpose and fittingness, which would be compared to purpose rationality in Weber. If Weber sees the purpose rationality and its ethical attitude in fittingness or elective affinity with economic rationality in terms of responsibility, Niebuhr relates a teleological ethics to the purpose rationality in terms of fitting and foreseeing consequences, which continues to play a significant role in his interpretation of human response.

Responsibility and fittingness require a hermeneutical reflection and skill, in which the fitting rationality needs to be involved in a particular situation. These are not acquired as an objective skill like a techne, because a moral being does not exist outside the particular situation, when he/she is interpreting what is going on.

Given this, I critically renew Niebuhr's response ethics in terms of hermeneutical reflection in order to safeguard its leaning to instrumental rationality. According to Alasdair MacIntyre, an Aristotelian theory makes a crucial distinction between what any particular individual takes to be good for him/herself at any given time and what is really good for him/herself as a human being. For the sake of the latter, it is necessary to practice the virtues by making choices about means 'according to right reason' in order to achieve that end. This practice requires judgment, and the exercise of the virtues needs 'a capacity to judge and to do the right thing in the right place at the right time in the right way.'[18]

The virtues find their significance in the life of the city-state in which the individual becomes intelligible only as a political animal. In the exercise of the virtues as dispositions according to

---

[17] Ibid., 63.
[18] MacIntyre, *After Virtues*, 150.

right reason, a choice issues in right action in harmony with other and is reproduced in harmony with the city-state for realization of the common good.[19]

A teleological virtue ethics can be renewed in hermeneutical reflection, because it has a lack of historicity, in which human response comes to terms with human prudence. A human being as a social being grows and interacts with one another in terms of the fundamental end of society based on the common good. Aristotle may retain a hermeneutical relevance in his ethics in which reason plays the significant role in moral action. Reason and knowledge are not detached from a being which becomes independent of Plato's metaphysics; thus, Aristotle takes issue with the Platonic idea of the good as an empty generality.

Aristotle's major concern is with the question of what is humanly good in terms of human action. The basis of moral knowledge in human being is striving (orexis) in the development into a fixed demeanor. Elaborating ethics, Aristotle bases virtue (arête) on practice and ethos. A human being becomes what he/she is through what he/she does or how he/she behaves. Making a moral action and decision means doing the right thing in a particular situation, understanding what is right within that situation.

If one encounters the good in the particular practical situation through right behavior, the hermeneutical problem is involved in particular situation; the interpreter belongs to the tradition or history that he/she is understanding and interpreting. Understanding is a historical event. For Aristotle moral knowledge (phronesis) is not objective in contrast to theoretical knowledge (episteme), since the moral knower does not stand outside or over against a situation, but is involved in it as an acting agent. It is also an intellectual virtue which enables

---

[19] Ibid., 149.

someone to know what is due to him/her and 'how to exercise judgment in particular cases.'[20]

Intellectual virtues are acquired through instruction, while the virtue of character comes from habitual exercise according to right reason. These two entities are not separated from each other like Kant's distinction between reason, understanding, and natural experience.[21]

Moral knowledge includes the task of application which is central in the hermeneutical problem. Self-knowledge, knowledge for oneself, features the self-knowledge of moral consciousness in distinction from theoretical or technical knowledge (the model of techne as a real ort and skill of the craftsmen).[22]

A moral agent is always already in the life situation when applying moral knowledge. A concept of equity as the correction of the law is a necessary supplement to law, because human reality is necessarily imperfect in comparison with the order of the law. The idea of natural law remains indispensable and has only a critical function in the question of what is equitable. In the nature of the thing, or 'natural law,' there would be a space for free play within the confines of what is right.[23] It would be changeable with respect to the imperfection of all human laws rather than unchangeable.

Given this, moral knowledge has not merely particular end, rather it pertains to right living in social, moral, and political realms, since moral knowledge requires self-deliberation. In Aristotle, the right means is sometimes related to the end. His ethics of virtue proposes the true meaning, which is to be observed in human behavior and life in response to the demands

---

[20] Ibid., 154.
[21] Ibid.
[22] Gadamer, *Truth and Method*, 314-6.
[23] Ibid., 319.

of the situation. Knowledge of a particular situation becomes a necessary supplement to moral knowledge, which embraces means as well as ends; this runs counter to technical knowledge based on purposive rationality and fittingness from which the responsibility comes. The self-knowledge of moral reflection is elaborated in the phronesis, the virtue of thoughtful reflection, besides which sympathetic understanding stands.[24]

At this point, ethics of responsibility is framed within sympathetic understanding in modifying the virtue of moral knowledge in dealing with the concrete situation. An ethical phenomenon provides a model for the problem of hermeneutics in correlating moral knowledge with understanding in the particular situation.[25]

This hermeneutical insight into moral knowledge reinforces Niebuhr's responsible ethics in terms of sympathetic understanding and interpretation in the particular situation. Niebuhr entails an important side of dialogue in the intersubjective relation. Our responsible actions are made in anticipation of answers of the Other to us. An agent's action is likened to a statement in a mutual dialogue in the intersubjective context, and it fits into the previous statement; it is made in anticipation of reply of the Other through objections, confirmations, and corrections.

The agent's action is involved in the whole conversation, becoming a part of it going forward, and it has meaning as a whole. In this communicative context, the agent's action accepts the consequences in the form of reactions, interactions, and anticipations. The agent is held socially accountable for his/her acts.[26] The accountability in the anticipation of reaction

---

[24] Ibid., 322.
[25] Ibid., 324.
[26] H. R. Niebuhr, *The Responsible Self*, 64.

of the Other to our reaction leads to the fourth element of responsibility, namely, social solidarity. Our responsible action in continuing interaction among agents forms a continuing society.

In sum, the idea of responsibility may be defined as the idea of an agent's action as *response* (the first element of the responsibility) to an external actions or events upon the agent. Then it is undertaken in accordance with the *interpretation* (the second element of the responsibility) of his/her action. With the agent's interpretation of his/her response, the agent's act is held socially accountable (*accountability* as the third element of responsibility). All of this is held in a continuing society of agents in terms of *social solidarity* (the fourth element of the responsibility).[27]

Hermeneutical Clarification

Niebuhr's ethical theory of responsibility implies public ethics in terms of accountability and social solidarity in the context of an intersubjective, communicative sphere. It holds an important moment of sympathetic understanding and interpretation in the hermeneutical sense. Considered in the hermeneutical perspective, an interpretation of one's response to external action or effect (history, society, and culture) upon one's life is involved in one's existence in life setting. Life is given. One's moral self is already constituted and influenced by history and society, when he/she engages in a proper response to the external events in a self-reflective manner. One's language, which mediates the realm of meaningful action in the past to one's present response, shapes and determines the idea of responsibility in an ethical context through discourse rationality or meaningful action.

---

[27] Ibid., 65.

Moral ontology is linguistically constituted and engaged in intersubjective dialogue.

One's response has been influenced under the effect of history and cultural tradition, and it is expressed and explicated in social context through language; the moral knowledge and the idea of responsibility is shaped in the intersubjective conversation or social events. Interpretation in a fitting, self-reflective manner reinforces meaningful action rather than focusing upon purposiveness or universally valid law of the duty. Fusion of horizons among agents is undertaken in the communicative action, and the dialogue partners approach the consensus for mutual agreement and recognition in terms of accountability and social solidarity for common good and what is right in an open, approximate manner.

My understanding is enriched in the sematic circle through dialogical process and the horizon of my life-world is retrieved, fused and enlarged for synthesis of meaningful, moral action. This implies an ethical deliberation of givenness of life, in which life-world becomes the source for sympathetic understanding, interpretative rationality, and moral virtue of phronesis.

Niebuhr draws attention to the social character of all human life in the idea of responsibility, and to be a self in the presence of other selves is primordial. Thus, the self is fundamentally social and reflexive in its response to others, in which self exists in relation to others through dialogue with them. Niebuhr concurs with George H. Mead, who maintains that the self is essentially within a social structure, arising from social experience.[28] Niebuhr's pragmatist leaning entails a hermeneutical dimension in dealing with the responsible self.

Niebuhr is concerned with relating the social structure of the responsible self in time and history. My past is with me in

---

[28] Ibid., 72.

the present, as conscious and unconscious memory influencing my response when I meet with other selves. The future is also present in my now in terms of expectations and anxieties, or in anticipations and commitments, or in hopes and fears. Being a responsible self means living not only in the form of purposiveness, but also expectation, anticipation, anxiety and hope toward the future. The three tenses of the time refer to dimensions of the time-fullness of the responsible self.[29]

The full-time existence is in encounter with others, by response to the challenge from the others. My responding in the present is interpreting what acts upon me as an historical being; being in time becomes interpretive being.[30] Interpretation of present external actions upon myself is undertaken with reference to the past as well as the future. Responsiveness is embedded with time-full reality, historicity of the human being. Self-reflexive interpretation in our responses seeks to make itself fit into circumstances, the larger context. Herein, the interpretation of the present events can be modified with respect to the fittingness or un-fittingness rather than rightness or wrongness (deontology), goodness or badness (teleology).[31]

A broader framework of interpretation would encompass interest of deontology (respect for autonomy and justice) and teleological position of good, the means, and consequential principle of utility for the sake of fitness. Interpretation of responsible being can be comprehensive in integrating diversity of hyper-goods and moving from different principles to cases in order to guide action in terms of fitness.[32]

---

[29] Ibid., 93.
[30] Ibid., 98.
[31] Ibid., 97.
[32] Beauchamp and Childress, *Principles of Biomedical Ethics*.

Niebuhr incorporates Mead's social psychology into Martin Buber's philosophy of personal relation in the distinction between I-Thou and I-it relations. I in I-it relations is not a reflexive being, but I in I-Thou relation lives in responsive relations to Thou, who displays constancy in the actions toward the self. The reflexive self seeks to interpret the others' action or anticipate their reaction to mine, involved in an interpersonal, social context.

Niebuhr distinguishes his notion of social self from Kant's universal moral law in the form of duty or demand in anticipated and predictable ways. Niebuhr's concern is with persons as Thous, members of a system of interactions, rather than moral laws. Thus, he undertakes to develop the social understanding of conscience through I-Thou relations within the ethos of the society.[33] "I live in the presence of, and in response to, a Thou who is not an isolated event but symbolic in his particularity of something general and constant."[34]

Niebuhr paves an insight into public ethics in a hermeneutical frame of reference, in which our social self is based on the interpersonal dialogue within the ethos of society. The self is born in the womb of society and grows in its experience of a common world through education, interpersonal relations, dialogue, and accountability.[35] We are responsive, time-full beings which seek to reinterpret the past, engaging with history and tradition for the sake of a reconstruction of a past toward freshness and fittingness.[36]

"In the life of the self," Niebuhr emphasize, "responding to action upon it [self] in the present, freedom from the past or

---

[33] H. R. Niebuhr, *The Responsible Self*, 77-8.
[34] Ibid., 77.
[35] Ibid., 73.
[36] Ibid., 103.

newness of understanding and movement toward more fitting response does not come through the rejection of the past but through its reinterpretation...as a being in three tenses, the reconstruction of our past can be a large part of our hope for the future."[37]

If the ethical is framed in a reinterpretation of the past, it should include the history of what has been excluded and subjugated, because it shapes ethical attitude or response toward the reality of the vivid present, which runs counter to what is taken for granted in society and culture. One's response seeking the interpretation of other's interaction is placed in a larger spectrum, which I call a hermeneutical or semantic circle. Responsible action is on the approximation through fusion of horizons in the intersubjective relation and communication among the responsible agents as moral subjects.

Unless a critical mediation is undertaken between transcendental normative ethics and historical hermeneutic, the normative would be reduced to the authority of tradition. Such critical mediation requires responsible critique and emancipation from prejudices and obscurities from the ossified tradition. That which is taken for granted and unquestioned should be placed under scrutiny and problematization. This perspective helps to overcome imitation in Niebuhr's response ethics, which tends to belittle a social scientific analysis of what's going on; he does not fully manage to uphold responsible critique of and emancipation from what has been sedimented from tradition and culture. Life is given in society and culture, in which life-world is reified and encroached upon by power mechanism and ideological interpellation.

---

[37] Ibid., 104.

Phenomenology of Discourse

Ethics of responsibility can be reframed within sociological inquiry and hermeneutical reflection, which recasts discourse ethical reasoning of intersubjectivity in the communicative context through problematization, critique, emancipation, and social solidarity. A transcendental normative position should be enhanced and described in dealing with the reality of a human being-in-the-discourse, as historically affected and socially located.

Discourse is impregnated with material interests (politics, social-culture sphere, economic, and mass media), which are imbued with epistemic legitimacy, rationalization, and power relations. This perspective takes issue with a type of "man-the-interpreter," because the latter would be vulnerable to reality of impersonal forces in the public sphere. It is important to undertake a type of man-the-interpreter in a loaded manner through social scientific analysis of what's going on in reference to what is to be done against external events and power. Interpretation comes to terms with scientific analysis of social discourse and power relations.

What is crucial in the historical, sociological analysis of discourse is to differentiate discourse of representation (as hegemonic type) from moral discourse (as prophetic, charismatic type) in religious context. A morally inspired reasoning entails an anamnestic position in deciphering the regime of the vanished, the margins, or the subjugated through thickly describing; it make a conceptual clarity in dealing with the procedure of how discursive formation is made and its practice would produce a corpus of knowledge-power through dissemination and penetration into the entire body of society.

An anamnestic moral reasoning is concerned with horizon for the search of rupture, mutation, and transformation in the analysis of episteme underlying the mode of representation as the dominant system in a given society. An archeological analysis of hegemonic discourse serves to mobilize a moral reasoning of innocent victims in light of the Christian symbol of the kingdom of God, which has broken into our midst as prolepsis in Jesus' solidarity with *massa perditionis* (public sinners and tax collectors).

A moral interpretation does not undermine a textual analysis of types of religious discourse and material interests invested in power relations, while exploring the ethical semantic significance with emphasis on the original text.[38] Discourse (written and spoken) remains an undercurrent in constituting an ethical stance, which is adopted and developed through social scientific analysis of diverse types of discourse with reference to life-world.

What is missing in Niebuhr's responsive self is, however, the significance of language and discourse in the textual world. We engage in the interpretation of the classic texts for reconstruction of their moral significance in our present and for the project of the future. A responsive, historical being is a linguistic being enabling the interpretation of the past and the present for the future. Language is not merely transmitted through tradition and history affecting human consciousness, but also it is conditioned and even distorted by its symbolic power and violence in the society stratified in hierarchical and unequal manner.

It is necessary for public theology to analyze social effects (politics, economics, and mass media) upon hierarchy of language and social discourse; it has a critical function in dealing with ideologically distorted ream of communication, its manipulation and privilege in terms of problematization and critical distance,

---

[38] Foucault, *The Archaeology of Knowledge*, 221.

and emancipation. Interpretation of religious text helps one to adopt a moral value in response to the external event. This aspect forms an indispensable part of public ethics in terms of a human being-in-the-discourse.

2. Responsible Self and the Other

The discursive perspective improves and relocates Niebuhr's reflection of responsible being as a moral being in recognition of the dignity of the Other in the light of God. To say 'God' means to say 'good' in our common speech and idiom, because the word 'God' implies the affirmer of our being.[39] In our interpretation of "in what society and in what time do we make our responses to immediate external events and actions upon us," we are related to the transcendent One, center and source of all existence.[40]

Our responsibility is in absolute dependence upon a Deity. Niebuhr's responsibility maxim maintains: "God is acting in all actions upon you. So respond to all actions upon you as to respond to his action."[41] The fitting act entails a religious dimension, when we as interpreting agents engage in the enlarging society and time-fullness of our historical being. One's religious thoughts and practices have come to me as a historical being in society through parents, society, church, and the culture, in which one's responses can be more fitting, as fit into in the whole spectrum.[42]

One's responsible self does not exist outside the givenness of society and time, but with its life-world. The responsible being finds its meaningful action and rationality in interpreting

---

[39] H. R. Niebuhr, *The Responsible Self*, 119.
[40] Ibid., 124-5.
[41] Ibid., 126.
[42] Ibid., 109. 119.

the meaning of the Others' action and allowing for the Others to speak of themselves. In Niebuhr's understanding of the self as social, "We respond as we interpret the meaning of actions upon us."[43] It can be reinforced and sharpened in a way that we respond as we interpret the meaning of the Other acting upon us in reference of God, while living in response-relations to other selves through dialogue, accountability, and social solidarity.

Niebuhr shows a parallel with Emmanuel Levinas' ethics of responsibility. Levinas articulates responsibility for the Other without waiting for reciprocity. I am in subjection to the Other. The structure of subjectivity in the essential, primary, and fundamental sense is defined in ethical terms, because the subjectivity is initially in hostage for the Other.[44]

In the substitution or hostage for the Other, Levinas articulates the heart of responsibility. Because transcendence is ethics rather than implying a transcendental I, subjectivity is defined as a responsibility for the Other, in other words, a subjection to the Other.[45]

To approach the Other in conversation is to welcome his/her expression in its ethical relation, and it is to receive from the Other; the idea of the infinity in me.[46] The saying in the conversation is a way of greeting the Other. According to Levinas, "ethics is not a moment of being," because "to be good is excellence and elevation beyond being," otherwise than being,[47] which refers to the glory of God. In this ethical reversal the transcendence

---

[43] Ibid., 63.
[44] Levinas, *Ethics and Infinity*, 95-101.
[45] Levinas, "God and Philosophy," in *Emmanuel Levinas Basic Philosophical Writings*, 140.
[46] Levinas, *Totality and Infinity*, 51.
[47] Levinas, "God and Philosophy," in *Emmanuel Levinas Basic Philosophical Writings*, 141.

of God is with an alterity, whereas God's illeity turns into my responsibility for the Other.[48]

Here, I observe that Levinas employs a basic feature of Jewish mysticism in which the faithful one begins by saying to God 'Thou' and concludes the prayer with 'He'. Levinas calls this 'He' the illeity of the Infinite. Ethics as substitution for the Other breaks up the unity of transcendental apperception (synthesis of the self and the objects through categories in Kantian sense) in conditioning and understanding all being and all experience. This position takes into account the inspiration and prophesying in which the Infinite passes and awakens in an ethical way.[49]

If ethics goes beyond human being and is seen in terms of the illeity of God, an interpretation requires freedom of God in solidarity with the Other. It refers to phenomenology of ethics concerning God *totaliter aliter* in the self-manifestation through the face of the Other in society and culture. The self is placed with the Other existing in the public networks of social relationships. God is met with my ethical responsibility for the Other rather than my ontological reasoning.

An ethical question turns into a question of how to interpret an expressing the moral self in the response-relations to the givenness of the Other. Moral self is bound to the face of Other in the intersubjective relation, entering into the social reality of situated interactions and validity. Moral reason is embodied in responsibility, and the self is situated in interaction with the Other; the responsible self has little to do with the transcendental subject, which is free of the life of the Other.

---

[48] Levinas, *Ethics and Infinity*, 106.
[49] Ibid., 146-7.

Communicative Rationality and the Other

Language or social discourse is socially stratified in a hierarchical and unequal manner, in which the social scheme of knowledge comes to terms with power relations. The Other under divine illeity cannot be reduced into communicative rationality in its ideal of speech act.

According to Habermas, the discourse theory of truth, morality, and law is comprehended as a response in the post-metaphysical stance in which participants engage in rational discourse as a form of communication. It is performed by the normative content of argumentation, with pragmatic presuppositions; inclusivity, equal distribution of communicative freedoms, trustfulness, and absence of contingent external constraints or within the structure of communication.[50]

The universal validity or the principle of universalization (U) becomes a general, transcultural binding force for practice of argumentation in which the communicative practice is realized only in the epistemic dimension of testing validity claims and trustfulness. Co-responsibility is sought in this rational discourse for the practice of argumentation.

Granted the four validity claims (claims for factual truth, moral rightness, veracity, and comprehensibility) are required for the consensual agreement in the process of communication, but communicative rationality should not be placed over anamnestic rationality, insofar as communication unfolds within the ethical frame of reference. Reason is constructed as an historical product, which is operative within life-world without dissolving it into historical relativism. The presence of the Other as victim (in the regime of effective history against marching dominant

---

[50] Habermas, *Between Naturalism and Religion*, 82.

history) takes issue with grounding reason in the trans-historical and universal structure of communicative rationality.

Language as social discourse is to be seen as a medium of power relations and symbolic domination in terms of the social conditions and hierarchy. For instance, a linguistic interaction between a WASP and a Black American is constrained in the structural relations (such as gender, level of education, class origins, ethnicity) intervened in communicative action.[51]

An invocation of the poor or the disadvantaged in the global South does not violate the transcendental normative position, but awakens the member of the privileged community and its self-critical rationality for undertaking responsibility, recognition, and solidarity with those who are not communicatively competent and disadvantaged.

However, theological ethics of responsibility is grounded in God's Saying rather than the post-metaphysical principle for universal validity and rational argumentation. The Other (the poor, the widow, children, the alien) is protected in divine command rather than invited to rational argumentations for validity claims. It shapes the communicative reason in accordance with the face of the destitute and disadvantaged in the public space. Givenness of the Other and their life-world de-transcendentalizes the self and its rational argument, because the Other is not shared with the life-world of the self, but marginalized and foreclosed in the historical march of rationalization on the part of the self.

As Levinas writes, "the exposition of the ethical signification of transcendence and of the Infinite beyond being can be worked out beginning with the proximity of the neighbor and my responsibility for the other (autrui)."[52]

---

[51] Bourdieu and Wacquant, *An Invitation to Reflexive Sociology*, 143.

[52] Levinas, "God and Philosophy," in *Emmanuel Levinas Basic Philosophical Writings*, 141.

His ethical perspective is of theocentric character, yet with an ethical commitment to the other in prophetic orientation. Our responsibility for the Other is a way of testifying to the glory of the Infinite through inspiration. Prophetism and inspiration underlying the responsibility answers for the Other, in which he elevates the responsibility to be God's revelation. The Bible is the outcome of prophecies with ethical testimony ("Here I am") which testifies to the Infinite and comes to terms with responsibility for the Other.[53]

God and the Prophetic Moral

The God of the Bible signifies the beyond being, in other words, transcendence of the God of Abraham, Isaac, and Jacob, who cannot be reduced to the ontology or philosophical rationalism.[54] Saying as testimony glorifies the glory of the Infinite, and bears witness to the other of the Infinite, which awakens me for the responsibility in the Saying. In this way, language earns an ethical significance rather than the doubling up of thought and being. Saying is the testimony of this responsibility for the Other prior to all experience, while the Infinite speaks through my mouth.[55]

If Levinas comprehends subjectivity or responsible self as the temple of the transcendence, his understanding of transcendence takes on an ethical meaning for responsibility in relation to God, prophetic testimony, and the Other. The Other is not idealized, but belongs to the realm of divine commandment ("Thou shall not kill"). This is a commandment in the appearance of the face, in which the Other as face is of ethical character in a straightaway

---

[53] Levinas, *Ethics and Infinity*, 115.
[54] Levinas, "God and Philosophy," 131.
[55] Ibid., 145.

sense. "In the access to the face there is certainly also an access to the idea of God."[56]

Ethics as a first philosophy comes to terms with theological deontology within the framework of God's illeity and the Other. It is required for moral interpretation in regard to responsibility, recognition, and social solidarity with deontological precept of non-murdering of the Other in the neocolonial context, which is beset by innocent victims and institutionalized violence. It is of trans-ontological character constituting language with ethical significance ("Thou shall not kill").

Levinas' phenomenological inquiry into ethics of the Other as the ethics of all ethics[57] relocates ontological ethics within a different index, coming into tension with Kant's metaphysics of the moral, while radicalizing its historical vision of hospitality from the standpoint of the Other. Ethical hermeneutics becomes feasible within the reinterpretation of responsible self in reference to Levinas and Kant, in which the Other occupies a central role under illeity of the Infinite or kingdom of God.

Levinas' responsible self is of a theocentric character within an ethical frame of reference through prophetic inspiration. It does not necessarily contrast with Niebuhr's radical monotheism underlying responsible self through interpretation, responsibility and social solidarity. The difference between Niebuhr and Levinas is rather seen in that the former is based on the rationality of fittingness in Jesus Christ, while the latter on the 'saying' action of God by awakening and inspiring me to ethical responsibility in the face of the Other. The transcendence of God begins in a cry of prophetic, ethical revolt which bears witness to responsibility.[58]

---

[56] Levinas, *Ethics and Infinity*, 92.
[57] Derrida, "Violence and Metaphysics," in *Writing and Difference*, 35-39.
[58] Levinas, "God and Philosophy," 147.

Levinas' ethic is biblically inspired through prophetic witness through Saying. But Niebuhr is philosophically informed and comprehends a biblical ethos which represents the historical form of the Christian life. In fact, Niebuhr's Christian moral philosophy is of a theistic character, and it is grounded in the biblical idea of radical monotheism. He is concerned with exploring the intentions of God in hiddenness yet present in the actions of Israel in relation to its enemy. He maintains that Israel sees and understands the action of God in everything that happens, and Israel makes a fitting reply.

Niebuhr affirms his basic principle of correlation in the life of Israel: "What is happening?" in connection with "What is the fitting response to what is happening?" This is relevant to Jesus in the New Testament, who teaches God's rule hidden in the manifold activities of plural agencies and interprets the signs of the times.[59]

3. H. R. Niebuhr: Sin and Salvation

Niebuhr advances his theological conception of sin and salvation in a theistic frame of reference. In the image of a human being-the-maker, he comprehends the human sinful condition as alienation, or hamartia (the missing of the mark). It has less to do with transgression of the law in the deontological sense than the perverse drive in human beings. The fundamental evil is conflict within or a life which is meant by its internal entelechy (or perfection through activity toward a goal). Its native drive is to be whole and complete whether in personal life, or social or universal realm.[60]

---

[59] Ibid., 67.
[60] H. R. Niebuhr, *The Responsible Self*, 132.

A human being wants to be like God by being his/her own maker, not merely in the knowledge of good and evil. Aspiration after godhead leads to self-destruction as well as the destruction of others. What distinguishes the teleological version of the Christian story of fall from the deontologist is a human surrender to the temptation to aspire after godhead. It has less to do with the disobedience to divine commandment or guilt than loss and confusion, which is the consequence of the first sin.

The ultimate form of good is lost to view, while the great attractive goal is removed. Salvation comes with the restoration of a goal in the vision of God to a human being that has been lost. That is the reflected image of God in the human being. The self, which is healed from its diseased powers, is granted to move again toward perfection. The self is enabled by the actualization of the power to see God and to live in God's likeness. The hope of eternal life, the vision of God and the image of God are communicated to the human self through word and sacrament. What becomes crucial in the teleological approach is characterized by God seen, known and loved as well as the perfection of the seer, or deification.[61]

Christian teleological interpretation, which is concerned with the life as aspiration toward the vision and the image of God, differs from the deontological position concerned with the problem of law and gospel. According to Niebuhr, the theory of teleology, whether Christian or philosophical, is grounded in the primacy of the human pursuit toward the ideal good. However, it is difficult for such direction to be reconciled with the primacy of *God*'s action, which reveals God's self by divine goodness rather than being found by the search. There is a contradiction at

---

[61] Ibid., 133-4.

the point to which the human being-the maker is combined into the image of God the creator.[62]

Niebuhr seeks to interpret Christian human experience as agents (sinful yet saved) in the analysis of response in order to cut through the limitations of teleology and deontology. When obedience to the divine commandment is seen as response to an action upon us, it would avoid the problem centering on law and gospel in the deontological sense. The problem of obedience and disobedience depends on how we interpret the intention of the commander rather than our understanding of the law itself. The gospel is the divine declaration which requires human response, and this response is defined as confidence and loyalty rather than obedience.

On the other hand, teleological problems would be overcome, insofar as we regard all human making as response to prior action; one takes the future-directed movement in human life in terms of eschatology rather than purely teleological. The conflict between "man-the-maker" and "man-the-citizen" (obedient man) would be resolved when they are regarded as responders. The interpretative scheme based on the human being-the-responder seeks to comprehend human being in sin and salvation.[63]

Reality of Impersonal Forces

What is distinguished in Niebuhr's analysis of response and responsibility is to avoid the reality of "the war of all against all," because he acknowledges that 'I' have many interests, many potential actions in relation to the world of the agents. Manifold interests and conflicts would make us irresponsible. Niebuhr draws attention to a biblical imagery of principalities and powers,

---

[62] Ibid., 135.
[63] Ibid., 136-7.

the rulers of the darkness of this world to whom humans are subordinated.[64]

In Niebuhr's account, such mythological reality refers to the system of impersonal forces (such as "the system of society, the customs and the mores, the large organizations of economic and cultural activities"),[65] which is powerful, neither good nor evil. We live in it and must adjust ourselves to it and be responsive to it. They are called vaguely "climates of opinion, or spirits of civilization." Considered in social systems, they are named as "feudalism, industrialism, capitalism, communism, [and] nationalism."[66]

The reality of "superpersonal forces of evil" (Walter Rauschenbusch) exercises dominion over us, but Niebuhr argues that they are not all evil powers nor devils. Thus, his recommendation is that we must adjust or accommodate our actions to these powers in terms of the fittingness into their action.[67]

Resistance and Impersonal Forces

Where do we find our responsibility in protest to the evil reality of the impersonal forces? Niebuhr seems to be despairing, because he sees the One always present to us even in our sin. This refers to his understanding of reconciliation. However, Niebuhr does not manage to comprehend the biblical meaning of reconciliation through Jesus Christ by differentiating it from the unreconciled reality of impersonal forces.

In theological conception of reconciliation and *theologia crucis*, public theology elucidates a prophetic ethics of reconciliation in

---

[64] Ibid., 138.
[65] Ibid., 139.
[66] Ibid.
[67] Ibid.

taking issue with the reality of impersonal forces in public spheres. The church must concentrate first the poor or the Other as the object of the primary concern and social justice in the political sphere through solidarity grounded in its greatest measure.

Certainly, we do not undermine the positive factors of capitalist revolution, which plays as the motor of society in becoming the hidden wire pullers in the great and small enterprise, movement, production, technological revolution. But there are also factors in the evolution and obstruction of the completely personal lives of individual humans. The reality of impersonal forces works in the field of politics, economic, culture, and ecology. Public theology engages with social scientific analysis of biopolitical governance, economic system of injustice, ideological interpellation, ecological sustainability, and racial justice in democratic, pluralist society.

On the contrary, Niebuhr has a lack of conceptual clarity regarding the biblical imagery of reconciliation. He simply argues that we live and move and have our being in a realm of the impersonal forces ruled by destructive power.[68]

Given this, I perceive that Niebuhr's theocentric stance, initiated by Paul's position before Areopagus, turns into an accommodation to the reality of unreconciled powers and principalities. "The One beyond the many is the enemy, the creative source whence comes destruction."[69] In sin we live before God as enemy which is unknown as God or good, and it is unrecognized as love-worthy and loving.[70]

However, Niebuhr's standpoint tends to betray the radical monotheist faith in God who entered through Jesus Christ into the realm of sin under the impersonal forces, as the victim. In the realm of sin, when we are enemies of God, God still loves us.

---

[68] Ibid., 140
[69] Ibid.
[70] Ibid., 142.

According to Paul, nothing can separate us from the love of God in Christ (Rom 8:38-39).

Niebuhr's theocentric stance is of a philosophical character imbued with the monism, rather than consistently grounded in a Christological sense. Certainly, Niebuhr is aware of three options: ignoring, fighting, and appeasing regarding the supernatural forces as enemy. The courageous fighting against such overwhelming power is rare, while an ignoring or forgetting attitude is most usual in our unreconciled existence in devotion to all the little gods. We practice our special cults and turn away from ourselves for appeasing to the power of destruction.[71]

Niebuhr perceives that all human righteousness in loyalty to societies or other causes has been infected with anxiety, defensiveness, and hidden rebellion against the One, but this network of interaction was ruled by fear of God the enemy. This body of death characterizes the wretchedness of the human condition in light of reconciliation.

Nonetheless, Niebuhr sees in the context of life-giving in a universal teleology of resurrection the possibility of redemption in his interpretation against the negative counterpart.[72] Our response to commandments is given with the promise of life, moving our interaction into destruction toward universal, eternal life. The ethics of life begins with open society and future by replacing the ethics of death.

Niebuhr maintains that we have been led to metanoia through the life, death, and resurrection of Jesus Christ. Death appears as act of mercy in the responsive and responsible existence. The process of reconciliation has begun through metanoia in transition of death toward life and its completion is our hope, telos, and eschaton. The responsible self in Christ is a universally

---

[71] Ibid., 141.
[72] Ibid., 143.

and eternally responsive I. The self responds "to the action of the One who heals all our diseases, forgives all our iniquities, saves our lives from destruction, and crowns us with everlasting mercy."[73]

The action in Jesus' life is going beyond all laws responsible and fitting action "into the context of universal, eternal, life-giving action by the One" for salvation.[74] If God's reconciliation took place and has begun with metanoia, wouldn't the responsible ethics of fittingness correspond to our discipleship in taking issue with the reality of impersonal forces?

In Niebuhr's transition from God the enemy to God the friend, I find it important to interpret the imagery of God the enemy in the relation between a human being and death-creating power of the law in accordance with Luther's teaching of justification and God's righteousness. Once we are justified, we are called to participate in the public realm by serving others. Law-gospel dialectics is imbued with God's universal reign in the reconciled world. *Theologia crucis* is more than fitting rationality, because it points to restorative justice in solidarity with the victim under reality of impersonal forces in late capitalism.

This perspective contrasts with Niebuhr's identification of God the enemy in principalities and powers. If the ethics of reconciliation has begun through Jesus Christ and our conversion to his gospel about the kingdom of God, Christian ethics brings home to us that Jesus Christ reins as the Lord of the world in protesting and defeating the reality of impersonal forces in light of the coming of God's kingdom. Reconciliation is an ethical basis for proleptic discipleship.

Indeed, Niebuhr acknowledges that Jesus Christ lives and reigns and is powerful over us and among us through the

---

[73] Ibid., 144-5.
[74] Ibid., 145.

resurrection. The responsible and fitting action of Jesus is based on forgiveness, healing, and everlasting mercy. Nonetheless, his theistic reasoning fails to locate Jesus' life-giving action and our responsible self within Jesus' eschatological history in fighting against the power and principalities in our midst; we are summoned to participate in his fighting history. A responsible self in faithfulness to Jesus' ethic needs to take into account eschatological hope for a new heaven and a new earth. The eschatological dimension of Christian ethics remains restrained in Niebuhr's theocentric stance.

Niebuhr's passivity is seen in his recommendation of human subjection to principalities and powers in the New Testament as systems of forces, politics, economy, society, culture, ethos, and nature. All of these are partly objective as well as partly subjective, referring to spirits of civilizations which exercise dominion over us. They are not all evil powers, but some forms of them can be called superpersonal forces of evil.

Niebuhr articulates reconciliation in ways that the Deity was and is always present to us even in our sin, at the same time as enemy. We live and move and have our being in a realm ruled by a destructive power. If the radical One beyond the many is the enemy to human being, the creative source comes from destruction.[75] We must adjust ourselves to One and are responsive to One as the maker as well as destroyer through appeasement. This monotheistic stance contrasts with the biblical notion of radical monotheism in the covenant history of Israel and in the revelation of Jesus Christ, which is prophetically inspired.

What Niebuhr sees through the reconciliation is the body of death, in other words, the wretchedness of the human condition ruled by fear of God the enemy. Through Jesus Christ we have been led to metanoia, because he lives and is powerful over us

---

[75] Ibid., 140

and among us. The ethics of the reconciled maintains that the process of reconciliation has begun, and the completion is our hope, telos, and eschaton. "The responsible self ...in Christ... is a universally and eternally responsive I" "to the action of the One who heals all our diseases, forgives all our iniquities, saves our lives from destruction, and crowns us with everlasting mercy."[76]

If so, shouldn't Niebuhr reframe the responsible ethics within a proleptic understanding of reconciliation through *theologia crucis* and resurrection, which calls for metanoia from impersonal forces and upholds discipleship to Gospel ethics? This perspective transcends the fitting rationality and response.

However, Niebuhr sees in Jesus Christ the fitting action, "which is fitted into the context of universal, eternal, life-giving action by the One."[77] In confronting the reality of impersonal forces, Niebuhr introduces three different attitudes: "ignoring, fighting, and appeasing"[78] In Niebuhr's account, reconciliation is not conceptualized as an ethical basis against the superpersonal forces of evil, but in terms of appeasement or adjustment to them. Niebuhr regards such attitude of fighting to be rare among us. It implies a despairing attitude, which is built on Niebuhr's responsible ethics

Concluding Remark

Christian moral philosophy has a sociological character and epistemological attitude calling for critical, scholarly research of human responses to external events. Under presupposition of givenness of life an ethic always implies the formation of an ethical tradition, and also involves the construction of such tradition in

---

[76] Ibid., 144-5.
[77] Ibid., 145.
[78] Ibid., 141.

a new and creative manner in response to social relevancy and contemporary pressing issue.

Considered in the phenomenological perspective, ethical thought can be articulated at the reflexive level as well as at the practical level by upholding the correlation between ethical consciousness and its meaningful action; this ethical epistemology remains an undercurrent in the relation between God *totaliter aliter* and the Other for moral semantic. Morality as a theoretical or reflexive science correlates with meaningful regime under influence of life-world, which is embodied as practice for and from the Other under God's illeity.

There is practical intentionality in regard to ethical meaning, which requires a meta-ethical stance for good beyond being. Moral self or its ontology is embodied in God's command in protection of the destitute, the poor, the widow, and the children. The good and the right attain the status of the meaningful discourse in terms of interpretation in social scientific frame of reference, as engaged in reality of human being-in-the-discourse.

A suspension of what is taken for granted concerning impersonal forces leads to problematizing what has been excluded and sidestepped by the self in relation to the Other, the irreducible. A social scientific analysis is undertaken in taking on discourse and material interests enmeshed in their power relations through institutional ratification, biopolitical governance, social economic rationalization, and judiciary legitimacy in diverse fields in civil society.

The Other is affirmed as prior, or anterior to oneself, because it refuses the irrational myth accompanying modernity and justifying its logic of colonialism in the name of development and capital accumulation. The life-world of the Other, which is displaced and silenced, comes to terms with trace under God the *totaliter aliter*, who continues to address through the face of the Other. It seeks to clarify the basis and ground of public theology and discourse ethics through the phenomenological method, in other words, ethical framework in phenomenological inquiry for semantic retrieval of responsibility, recognition, and emancipation.[79]

The Other should be an Indian, an Africa, and an Asian in their respective concrete manifestations. The reality of victims is seen as inflicted by Stalin, Hitler, or totalitarian figures who continue to perpetuate its logic of violence upon the Other in the periphery in postcolonial condition. Against this domination, the Hebrew word *dabar* (speak, talk, and reveal) entails prophetic reasoning in its anamnestic solidarity with those afflicted. *Analogia verbi* in God's speech act comes to terms with *analogia fidei* in its discipleship to the gospel of reconciliation, which is grounded in anamnestic frame of *theologia crucis*.

It is important to synthesize a meta-ethical position of interpretation with social scientific analysis of social discourse and power relations. Ethics of responsibility finds its significance in taking issue with the represented Other in Eurocentric discourse as inferior, backward, and irrational. It reacts against the Christian form of missionary universalism, as obviously seen in the Spanish *conquistadores* with the indigenous American culture, or modern politics of imperialism.

Dussel writes: "The Philosophy of Liberation affirms reason as a faculty capable of establishing a dialogue, an intersubjective discourse with the reason of the Other as an alternative reason. In our time, it is this reason that denies the irrational moment of the 'sacrificial Myth of Modernity,' in order to affirm (take up into a liberating project) the rational, emancipatory

---

[79] Ferrarello, *Husserl's Ethics and Practical Intentionality*, 4.

moment of the Enlightenment and of Modernity, but now a Trans-Modernity."[80]

In fact, the dialectics of enlightenment carried out an irrational myth producing under-modernity in the peripheral colonial world. Exploited victims are covered with an argument for the myth of progress in terms of rationalization and modernization at the expense of the Other. A project of liberation must transcend and deconstruct such a myth of capitalism and its neocolonialism in preference for a trans-modernity, which is featured by ecological civilization, popular democracy, civil society, and economic justice.

Unlike Liberation philosophy, however, I look for moral epistemology by appropriating phenomenological attitudes and its dialectical character, in other words, in the problematic way of thinking. For Husserl, ethical consciousness and practice can be constituted from the regime of the Other (the unthought), which entails an epistemology of liberating our ethical attitude from obscurities and prejudices 'arising out of a sedimentation of tradition.'[81]

It implies the ethics of responsibility and emancipation on the basis of self-reflection and critical attitude in dealing with the human being-in-the-discourse in history and society. Thus, we are "to carry out a responsible critique...which has its ground in these historical, personal projects, partial fulfillments, and exchanges of criticism."[82]

Along with the ethical tradition, ethical theory always implies a social world in its openness to differing interpretations, in which our moral consciousness and practice are interrelated with and

---

[80] Dussel, *The Invention of the Americas*, 203; see Barber, *Ethical Hermeneutics*, 76.
[81] Husserl, "Elements of a Science of the Life-World," in *The Essential Husserl*, 362.
[82] Ibid.

moves within the influence of life-world. The general question of 'what is going on' should be met with the specific question of 'what is God doing in society and world' for recognition, responsible critique, self-reflection, and emancipation.

A biblical discourse of reconciliation has little to do with accommodation to the pathology of impersonal forces in the teleological sense of fittingness but is of deontic character in response to God's grace and justice through the proleptic discipleship in the anamnestic frame of *theologia crucis*. The face of the Other colonized and reified awakens the self to recognition, solidarity, and emancipation in dealing with neocolonial condition between metropolis and periphery.

Chapter 3.

Colonialism, Hegel's Dialectics, and Empire

A postcolonial study of Hegel finds its significance in a global theory of Empire in which Christian public theology can be featured in an ethical discussion of life-world and effective history for and from the subaltern. This chapter begins by examining Frantz Fanon's reading of Hegel in an Algerian context, focusing on a dialectical model of struggle between master and slave in terms of recognition and struggle. In furthering a sociological reading of Hegel's texts, I bring him to dialogue with Foucault, while characterizing Hegel as the intellectual 'Caliban' for Christian public theology.

In so doing, I enter into an interrogation with Hegel through the anamnestic reasoning of *theologia crucis* and effective history. This endeavor seeks a hermeneutical skill in critically synthesizing Hegel's theory of recognition with Walter Benjamin's messianic rupture.

In the discussion of the biopolitical approach, it is useful to appropriate Foucault's genealogy in explicating the colonial order of things. Hegel's dialectics of recognition can be complemented in biopolitical formation in which I undertake a sociological, genealogical explication in scrutinizing problems, such as colonial racism, slavery, and death politics in African apocalypse (*Heart of Darkness*—Joseph Conrad). Further discussion is made to analyze the Black experience of racism and biopolitical lynching in the American context.

At last, I am concerned with the significance of Hegel's dialectics and hegemony with reference to a global theory of Empire. Hegel's negative dialectics should be emphasized in critical interrogation with theory of hegemony (Antonio Gramsci) and dictatorship. Then I deal with Rousseau's reading of Machiavelli with republican democratic significance, seeking to mediate Hegel's theory of State and popular legislative model (J. J. Rousseau) for the sake of postcolonial civil state. Excursus is a critical study of religion and colonialism by involving the legacy of Bartolome de Las Casas (1484-1566) for Christian public theology with postcolonial implications.

1. Postcolonial Hegel: Recognition and Struggle

Hegel is read in the French colonial context in Algeria. By 1848 the French government of the Second Republic occupied nearly all of northern Algeria and organized it as French local administrative units under a civilian government. A French person born and living in Algeria during the period of French rule was called a 'colon' (colonist) or, more popularly, *pieds noirs* (literally, black feet). This refers to a French type of settler colonialism in Algeria (between 1830 and 1962), and within the first three decade (1830-1860) it is estimated that between five hundred thousand and one million Algerians were killed on account of war, massacre, disease and famine.

During and after the Algerian War (1954-62), about one million *pieds-noirs* (including Algerian Jews) were evacuated to mainland France. This community continues to appear as the boomerang effect in French society today.¹ Politically, the Muslim Algerians (nearly nine million versus roughly one million *pieds-noirs*) are disposed, displaced, and depersonalized, and had no representation in the French National Assembly until 1945.

In 1953, Fanon became head of the psychiatry department at the Blida-Joinville Hospital in Algeria, where the war for independence broke out. Fanon was horrified by the stories of torture from his patients — both French torturers and Algerian torture victims. Social antagonism in the colonial order of things led Fanon to realize impossibility of his work as a colonial psychiatrist. "If psychiatry is the medical technique that aims to enable man no longer to be a stranger to his environment, I owe it to myself to affirm that the Arab, permanently an alien in his own country, lives in a state of absolute depersonalization…The social structure existing in Algeria was hostile to any attempt to put the individual back where he belonged."²

In 1956 he resigned his post with the French government to work for the Algerian cause. Fanon explores Hegel's dialectical model of struggle between master and slave for recognition, emphasizing an aspect of struggle based on life and death. An indispensable moment of mutual recognition is out of question, because colonialism creates Manichean delirium with its binary opposition. However, recognition in Hegel's genuine concern should be undertaken on the part of the colonized after the overthrowing of the dominant. What does the Black man want in relation to the white master? This desire requires dis-alienate him effectively from political, social, economic, cultural realities in settler colony, which continues to produce the inferiority

---

1   Hubbell, *Remembering French Algeria*, 7.
2   Fanon, *Black Skin*, ix.

of the black, in other words, the epidermalization of the black inferiority.[3]

In the discussion of the Negro and Hegel, Fanon is concerned with recognition by the other being that one's own human worth depends. "At the foundation of Hegelian dialectic there is an absolute reciprocity which must be emphasized."[4] For the right of recognition, the master and the slave are engaged in a fierce struggle by risking life and death for freedom, recognition, and emancipation. The struggle in creation of the reciprocal world of mutual recognition is featured in a direction toward alterity in rupture, conflict, and battle.[5]

Hegel accentuates the significance of prestige struggle in the process of humanization. In the historical progress a human being would be able to eliminate such system of domination and comes to realize the ideal of freedom. The citizen of the universal homogeneous state has not yet reached its satisfaction in the desire of recognition, nor is it identical with the last man in the fashion of Nietzsche.[6]

The colonial reality is characterized by the boomerang effect in counter violent or aggressiveness against the European subject. The boomerang effect reacts against the colonial perpetuation of the violence from above.[7] Its effect continues to appear in the aftermath of colonialism in the community of *pieds noirs* in suffering desire for a lost homeland in Algeria.

To combat the dialectic of colonialism, the colonized are given a space for themselves to understand their existence, dignity, and otherness with respect to language and cultural formation under their own life-world. One's world is expressed by the language,

---

[3] Ibid., 13.
[4] Ibid., 217.
[5] Ibid., 222.
[6] Kojeve, *Hegel*, xi-xii.
[7] Hardt and Negri, *Empire*, 131.

because it is 'the god gone astray in the flesh' (Paul Valery).[8] Language is a tool of power and cultural prejudice in dependence on color of skin.

Hybridity and Mimicry

Postcolonial legacy continues to address the colonial hangover in our midst, in other words, it refers to boomerang effect or colonial nightmare. We have seen a reality of colonial racism in Fanon's analysis of black skins and white masks, in which the black has a desire of mimicry to become like the European white. French colonial modernity in Algeria is undertaken in a violent project of massive destruction, transformation, and replacement in the multi-layered ways.[9] If postcolonial theory is concerned with the dialectic of recognition in the effective history of the margins, the racially mixed groups are important signifier in a better understanding of process of colonialism and decolonization toward the postcolonial society of recognition and difference.

The French reality of *pieds noirs* is buried in collective amnesia in erasure of traces in the past colonial condition between parentheses in modern period of the French society (1963-1981). Their collective memory in modern France and their movement in literature, film, association, and communal memories have de-stabilized postcolonial French society from 1962 to the present. Their suffering reality for a lost homeland, return, and recognition can be in no way generalized into a parasite type of existence of the settler broker in imperial vocation in universal-abstract sense.[10]

---

[8] Fanon, *Black Skin*, 18.
[9] Hannoum, *Violent Modernity*.
[10] Hubbell, *Remembering French Algeria*, ix. 5-6.

On the other hand, British colonialism has also left its fissure or traces on the British Indian diaspora or Anglo-Indian community of the mixed race between Indo-European population, which has arisen out of the European trading and imperial presence in India. The British Indian community is vulnerable to postcolonial British discrimination. Anglo-Indians were placed in an intermediary position between Indians and Domiciled Europeans within the Raj's socio-racial hierarchy.[11]

A developmental-assimilating logic of colonial modernity and its imperialist capitalism was crucial in British colonial rule in India. India was a great market and provider of raw materials for the British Empire to solve the problem of overproduction through the industrial revolution and expand its subsequent capitalist revolution.

In the technological annexation of India to the western world, the internal dynamic net of railways, locomotion, machinery, irrigation, and communication system among other things are all established in infrastructure by destruction of Indian society to replace. India was endowed with the railway-system—the forerunner of modern industry—with an exclusive view to "extracting at diminished expenses the cotton and other raw materials for their manufactures."[12]

In the settler colonialism, it is worthwhile to unveil "the profound hypocrisy and inherent barbarism of bourgeois civilization," to the naked colonies. An exploitative system of the East India Company would face a boomerang effect, which is connected with an expectation of a great social revolution. Human imperialist progress must "cease to resemble that hideous

---

[11] Charlton-Stevens, "Decolonizing Anglo-Indians, 355.
[12] Marx, "The Future Results of British Rule in India," *Karl Marx Selected Writings*, 334.

pagan idol, who would not drink the nectar but from the skulls of the slain."[13]

Along with this colonial project of modernity, the Christian religion and the Social Darwinist version of imperial racism (White man's burden) become the theoretical, practical background for the civilizing mission and for capitalist imperialism. Queen Victoria's famous proclamation (1858), in which a new British policy was addressed for perpetual support and nonintervention in matters of religious belief, became the backbone for imperial deception with its ideological interpellation. The Great Indian Famine (1876–1878) under the British Raj was followed by British policy of 'divida et impera'. British imperial logic and model were imposed on Indian reality in the colonialist creation of an Indian history and social cultural formation.

An imperial type of settler colonialism unveils how the darkness of the enlightened despotism has looted India and ignored experience and feeling of the subjugated. The British colonial state in India is described as "a totally amoral, rapacious imperialist machine bent on the subjugation of Indians for the purpose of profit."[14] Its imperial logic of subjugation can be revealed as a drain theory in the expropriation of Indian wealth and natural resources to serve British growth and economic prosperity.

In the discussion of postcolonial India, Homi Bhabha engages with Fanon's anti-colonial position, developing Hegel's significance in the psychological sense of mimicry. A mimic person is elevated as an interpretive function of mediation with or intermediary for the colonial authorities in regard to the

---

[13] Ibid., 336.
[14] Tharoor, *The Looting of India*, 222.

dominated. The mimic person is Indigenous in blood and color, while Western in taste, in opinions, in morals, and in intellect.[15]

However, it can be argued that this psychological desire of mimicry and its camouflage tends to exonerate crime and guilt on the part of pro-colonial agents. A psychological notion of mimicry discards a basic assumption in Hegel-Fanon, because an imperial system of flattering language characterizes the mimic person as elitist collaborator.

Against the desire of mimicry, concrete universality in Hegel's philosophy helps to draw upon the relational whole of life which is associated with a conceptual sense of sublation underlying the fresh greenness and reciprocity of life-whole. In the drama of phenomenological journey is a hope expressed for the dominated in terms of creativity, freedom, and non-violence against the unhappy consciousness of the mimic.

The life of the subjugated is not lost forever, but retrieved to the regime of effective history for vivid present. "There is nothing more foreign to Hegel than a lamentation for the richness of reality that gets lost when we proceed to its conceptual grasp."[16] In the colonial order of things, consciousness of resistance still survives, as it were, in an abridged or subjugated edition, which is torn out of its context of the whole, or life-world.

Sociological Interpretation of Hegel: Civil Society and Colonialism

Hegel's life was contemporary with the most revolutionary epoch in France and his philosophy was in continual dialogue with, and in response to, this world historical event. With Napoleon at the very gates of the city, Jena, Hegel's *Phenomenology*

---

[15] Bhabha, "Of Mimicry and Man," in *Discipleship*, 125-33.
[16] Zizek, *The Sublime Object of Ideology*, IX.

(1806) is imbued with expectation for Napoleon (the soul of the world) to modernize the constitution of Germany. His dialectic of recognition between the dominant and the subordinated is elaborated in his reflection of French Revolution.

In the dialectical dramaturgy Hegel becomes an 'intellectual Caliban,' an important character as half human and half monster in William Shakespeare's play *The Tempest*. His figure is a symbol of the indigenous people suffering under colonialist oppression. His symbolic meaning can be taken up in his dialectical phenomenology, which promotes resistance to European colonialism and affirmation of the non-European desire for recognition and emancipation.[17]

Along with this lead, I undertake a sociological reading of Hegel's texts in the discussion of economic issue, morality, and civil society, as seen in the *System of Morality* (1802) (its draft known as the *Philosophy of the Spirit*) and the lectures of 1803-1806 in Jena. The civil society becomes the realm in which the struggle for recognition would lead to emancipation of humanity from the state of nature. Here, we observe that there is a strong criticism of capitalist order in the economic world; the accumulation of wealth leads to the opposition between wealth and poverty in the modern world. In the new constitution of civil (or bourgeois) society—the capitalist society is denounced as blind movement leading to losing their freedom and human dignity.[18]

In Marx's account, Hegel conceptualizes labor as the essence of humanity and his greatness can be seen in his comprehension of the self-generation of the human being as a process; process implies objectification as confronting objects, in other words, externalization and the critical integration of

---

[17] Hardt and Negri, *Empire*, 81-2.
[18] Lukacs, *The Young Hegel*, 323.

the externalization.[19] But, Marx still states that Hegel does not see the negative side of alienated labor. Instead, Hegel does not dismiss the deteriorating consequence of human labor in civil society, because its antagonistic structure is dominated by the capital. In this dialectical system of needs and satisfaction, the state is required to intervene to regulate the self-regulating system of capitalist economy, while circumventing inequality, contradiction, and destruction.[20]

Hegel's sociology in his description of struggle and recognition entails the importance of practical reason, in other words, universal self-consciousness in the foundation of moral, social and cultural life. This refers to the ethical world (in the sphere of objective spirit). Hegel's dialectics entail social typology in historicizing configurations of consciousness in its process of externalization in society, culture, and civilization. In other words, it indicates a system of the satisfaction of needs and social change through work, struggle, and politics of recognition. Hegel acknowledges that the dialectic of the externalization (labor, human activity, and social praxis) is incorporated into the society of commodity, while subordinated to it.[21]

More than that, Hegel in *Philosophy of Right* introduces certain normative conditions to the market economy in order to transform individual selfishness into satisfying the needs of everyone as the normative conditions for mutual recognition and self-respect to contribute to the common good.[22] In the ethical world (conscience, harmony of moral duty and happiness, and forgiveness), Hegel seeks the incomplete middle state within God's grace.[23]

---

[19] McLellan, *Karl Marx Selected Writings*, 101.
[20] Marcuse, *Reason and Revolution*, 58-9.
[21] Lukacs, *The Young Hegel*, 483-4.
[22] Honneth, *The I in We*, 64-6.
[23] Hegel, *Phenomenology*, 358.

Now, he retains a dialectical view of ethical position of reconciled grace in dealing with civil society. Though fraught with competition and antagonism, it still has an inherent moral aspect in mutual respect and recognition. Formation of civil society is imbued with willingness to work for the satisfaction of the needs of everyone else, universal resources and the common good. Self-interest in earning the living creates a system of mutual dependence and its public moral significance of recognition in the market society. A moral significance of labor can be critically reformulated under the sociological precondition of universal recognition and self-respect; it requires an institutional, integrative model (trade associations), which facilitates correction and renewal of the problem of the economic system.[24]

Colonialism, State, and Liberating Discourse

In *Philosophy of Right*, Hegel is aware of the capitalist society and its overseas expansion and colonialism (§ 247). In the wider connection and communication through the sea, a means is made for colonization, in which civil society finds itself impelled. Capitalist expansion in civil society leads to "sporadic colonization [that] is particularly characteristic of Germany."

The second and entirely different type of colonization is the systematic; the state undertakes it and is aware of the proper method of carrying it out and regulates it accordingly. "This type was common amongst the ancients, particularly the Greeks...In modern times, colonists have not been allowed the same rights as those left at home, and the result of this situation has been wars

---

[24] Honneth, *The I in We*, 67.

and finally independence, as may be seen in the history of the English and Spanish colonies." (§ 248)[25]

Hegel has in mind a settlement type of colonialism, which traces back to his consideration of colonial age of discovery, as seen in his *Philosophy of History*. He characterizes the colonial age of discovery in terms of "the chivalrous spirit of the maritime heroes," which is originated in Portugal and Spain. They "opened a new way to the East Indies and discovered America." In Hegel's view, Columbus was by no means driven by a merely secular aim. Instead, he presented "a distinctly religious aspect." Hegel interprets that "the treasures of those rich Indian lands… were destined in his [Columbus' discovery and] intention to be expended in a new Crusade."[26]

Crucial in Hegel's analysis of the modern time is the colonial discovery of America imbued with a new crusade and the passage to India by the Cape. Hegel's analysis of colonialism as a modern European crusade helps me to treat his dialectical theory between the master and the slave against the historical backdrop of European colonial expansion in the enslavement of Africans, in the plundering of Americans, and in the exploitation of Asian people. Hegel distinguishes a colonial type of civil society (Bourgeoisie-dominated economic society) from the morality-enhancing type of civil society.

The latter is made part of the rational, universal state, which guarantees freedom, protection, and moral progress. "The state in and by itself is the ethical whole, the actualization of freedom; and it is an absolute end of reason that freedom should be actual." (§ 258)

In dealing with the colonial type of civil society, Hegel draws attention to language and cultural formation in the social model

---

[25] *Hegel's Philosophy of Right*.
[26] Hegel, *The Philosophy of History*, 430.

of the dominant and the dominated with reference to political domination and economic property and wealth.[27] Crucial in his conceptual reflection of this problem is alienation, liberating discourse, and struggle, finally revolution.

In Hegel's analysis, the attributes of nobility find themselves in accord with the public authority of the state. The noble consciousness is adequate both to state power and to economic wealth. It renders obedient service to the interest of the state and respects inner reverence toward it, while finding its satisfaction and enjoyment in wealth. It refers to the mind of aristocracy and its equality and cultural honor with no revolutionary aspiration.

In the sociological context, two types of self-consciousness are produced in the capitalist externalization and its alienation of the base consciousness in social and personal life. Here, it is worth considering the extent to which Hegel analyzes the internal struggles within French absolutism in regard to conflict between wealth and the power of the state.

"Hegel shows how once-independent vassals degenerate into sycophantic courtiers and how the 'noble consciousness of the feudal lords (another echo of Montesquieu) had been translated into mere flattery of the monarch. This process involves, at the same time, the transformation of the 'state-power' into 'wealth'..."[28]

At this point, the revolutionary character of Hegel's dialectic is unmistakable, and its implications can be elaborated in terms of 'I-We' unity in universal recognition among equals. In the dialectical dramaturgy a postcolonial significance of Hegel as an intellectual Caliban can be found in the politics of recognition and difference in terms of economic justice of distribution and reparation underlying an ethic of life-script on the colonized

---

[27] Hegel, *Phenomenology*, 288.
[28] Lukacs, *The Young Hegel*, 492.

community. This epistemic stance focuses on the attribute of baseness, which is in discord or disparity with dominion and wealth.

Looking at political dominion as a chain, it is in enmity with the ruler, obeying only with secret malice, while standing ready to burst out in rebellion. The disparity between these two types of self-consciousness reiterates and reinforces the dialectics between master and slave at a higher level in the world of culture in his articulation of liberating discourse. In the oppressive order of things occurs the social struggle for freedom, independence, and universal recognition on the part of the dominated in challenging the power mechanism.

Now, Hegel takes a step further in underlying social discourse as critique in regard to state power, economic wealth, and cultural injustice. Individual self-existence in the case of the base type of consciousness "is the inner secretly reserved spiritual principle of the various classes and stations."[29] Discordance of the subaltern reacts against the political domination of the state and arrives at the point of breaking out into rebellion.[30] Language as discourse has the power of utterance through speaking out against the state power, an abstract universal. Speech alone expresses 'I' itself, because ego becomes intersubjective ego in its particular and universal form.

In the face of the discourse of discordance and rebellion, the noble consciousness produces a language of flattery in defending their privilege and prestige; "the heroism of dumb service passes into the heroism of flattery."[31] Through this flattering system of discourse the noble consciousness serves the state power of an unlimited monarch, giving the monarch his proper name

---

[29] Hegel, *Phenomenology*, 297.
[30] Ibid.
[31] Ibid., 300.

(in written legal documents) and elevating this state power into universality. The spirit of flattering and gratitude serves as the haughty vassal, while placing the monarch on its pinnacle, turning the dominated into the condition of humiliation; they feel the deepest revolt. "Wealth shares repudiation with its clientele, but in place of revolt appears arrogance."[32]

In the pure disintegration the self becomes sheer internal discordance, such that all oneness in concord is taken asunder; the respect for the benefactor is shattered, standing in front of the abyss. It cleaves the bottomless pit in which every solid base and stay has vanished.[33]

In the discussion of the state, Hegel affirms the significance of resistance discourse against the flattering language of the upper class, which is allied with the state—its non-rational and dictatorial form. Flattering discourse implies a political type of representing the power mechanism, economic wealth, and cultural inequality in its service of rationalization, material advantages, and social prestige. It refers to language expressed in the abstract universal (called universal best), which maintains its inherent nature of self-respect and honor under the unlimited monarch.[34]

The world of culture is that of alienation, and the body politics is corrupted by economic wealth, especially with respect to the contradiction, poverty and discordance; these are expressed in language of laceration and absolute disintegration underlying unhappy consciousness in the pre-revolutionary stage.

In Hegel's dialectical drama, an exchange occurs so strikingly that noble consciousness turns base and abject, while abjectness changes into the nobility of self-consciousness. In this social

---

[32] Ibid., 304.
[33] Ibid.
[34] Ibid., 299-300.

drama, Hegel's vision of the future state can be seen in the state of citizen with equality of rights and democracy, which has little to do with class dominion or monarchical ruling. Hegel's ethical state remains an alternative to Greek idea of city-state (god-society equation: The goddess Athena as Athens itself). He observes that a historical collapse of the Greek (incarnation of ethical life, or "a self-completed ethical order"[35]) has provided room for more externalized modern civil society. The Greek ethical life, though lost, remains an ideal type for Hegel's theory of civil society and state

The Logic and Conceptual Principle

Hegel's *Logic* is the science of the Idea, in which God's intellect is revealed to us, living in our thought. The logic involves the inner life of God through language. "*This realm is truth unveiled, truth as it is in and for itself.* It can therefore be said that this content is *the exposition of God as he is in his eternal essence before the creation of nature and of a finite spirit.*"[36] This exoteric language indicates that Hegel stands in Aristotelian tradition of God, the Intellectual totality of all beings.

God's internal life is conceptually apprehended in the free subject as the Idea of the truth, good, and freedom. The *Logic* credits conceptual principle with the Idea. In the Idea, Hegel seeks the unity of cognition (knowledge of the Truth) and moral action (the realization of the Good), while articulating the latter as a higher than the former in a move toward logical discourse of perfect freedom. "The idea of the good can therefore find its completion only in the idea of the true."[37] Hegel cuts across Platonic Idea of the Good built in its potentiality.

---

[35] Ibid., 267.
[36] Hegel, *The Science of Logic*, 29.
[37] Ibid., 731.

By doing so, Hegel does not begin with the absolute knowledge, which has come to attain itself as the final stage in *Phenomenology*. But he starts from being, in dealing with the passage from being to nothingness and then from nothingness to being (being-nothingness-becoming).[38]

This category appears as the relational whole, an expression of the Absolute itself (being-essence-concept). Essence emerges in the process of negation and mediation. It refers to subjective reflection of the actual structure of being as the unity of opposites. The ontology of being or all reality is grasped in self-contradictory and self-different terms. Remarkable in the character of essence is a dialectical position of contradiction as the source and root of all life and movement. The essence denotes the ground of reality, in which contradiction is taken as necessary development at the deeper and more essential level.[39]

Hegel develops Kant's notion of an intellectual intuition, which is created with the thought, as independent upon external reception. Hegel's logical discourse of immanence is concerned with universal being in itself and for itself by penetrating to and transcending Kantian's realm of thing-in-itself ineffable and unknowable.

For Kant, Idea or reason is the regulating principle (as goal or archetype) of understanding, while having no adequate empirical application. He appropriates the concepts of reason in order to comprehend our perception of the external objects in terms of categories. His position remains in the external reflection because of his pictorial or mere presentation of them.[40]

In fact, Kant has limited the knowledge in order to leave room for faith. However, for Hegel reason is the common

---

[38] Hyppolite, *Logic and Existence*, 64.
[39] Taylor, *Hegel*, 262.
[40] Hegel, *The Science of Logic*, 671.

source of sensibility and understanding, and it mediates these for the dialectical unity between thing-in-itself and for itself. He preserves the Idea (unlike Kant) for objective and real concept, and he thinks of the internal life of God a la Aristotle. Indeed, Hegel has limited the faith in order to leave room for knowledge.

In Logic as the discourse of Being, being becomes its own other by becoming the subject and object in self-contradiction and negativity; it is expressed and synthesized as affirmation of negation in and through dialectical discourse in the world of signification. For Hegel, the Concept, a part of system of subjective logic, implies a logical foundation of being and essence, and freedom is its relational mode. The kingdom of freedom is revealed in the Concept in its character of negation of determination, which is defined as a totality of the universal and the singular (individual personality).[41]

Kant constitutes the unity of the "I think" (self-consciousness) as the essence of the concept, while bringing manifold of given representations to the unity of consciousness; they are recognized in the original synthetic unity of apperception by virtue of categories. Kant's original synthesis of apperception contains the initial stage of a true apprehension of the concept.

Given this, Hegel values Kant's position as "the profoundest and truest insights" in the *Critique of Reason*.[42] However, Hegel maintains that a conceptually comprehended apprehension of the external reality or insight into it is at the root of reality. Thus, the conceptual sense is the relational totality, which is moving by contradiction, deduction, and dialectical discourse of mediation; it transforms externality into universality according to the cognition of what is true.

---

[41] Ibid., 513.
[42] Ibid., 515.

The universality of the Concept is seen in its absolute self-identity, or pure self-reference with creative power, which refers to the total reflection (immanent and external); it is the negation of negation or the infinite unity of negativity with itself.[43]

The Concept is of sociological character, because it is the soul of objective reality, or universality. The Concept has power to develop particularity, perpetual reproduction, self-transformation and actuality of the free subject through progress of self-consciousness of freedom and knowledge of the truth. This aspect implies that the universal is free power; it is reaching out to its other, embracing it, at rest in the other, "but without doing violence to it." It is called "free love and boundless blessedness."[44]

The Concept is bound up to sociology of externalization, while guiding the external world toward self-realization in accordance with creative power, freedom, and recognition. The highest form of this self-realization is called the Idea, the unity of the concept and reality. The Idea, based on the freedom, the true, and the good, "has the most stubborn opposition within it; its repose consists in the assurance and the certainty with which it eternally generates that opposition and eternally overcomes it, and in it rejoins itself."[45]

Concept, which corresponds to the multitude of things, designates the rational structure of being, the world as Logos, reason, which underlies the actual basis and content of the Logic. Conceptual principle has its creative power, because Hegel comprehends creativity "only in the concept's innermost core."[46]

---

[43] Ibid., 530.
[44] Ibid., 532.
[45] Ibid., 674.
[46] Ibid., 534.

In the totality of the conceptual whole, diversity passes over into opposition, into an immanent connection of diverse moments, and it is the essential principle in characterizing the relation of self with the other through free power, mutual love, and blessedness, without doing any harm to the other.

A critical theory of the conceptual whole denotes the final penetration of the world by freedom, love, creativity, and reason. The conceptual principle is to be realized in the universal construction of the rational social organization in accordance with the principle of mutual recognition,[47] as seen in sociology of externalization. Social totality or formation is generative, contradictory, immanent (analytical), and synthetic in terms of a relational whole.

Along with the principle of recognition, social formation should be pervaded through the conceptual principle, in which society is based on freedom, love, creativity and blessing, with no violence to the other at all. Everything is in a teleological dependence upon Reason or the Idea (spirit or the Concept), because the latter as the ground of social cultural reality produces a real world out of its conceptual principle.

To know oneself through reflection is to contradict oneself through the synthetic whole. Dialectical thinking is of problematic character striving to realize the external world in accordance with the reason. Synthetic totality is Not-All, but conceptual whole according to creativity, freedom, and mutual love.

The principle of universal recognition is fulfilled in the Idea of the triad (the Truth, the Freedom, and the Good), which is articulated in the absolute Idea (the complete totality of the concepts, or the identity of the theoretical and the practical idea); it is conceptualized in the process of unification of opposites

---

[47] Marcuse, *Reason and Revolution*, 161.

through the negation of negation. Thus, "the absolute idea alone is *being*, imperishable *life, self-knowing truth*, and is *all truth*."[48]

Hegel and Foucault

In *Phenomenology* Hegel indicates a possibility of epoché through dialectical discourse. He puts 'man' (a natural *Dasein*) into bracket toward an enriched regime of meaningful world and understanding. This phenomenology is enriched and deepened in terms of conceptual ontology in the discourse of the *Logic*.[49] In Hegel's logic "there has language penetrated, and everything that he transforms into language and expresses in it contains a category, whether concealed, mixed, or well defined."[50]

In Foucault's assessment, an attempt at escaping Hegel is indebted to Jean Hyppolite, a great French commentator of Hegel, "whether through logic or epistemology, or whether through Marx or through Nietzsche." In his disloyalty to Hegel, Foucault still pays appreciation to Hegel to dissociate his theory of discourse from Hegel's phenomenological dialectics. Hegel's theory of knowledge allows for Foucault to think and react against Hegel.[51]

Although Foucault's anti-Hegelian stance treads an anti-metaphysical path a la Nietzsche, Hegel's negative dialectic of diversity and difference shows a different angle, while facilitating an epistemic skill in deciphering the particular, the marginal, and the subjugated for the sake of effective history in contrast to the marching history of progress of Reason and its meta-discourse.

According to Foucault, a human being is governed by labor, life, and language, in which his/her concrete existence finds its

---

[48] Hegel, *The Science of Logic*, 735.
[49] Hyppolite, *Logic and Existence*, 42.
[50] Hegel, *The Science of Logic*, 12.
[51] Foucault, *The Archaeology of Knowledge*, 235.

determinations. If human knowledge is finite, a human being is trapped within the confinement of language, labor, and life, as seen at the archeological level, "which reveals the general, historical a priori of each of those branches of knowledge."[52]

This is socially established generality of knowledge system (episteme) as the site of constituting 'man' as its object. In the threshold of the modernity a human being is constituted as 'man' entitled with transcendental capacity of reason and empirical experience, such the empirical and the transcendental coincide "in a strange empirico-transcendental doublet."[53] Based on such epistemic order of things, 'man' is embedded within labor, life, and language, while acquiring his own historicity. Thus "all differences, all dispersions, all discontinuities would be knitted together" into "a single point of identity."[54]

Foucault holds that phenomenology has allegiance to the discovery of life, work, and language, but an ontology of unthought short-circuits and even fails the primacy of cogito. In the apprehension of the unthought, Foucault argues that all knowledge is historically rooted in a life, a society, and a language. He acknowledges a certain methodology in the element of *Lebenswelt*, intersubjective communication, or hermeneutics. These historical social sciences "will never raise themselves to the status of absolute totality."[55]

If labor, life and language appear to be a transcendental site by which making possible the object knowledge of living beings and their experience, their region of problematics belongs to Hegelian phenomenology. Here, "the totality of the empirical domain was taken back into the interior of consciousness

---

[52] Foucault, *The Order of Things*, 318.
[53] Ibid., 318.
[54] Ibid., 239-30.
[55] Ibid., 373.

revealing itself to itself as spirit, in other words, as an empirical and a transcendental field simultaneously."[56] In fact, Hegel relocates the Kantian doublet of empirico-transcendental 'man' in the dialectical relationship between externalization and its social cultural product. Here, a triad 'life, labor, and language' can be explicated in terms of political power, economic wealth, culture, and discourse formation. In Hegel's view, the Kantian mode of representation fails to clarify the unknowable with reference to the other, unthought. This conceptual problem is already explicated in the sociological interpretation of Hegel in *Phenomenology* and the *Logic*.

By doing so, Hegel is insidiously relevant to Foucault's theory of knowledge and power relations. Foucault acknowledges Hegel's philosophy as "a reassuring universe, or "philosophy as a totality ultimately capable of dispersing and regrouping itself in the movement of the concept."[57] Totality does not necessarily mean totalization of the alterity into the sameness through contradiction and negation. Hegel's phenomenology resides in restless activity and struggle in society, culture, and history toward the principle of recognition and conceptual clarification. Language is imbued with life-world and shapes and brings human consciousness to a higher level of synthesized totality through dialectical discourse of mediation and contradiction.

Life-world of language (the absolute Idea) is not exhausted into dialectical discourse of mediation, rather it becomes the source of understanding (recognition) and conceptual whole (the freedom, the truth, the good) together with non-violence. An epistemic movement is characterized in terms of conceptual problematic, continuous recommencement, rupture (in different languages), and semantic retrieval of relational whole. If Hegel

---

[56] Ibid., 248.
[57] Foucault, *The Archaeology of Knowledge*, 236.

features the concept as the subject matter in which it is the content of thought in expressing the truth of things, language is an indispensable part of the logos. This linguistic stance can be reinforced by discourse analysis of power and knowledge interplay. Concept formation is historically influenced in its power relations and struggle-recognition and socially represented as discourse in regard to political power and economic wealth.

With this said, Foucault's genealogy of discourse in power relations is not far removed from Hegel's generative phenomenology, which is undertaken in terms of negative reflection, becoming, contradiction, mediation, and sublimation. A dialectical totality is not-All in its absolute sense, but its journey strives to attain mutual recognition in concrete universal sense, or an ensemble of relations. A phenomenological analysis is cast upon consciousness-discourse relations in the world of externalization concerned with the relational whole of recognition and conceptual sense. It takes into account problems such as labor, life, and language in dealing with a prestige struggle for recognition, as well as conceptual principle (creative negation, freedom, and love).

Hegel starts off with the necessary articulation of opposites and contradictions to attain a relational whole in terms of manifestation of rational necessity and conceptual totality. Here, a question can be seriously raised whether Hegel acknowledges a regime of incommensurability in the life of significant Other, which would be excluded by the power relations.

It is worth taking into account a critical genealogy of those subjugated in the life of undetermined multitude with no articulated totality. It is also worth featuring the dialectical way Hegel comprehends consciousness-discourse relations in the web of reconciling power on the part of the dominated, while indexing the significant Other and the unthought through revitalizing no-harm principle.

2. Christian Public Theology and Hegel

In our sociological interpretation of Hegel, it is fair to credit Hegel as one of the most distinguished philosophers who allies with Christian public theology and its discourse ethics of *parrhesia*. This is the Christian tradition of promoting a verbal activity in which a speaker expresses his/her personal relationship to truth.

The *parrhesia* articulates criticism instead of flattery and moral duty instead of self-interest and moral apathy. For full recognition, the dominated adopts language as critical discourse in revolt and disintegration. The cultural aspect of language is utterance for the entire realm of spiritual culture and development, and it remains an undercurrent in befitting rebellion in the shape of the absolute self-identity against absolute disintegration.[58]

In Hegel's scheme, we are a vehicle of the Idea and have an Ideal of knowledge, freedom and truth (as not fully attained), while striving toward the good (as yet unfinished). The absolute Idea is the synthesis of knowledge (the true), life (embodied as locus of inner teleology), and moral striving. The conceptual position comes to terms with the principle of recognition, while seeking the perfect freedom and emancipation with no harm principle. But, in Hegel's philosophy, the Aristotelian God is fused with the Christian God of reconciliation; such fusion between the unmoved Mover and the *theologia crucis* becomes the regime of problem for Christian public theology.

---

[58] Hegel, *Phenomenology*, 305.

Indeed, Hegel's panentheistic logic discourages him to think of God *totaliter aliter* seriously in the death of Christ, so he has not managed to challenge the finite reality in the radical side of evil (holocaust, colonial genocide, apartheid, and Palestine).

In Hegel's dialectical experience evil appears to be the first actual expression of the self-concentrated consciousness in Adam's fall. Hegel traces its potential form of evil back to the divine Being in its assumption of human flesh. God is reconciled with the evil in divine emptiness (kenosis) in assumption of human flesh through forgiveness of sin. In the complete reconciliation, it is argued that evil constitutes the essential moment of the divine Spirit, belonging to the divine Being in the sense of Quarternity.[59]

The nothing itself outside its essential being (God) is self-centeredness, and it is the principle of evil in opposition to spiritual unity, but the universality of self-consciousness is finally seen in the reconciliation with the reality of evil. "The dead Divine Man, or Human God, is implicitly universal self-consciousness."[60]

The death of the divine Man is allied with his factual (or spiritual) resurrection in which God's individual self-consciousness (Christ) becomes the universal self-consciousness through the sublation and transfigured into the universality of the spirit, which lives in its own communion.

Against Hegel, however, reconciliation in the biblical context is not conflated with final consummation, but points to its future in terms of faith, love, and hope. Forgiveness of sin comes from God's grace of reconciliation and encourages us to take part in prophetic history of fight against irreconcilable reality of the nothingness, as resurged in crusade, colonial apocalypse, slave trade, holocaust, world wars, and apartheid, and so on.

---

[59] Ibid., 455.
[60] Ibid., 457.

This prolepsis of reconciliation comprehends effective history of the dominated in the light of the crucified God, by requiring recollection and the anamnestic reasoning of the innocent victims in history, society, and culture. It embodies (or translates) the principle of universal recognition among equals in history, culture, and society in accordance with dialectical logic of the concrete universality through conceptual clarification. Hegel does not simply replace Christian religion with absolute knowledge, because the regime of absolute knowledge is shared with a biblical idea of reconciliation, which implies the concrete universal in the death of Christ.

In Hegel's account, our experience of the absolute Spirit implies "the unity of different self-related and self-existent self-consciousness in the perfect freedom and independence of their opposition as component elements of that [absolute] substance." "Ego," Hegel holds, "is 'we,' a plurality of Egos, and 'we' that is a single Ego."[61] Hegel's major concern lies in comprehending the universal recognition among equals (I-We unity).

However, religious meaning of reconciliation could be only partially feasible in the inwardness of individual conscience and mystical contemplation of beautiful soul, in which divine nature is intuitively apprehended in the sphere of figurative thought. It is "not yet the universal of understanding."[62]

Universal recognition (or reconciliation) is the subject-matter, which is not exhausted in a lifeless universal, but it works the matter out to attain the concrete whole, or its concrete realization. A mutual, universal recognition does not exist in metaphysical world of thing-in-itself. It also reacts against Spinoza's un-dialectical notion of God or Nature (*deus sive natura*) of which I am a part, as caught up in its pan-en-theistic determinism.

---

[61] Ibid., 104.
[62] Ibid., 447.

In this phenomenological journey, understanding is the strenuous intellectual activity of penetrating into the very depths of the meaning of a living experience with divine reconciliation grounded in the very Being of the Absolute itself. It is the most astonishing power, which is "to comprehend the concrete riches and fullness contained in its various determinate qualities."[63]

The theological subject matter of reconciliation is appropriated and has become in-and-for-itself in philosophy, in the form of absolute knowledge. For Hegel, God is conceptually comprehended, and "attainable in pure speculative knowledge alone," which is "furnished by revealed religion."[64] But the absolute knowledge within the framework of understanding must be elaborated at a higher level through conceptual apprehension, in which the principle of recognition is grounded in creativity, freedom, and non-violence. Conceptual clarity of recognition provides Christian public theology to critically involve Hegel as a sociologist, with reference to effective history in the anamnestic reasoning (Walter Benjamin).

Anamnesis and Dialectical Experience

Anamnestic reasoning of history constitutes a form of metanoia breaking through 'the way it really was' (Ranke). Herein, there is no place of the insignificant and the different as subjugated under European reason as power.

A notion of progress is severely challenged: "But a storm is blowing from Paradise" and "irresistibly propels him into the future to which his back is turned, while the pile of ruins before him grows skyward. What we call progress is *this* storm."[65] Sociology of externalization in this regard emphasizes an aspect

---

[63] Ibid., 3.
[64] Ibid., 446.
[65] Thesis IX, in Benjamin, *Illuminations*, 257.

of internalization, or radical self-reflection in expressing the reversal of the progress in the externalized world.

The radical reflection in anamnesis should be the retrospective process of effective history with counter memory by critically testing the extent to which the marching progress of the externalized history would become a regime of self-concentration in exclusion of the significant Other; history of absolute knowledge can be scrutinized in the life-world of constellations in terms of negation, difference, and rupture with the externalized world and its historicized episteme. History as life-world in constellations requires archeological analysis of discourse and its powerful logic of representation in history, culture, and society, while reinforcing conceptual problematic to sharpen recognition in terms of no-violence principle and reparative justice. The principle of the concept remains a source of immanent critique in an archaeological analysis of discourse and its hegemonic mode of representation and exclusion.

A phenomenology of constellations brings dialectical experience of the relation between the dominant and the dominated in a concrete-universal sense toward a principle of mutual recognition, difference, and creative freedom. Symptoms in historical marching of metanarrative are discarded as meaningless and insignificant traces, and their meaning requires an epistemic skill of deciphering its region, as archeologically excavated from the hidden depth of the past; it is latent and hidden in discourse of representation in the network of material interests and power relations. In retroactive construction an epistemic skill is concerned with that which has been marginalized and foreclosed as the incommensurable in the progression of reason to the absolute knowledge.

The latter must be accorded with non-violence principle in conceptual problematic through the mode of radical reflection of the past in accordance with the vivid present. Epistemic practice of effective history seeks to engender the meaningful discourse of truth and the good in the true sense of recognition of difference and freedom.

Thus I incorporate Hegel's position of recognition and conceptual principle into the regime of effective history as the source of the immanent critique regarding the metahistory. It is important to explicate elective affinity in dealing with religious ideas and material interests in an archeological and thickly manner.

It takes into account an epistemic legitimacy of structural coupling of discourse and symbolic material systems in its governance of multiple realities within civil society. This social scientific approach unveils the extent to which social systems, episteme, and history would be differentiated, specialized, and stratified in the networks of recognition struggle, power prestige, and privilege among agency.

Ethical problematization involves in intersubjective or socially established consensus process in terms of interpretation and peaceful and meaningful discourse; it seeks to reformulate recognition, common good, and conceptual principle in the structural articulation of networks of differentiated multiple realities in pluralist, democratic society.

The signifying discourse assigns the symptoms to their symbolic place and meaning. In the symbolic material order of things, the past is not always present in the form of historical tradition and the present. The meaning of these traces is given through anamnesis reasoning which de-centers the truth regime of representation in the network of the signifier and power relations.

Such archeology brings every historical rupture and every advent of a new master-signifier into genealogy of effective history and ideological extrapolation, restructuring the narration of the past; archeological skill makes the region of the subjugated readable and translatable in another significant way. This epistemic stance does not contrast with dialectical phenomenology, which is concerned with the regime of the dominated in the struggle for recognition and freedom.

A critical theory of constellations in a life-world framework features anamnesis reasoning in the conceptual as problematic, always decentering and dethroning the personality cult in the pseudo-region of absolute knowledge. Absolute always remains relative in connection with effective history of the subjugated, which waits to be rediscovered for the sake of the vivid present and recognition.

This epistemic skill gives a new impulse to *theologia crucis* as the controlling principle of reconciliation to cut through a religious figurative representation of the reconciliation in purely inward sense. It seeks to reconfigure the effective history of the subaltern by exegetically engaging in the living, emancipatory Word of God in terms of immanent critique, metanoia, democratic, reparative justice, and proleptic eschatology in the messianic history. A messianic history requires a genealogical rewiring of history from the anamnestic standpoint of those suffering or for and from the vanquished.

God and Vivid Present

If history is to seize hold of a memory in the radical sense of re-collection, it flashes up at a moment of danger in the prolepsis of God's in-breaking into our time (vivid present). It entails the image of the past fraught with brutal reality of the innocent victims in the history of fascism or colonialism. God *totaliter aliter* comes into alterity through reconciliation with the world in which the alterity finds its place of recognition in the true sense of concrete universality. So, its vivid present is expressed in Christian ethical practice imbued with divine time of kairos. It breaks into our midst by halting the marching (pseudo) progress of reason in universal, abstract sense.

The history as danger "affects both the content of the tradition and its receivers," because the past of the innocent victim is not actively present in our midst. It keeps the history aloof from conformism or from becoming a tool of serving the ruling classes.

History as the constellations has multiple references to history as meaningful effect (horizon of life-world), the effective history (genealogy of power relations), and archaeological analysis of discourse (episteme) and the semantic retrieval of the subjugated knowledge in anamnestic reasoning.

This epistemic skill characterizes archaeological-semantic enquiry in dealing with history, culture, and society. The vivid present is not identical with unbroken, homogeneous present in diachronic-emanationist sense of the absolute knowledge, but it indicates conceptual problematic of real differences in history as constellations embedded with many diverse instances, differentiations, and registers.

A reality of effective history in divine kairos bursts apart the continuum of colonial history along the faulty path of progress and domination on the march, bringing up that the whole past of the innocent victims is present within our present. This implies a prototype and anticipation of the messianic time of eternity, and it implies vivid present of *theologia crucis* to be ethically embodied in history and society; it inaugurates a divine time in protest to evil of impersonal forces, in other words, irreconcilable reality in the world.

This position radicalizes Hegel as an intellectual Caliban, while reshaping dialectical reflection and practice into problematic way of thinking and vivid present of effective history. An archeological-semantic stance is undertaken at a micro-analytical level, thus it is worth explicating the extent to which the ensemble of public spheres and their intersectional variations (race, gender, sexuality, culture, religion, and ethnic nationalism) would be stratified and reified in postcolonial civil society.

By doing so, Christian public theology journeys together with Hegel and beyond him, while accentuating social practice for the margins and from them, in other words, ethics of life-world. This perspective seeks to reformulate Hegel's critical insight into the recognition struggle in a broader spectrum in explicating the extent to which discourse would be embedded with material interests and power relations in social formation.

3. Biopolitical Formation: Colonial Racism and Sovereignty

In the discussion of Christian public theology and Hegel, we focus on political technology of body and racism in colonial context as a new mode of crusade. The slogan "expansion for expansion's sake" is the central political idea of imperialism. It is an entirely new concept in the long century of political history, because its originality lies "in the realm of business speculation, where expansion meant the permanent broadening of industrial production and economic transactions characteristic of the nineteenth century."[66]

A genealogical analysis of colonialism and racial injustice requires conceptual clarification in terms of correlation between hegemony and political sovereignty of human body and racial hierarchy. For example, in the mercantilist context, it

---

[66] "Expansion," in *The Portable Hannah Arendt*, 107.

turns into necropolitical power through colonizing genocide. "The politicization of bare life constitutes the decisive event of modernity."[67]

This perspective remains an undercurrent in the political technology of subjugating the body of the colonized race and its totalitarian policy of race cleaning. The biopolitical type of colonial sovereignty can be seen in Spain's mercantilist colonialism of the indigenous Amerindian in the aftermath of Columbus' discovery. Mercantilism was made possible as mode of struggle among empires or nation-states within the European world-economy (from the 16th to the 18th century).

Religion, Origin of Race, and Its Ideology

In the discussion of biopolitical power and its racial ideology, it is critical to begin with Transatlantic Slave Trade, which was undertaken between the sixteenth and nineteenth century on the part of Portugal (1441-1869), Spain (1441-1886), the Dutch (1596-1863), the French (1658-1848), and the British (beginning in 1500s and lasting until the Slavery Abolition Act of 1833). Nonetheless, we cannot sidestep a dark side of Renaissance Europe in the late medieval period in which slavery was a common phenomenon as practiced by both Muslims and Christians.

A society of Renaissance humanists across the Mediterranean and southern Europe was reliant on human trafficking and slave trading. Genoa was an important city state and its merchants used the Black Sea port of Caffa (modern day eastern Crimea) in the late 13th century as a slaving hub, through which enslaved people were transported to southern Europe.[68]

---

[67] Agamben, "Introduction to Homo Sacer," in *Biopolitics*, 136.
[68] Hannah Skoda, "How slavery thrived in Renaissance Europe."

From 1415 onwards, Portuguese expeditions to west coast Africa brought more African slaves to be traded between north Africa and Europe. As Portugal and Spain established colonies in Africa and the Americas, they began with enslavement in 1441. In 1462, Portuguese slave traders were operative in Seville, Spain, in which the Christian assumption was entangled with the origins of race. Such correlation undertakes a project of Christian social imagination in unveiling how a theological assumption undergoes colonial order of things in terms of slavery and racism.

Prince Henry of Portugal, the Navigator (August 8, 1444), was sitting on horseback, waiting for the number of slaves, 235 at the port of Lagos. Gomes Eanes de Azurara (or Zurara), Henry's royal chronicler, was a Christian intellectual in a Renaissance pattern of learning. He recounts the ritual of slave capture and auction (August 8, 1444) as beginning with prayer:

"O, Thou heavenly Father…I pray Thee that my tears may not wrong my conscience; for it is not their religion but their humanity that maketh mine to weep in pity for their suffering. And if the brute animals, with their bestial feelings, by a natural instinct understand the suffering of their own kind, what wouldst Thou have my human nature to do on seeing before my eyes that miserable company, and remembering that they too are of the generation o the sons of Adam?"[69]

A theological assumption is colored and expressed in the Christian pity on suffering of the brutal animals, which are still offspring of Adam. It takes divine providence for Portuguese Empire to civilize the slaves into a Christian fashion for African salvation. Zurara's narrative is seen in his religious sanction of biopolitical deployment over slave bodies, while justifying colonial discipline, servitude, and control. Christian discourse of biopolitical displacement of slave bodies deeply distorts Jesus'

---

[69] Cited in Jennings, *The Christian Imagination*, 17.

compassion and solidarity with the lowest of the low; it turns a colonial hermeneutic of forced servitude into religious sanction of racism and sale of the slave as a commodity in the name of civilizing mission.[70]

In the colonial age of discovery, Indian populations were almost devastated. To meet the labor shortage, the trip called Middle Passage involved the slave trade in Africa to sugar plantations in Americas. The trip of the Middle Passage was notorious for its brutality and abuse by the captors as well as unsanitary brutal condition, over-crowded captives, chained together on the ships. The slave becomes a form of commodity as fascination and religious mission, becoming the doublet of labor and commodity (sale value).

Sugars, tobacco, and other products were imported to Europe; raw materials were produced as manufactured goods (arms, textiles, wine) for expansive sale, and slaves were captured in Africa. What is crucial is a settler theory of colonialism, which is based on slave trade and plantation works. This leads to the disappearance of the indigenous inhabitants.

Furthermore, the colonial theory of racism finds its sophisticated form in the modern context, for example, in Gobineau's pre-Darwinian theory of race, which finds its historical and genealogical apex in the political racial ideology in German National Socialism and its anti-Semitism. In Gobineau's writings in the 1850s, the French aristocracy is claimed to be originally of Germanic extraction, while the mass of the French people were Gallic or Celtic.

His assumption of the superiority of the Germanic race is created to thwart the rising ascendency of democratic movements after the French Revolution. Several decades later, it was taken up as the starting point of modern German racial ideology in the

---

[70] Ibid., 22.

circle of the exponents of National Socialism. Around that time in Britain and America "the White Man's burden" was fabricated to justify Anglo-Saxon world domination and its orientalist colonialism.[71]

The social Darwinist worldview reinforces the worldwide competition for the benefit of the whole of humankind, leading to the progress of civilization. In the midst of imperial undertaking Rudyard Kipling (1865-1936), English journalist, poet, and novelist, was awarded the Nobel Prize in Literature and published his poem, entitled "The White Man's Burden" (1899), which was widely reprinted in American newspapers.

It was a summons to the American war for colonial control over the Philippines (the Philippine-American war, 1899-1902); in this poem the concept of social Darwinism is politically charged in a white supremacist framework. In the power of the civilizing language of the colonizer, the reality of colonialism creates alterity and identity in terms of the denaturalization of racial and cultural difference. Colonial *"reality is not dialectical, colonialism is"* [72] of dialectical nature by defeating recognition through commodity fetishism, reifying of the slave, and apocalypse of death politics. Colonialism as modern crusade reinforces a political logic of resolving the contradiction between the colonizer and the colonized by excluding the intermediate or mediation by biopolitical sovereignty (sharpening Aristotelian law of excluded means).

This perspective improves on limitation of Hegel's logic of negation and contradiction through mediation for synthetic whole, because the law of excluded middle still plays a significant role in the context of racial struggle and biopolitical governance. The racial struggle for recognition implies the death of the

---

[71] Sweezy, *The Theory of Capitalist Development*, 311.
[72] Hardt and Negri, *Empire*, 128.

subjugated with socio-political and cultural discrimination in the colonialism. Genealogy of racism cuts through limitation of class struggle in an economic field.

Biopolitics and African Apocalypse

Religion and death politics remain an important ideology of alliance between throne and altar in justifying this economic exploitative type of colonialism, and religion turns out to be a flattering system of discourse. A discourse of representation for the "Scramble for Africa" is closely bound up to the European position of a civilizing mission, in which discourse of social Darwinism appears to be the main ideology of colonialism, racism, and slave-commodity while establishing and distributing racial injustice in African society and culture.

In the type of extractive colonialism, the 'White Man's Burden' turns into the 'Black Man's Burden,' as seen in the historical reality of the Scramble for Africa. The civilizing mission turns into savage mission and death politics was executed in Leopold II's sovereignty in the Congo Free State (1885-1912).

This historical type of extractive colonialism is concerned with a raw material in a particular locale (ivory, rubber, gold, etc), while destroying indigenous inhabitants. It depends upon native mediation, environmental knowledge, and forced labor, but it does not necessarily entail permanent settlement. Its economic greed and looting are bound to biopolitical technology of the slave body and racism leading to necropolitical genocide.

This historical reality of colonialism qualifies Hegel's dialectics of master and slave in the sense that death fear of the slave is deployed by biopolitical technology of colonial bodies, in other words, a death politics of terror. The slave is reduced simply to usable things as such, and their labor is not recognized to keep their life as survival. Death politics of terror characterizes a colonial dialectic between the white master and the black slave.

Biopolitical power depreciates the life of survival and eliminates struggle of the slave at the risking of life and dead. Finally, political technology of the slave body leads dramatically to mutilation of body, terrible punishment of atrocity, and brutal violence. The fascistic logic of racism, commodity fetishism (utility and sale) and death power find completion in modern crusade of colonial genocide, which reinforces a phenomenology of struggle between the master and the slave.

Heart of Darkness

A postcolonial approach to effective history in the colonial time contrasts with a Eurocentric position of justifying meta-discourse of a marching history of Western progress, scientific technology, and capitalist modernity, which can be obviously seen as the European project of the Scramble for Africa.

It appears already in David Livingstone's (1813-1873) slogan: "Christianity, Commerce and Civilization." This implies a type of trade colonialism, as seen mainly in the British colonies controlling over trade relationships. The colonial periphery provides the metropolis with raw materials, while the latter's manufactures (guns, cloth, and other goods) are sold in its colonies. Trade coercion in the case of the British Opium War with China (the first, 1839-1842 and the second Anglo-French War, 1856-60) exists in the intermediary network outside of imperial center.

The Scramble for Africa was undertaken in the project of Western European colonization (1870-1914). A genealogy focuses on regime of problems: the Berlin Conference of 1884-1885 and its granting of Congo to Leopold II of Belgium, who was made with the service of Henry Morton Stanley to possess the Congo Free State. Such historical type of extractive colonialism led finally to the heart of darkness and mass murder.[73]

Heart of Darkness (Joseph Conrad) assists us in bringing up a reality of extractive colonialism in dealing with political form of subjugation of life to death; it is intersected with religious discourse, cultural hegemony, material interests, and death politics. Nevertheless, *Heart of Darkness* was under fire by Nigerian novelist Chinua Achebe, who accused Conrad of being a bloody racist, because of his de-humanizing portrayal of Africans. In contrast, Maya Jasanoff, a professor of history at Harvard, tolerates a dated prejudice at his time because there is coexistence with some "elements of exceptional clairvoyance."[74]

As a rule, such literary critical response tends to sidestep what sets the colonialism into motion and what typology is operative in different approach to colonialism among the colonial agency.

Congo Free State was driven by extractive type of colonialism espoused with slave as labor (enslaved to intensification of productive forces), reified commodity, and religious parlance of civilizing mission, whereas British colonialism centered a free trade type with monopoly and political sovereignty, and religious sanction of British exceptionalism.

What is decisive in a Belgian type is seen in the rubber concessions for extraction of natural resources or ivory collection from a district allowed for individual entrepreneurs of European nations. With Berlin Conference's support, King Leopold undertook an indirect rule through rubber companies or individual entrepreneurs, while leading to economic exploitation

---

[73] Conrad, *Heart of Darkness*.
[74] Jasanoff, "How Joseph Conrad foresaw the dark heart of Brexit Britain."

and mass killings in modern African history; an estimated 10 million people died between 1880 and 1920.[75]

A European dialectic of enlightened despotism degenerates into a colonial dialectic of barbarism with its biopolitical genocide; this regime refers to the significant problem for African public theology in undertaking genealogical analysis of how political control of the slave body is operative in the economic mechanism of extractive colonialism; it elevates the white master to be a place of God, but finally ends up to its death politics of apocalypse. In the dialectics of lordship and servitude, commodity fetishism is bound up to colonial reality, in which the master is deified as the place of fetishism, whereas the slave degenerates to usable thing. Deification–reification relation comes into a fetishistic inversion, in which a white god kills a reified slave (commodity).

Colonial history of innocent victims shapes public theology in its anamnestic reasoning, in which a project of decolonization is made in accordance with African identity of independence, cultural authenticity, and ethical performance of life-script through their narrative.

A genealogical position raises a serious question about the *Heart of Darkness*; what defines extractive colonialism by enabling it? What makes it really happen? If European powers are involved in African colonization, their colonial motivations at the Berlin Conference should be individually addressed, while taking on British, French or German involvement within the world system framework.

But Conrad remains silent about political technology of colonial body and extractive type of economic exploitation, and destruction of its social formation and ecology; it was built on the cooption of local leadership and militia's brutal violence tactics together with the European agents in the local posts

---

[75] Vansina, *Being Colonized*.

for the sake of collection of rubber or ivory. The white master becomes deified, while the slave is reified as laboring commodity. Deification and de-recognition characterize a colonial logic, which reproduces dialectics of master and slave into biopolitical politics of terror.

Racism and Body Politics in America

A colonial regime is a biopolitical regime of terror and genocide, and its civilizing mission remains the historical burden of Black people, a symbol of the Lamb of God. It is perpetuated into apartheid in South Africa in the struggle at risking life and death, and also the African-American experience of terror and slaughter in the lynching tree.

According to Thomas McCarthy, Social Darwinism occupies a central place in American policy in the establishment of a racial caste system of African slavery in the South, while completing Indian removal from American life in the West. Then a shift occurred from the nationwide expansion to international war with Spain.

World–historical mission of America is seen in its expansion of the empire of liberty, which is religiously sanctioned as manifest destiny in the providential sense along with the hierarchy of racialization.[76] Throughout the 17th and 18th centuries European settlers in North America turned to enslaved Africans. They were forced into slavery in the British colonies of Jamestown, Virginia (1619). Six to seven million enslaved people were estimated to be imported to the New World during the 18th century.

Although the African slave trade was outlawed in the U.S. Congress (1808), the institution of slavery remained vital

---

[76] McCarthy, *Race, Empire, and the Idea of Human Development*, 76.

and even flourished in the South until 1860. The abolitionist movement from the 1830s to the 1860s gained strength but provoked a great debate over slavery, tearing the nation apart into the civil war (1861-65). Despite freedom for the nation's four million enslaved people through the Union victory, constitutional abolition of slavery (1865) remained problematic during the Reconstruction period (1865-1877); a price is paid for reunion in its establishment of white supremacy in the states of the former Confederacy.

The first Ku Klux Klan was established as an American white supremacist terrorist group in the aftermath of the American Civil War, while defining an organization of the Reconstruction era in 1865. Racial justice is lost out to reunion; subsequently, a colonial policy ensued and was followed by Jim Crow laws, white terrorism, and the barbarous festival of the lynching tree.

A reversal of the post-Civil War requires a skill of effective history to write the history of the vivid present on the part of the Black historians. In the interest of reconciliation with the antebellum South, the history of slavery, the Civil War, and Reconstruction were dominated by pro-Southern, anti-black scholars who had obliterated the black experience in textbooks of American history until after World War II. And arguably are they trying to obliterate the Black experience today when we look at the debate about teaching the American history of slavery and the black experience in the elementary and high school classroom.[77]

Against this propaganda, W.E.B. Du Bois contends that the story of slavery, the Civil War, Reconstruction, and the post-Reconstruction are not certainly the truth, as written in the chapters of the textbook. But "beyond that [such propaganda] is dangerous."[78]

---

[77] Ibid., 107-8.
[78] Du Bois, *Black Reconstruction in America, 1860-1880*, 723.

Unfortunately, Jim Crow laws ensued in the U.S. Supreme court decision in *Plessy v. Ferguson* (1896). They were legislated in Southern state, officially segregating Black people from the White, enforced until 1965. On the other hand, it is estimated that 4743 lynching cases occurred in the South from 1882 to 1968 according to records by NAACP.[79] "They put him to death by hanging him on a tree" (Acts 10:39). While the public spectacle of lynching may have stopped, the execution of Black bodies by police could be considered modern day lynching. Many stories that we have read in the past few years of Black people killing themselves by hanging might not be suicide given the robust history of lynching in the USA.

The biblical statement above finds the Black experience of burning, mutilation, beating, torture, and shooting as symbolized in the racial terror on the lynching tree. "Southern trees bear a strange fruit, blood on the leaves and blood at the root. Black bodies swinging in the Southern breeze, strange fruit hanging from the poplar trees."[80]

The analytics of sexuality and the symbolics of blood are grounded in the distinctive regime of biopolitical racism (on the false accusation of sexual aggression of the Black against White women). It has public deployment and spectacle, which was attended by the White community in the gloomy festival of White supremacy.

A political technology of racism is allied with statist form and mob lynching in intervention at the level of body and its color, while a mythical concern is seen in protection of the purity of blood, sexuality, and triumph of race.[81] A fascist ritual of racism

---

[79] Anti-lynching protestors like Ida B. Wells composed newspaper columns to denounce the atrocities of lynching.

[80] "Strange Fruit" was written by Abel Meeropol and recorded by Billie Holiday, a jazz and swing music singer in 1939.

[81] Foucault, *The History of Sexuality* I: 149.

in the relation between the White and the Black combines the symbolics of the blood with purity of sexuality, demonstrating a mechanism of punishment, torture, and terror as a public spectacle of the lynching tree.

This fascist bloody spectacle implies the doublet of power-racism, which articulates a terrifying mechanism of body politics in securing the purity of blood and sexuality. A doublet of power-race comes to terms with power-knowledge relations, while sharpening the political technology of body and race in terms of violence and death. A biopolitical racism appears to be exclusion of the means, to the extent that the White is deified, while the Black is reified to a usable thing and lost into terror of lynching tree.

The public execution in its horrifying deployment dethrones God on the cross of Jesus, but God is allied with those crucified on the lynching tree. In fact, the profound meaning of divine suffering is culminated in the Black experience with death politics.[82] Effective history of power and racism are an archaeological way of rewriting the history of vivid present in terms of excavating the past, which is buried and subjugated. The legacy of slavery continues to shape and influence American history from the Reconstruction to the civil rights movement, up to social movement of Black Lives Matter (2013-present).

The Black body in its colonial enslavement is now stratified and oppressed in political technology of body, blood, and sexuality in administration of racial hierarchy, while justifying brutal management and violence of the state functionary (police or army) upon its life through its bureaucratic administration.

---

[82] Cone, *The Cross and the Lynching Tree*.

4. Global Racism, Negative Dialectics, and Dictatorship

In the postcolonial discussion of global Empire, Michael Hardt and Antonio Negri elaborate their global theory of sovereignty and capital in the sociological schema of international networks of power and information. They appropriate Foucault's idea of disciplinary society toward the biopolitical nature of the new paradigm of power.[83]

Power becomes entirely political control of the body, and society is subsumed within political governance. It is expressed as a control; it extends throughout the depth of the consciousness and bodies of the population crossing the entirety of social relations.[84] Along with global expansion, a new form of imperial racism resurges and progresses, as seen in a passage from the end of slavery to decolonization, civil rights movements, and the end of apartheid. In a modern imperial context, subordinated people are categorized into a different order of being, culture, and things. Social and cultural forces remain more crucial in social construction of modern imperial racism than essential biological difference and determinism.[85]

European racism is not based on modern practices of racial superiority or exclusion but operates in relation to the White-Man face, which is yardstick in determining the degrees of deviance. It underlines "a strategy of differential inclusion," which has less to do with binary division and exclusion.[86] In the discussion of sovereignty, Foucault focuses on a specific technology of power in contrast to the juridico-institutional theory. He is concerned with

---

[83] Hardt and Negri, *Empire*, 245.
[84] "Governmentality," in *The Essential Foucault*, 24.
[85] Hardt and Negri, *Empire*, 191-2.
[86] Ibid., 194.

a historico-political discourse about war which is "the permanent basis of all the institutions of power."[87] Political hegemony and economic exploitation were established and rationalized through technological procedure of racial discourse and its imperialist mode of representation in determining the relation between the dominant and the subordinated.

In a like manner, negative dialectics is characterized by struggle, resistance, and freedom in regard to the colonial order of things, and returns as effect of boomerang to the colonial master and its parasite agents. The state power (coercive ideological apparatuses) in the fascist-colonial context absorbs civil society, and a hegemonic element of sovereignty becomes indispensable in investigating imperialist or state socialist politics within the crisis of modern sovereignty.

Accordingly, Gramsci emphasizes the significant role of the hegemony as practiced in the sphere of civil society (such as the church, trade unions, schools, the mass media, or political parties). But *force or coercion* involves the use of repressive apparatus to bring the mass of people into conformity or dictatorship.[88] At issue is to build an integral state until the coercion would be removed and disappear (the regulated society in re-absorption of political society into civil society; worker's councils).[89]

Gramsci's philosophy of praxis is based on a culture of common sense and seeks hegemony as the epistemological primacy. This epistemic position (so called absolute historicism) makes it difficult to accept critical theory as scientific philosophy in its dialectical reflection of empirical reality and ideological apparatuses. There is no dialectical epistemology based on

---

[87] "Society Must Be Defended," in *The Essential Foucault*, 295.
[88] Jessop, *The Capitalist State*, 145. 149.
[89] Gramsci, *Selections from the Prison Notebooks*, 253.

conceptual sense and problematic in Gramsci's theory of praxis for hegemony.

Negative Dialectics and Dictatorship

Unlike Gramsci, however, Lenin still includes significance of Hegel's negative dialectics in his *Philosophical Notebooks* (1914-15). His provocative aphorism is expressed: "It is impossible completely understand Marx's *Capital,* and especially its first chapter, without having thoroughly studied and understood the *whole* of Hegel's *Logic.*"[90]

Hegel's dialectical question of universality and individuality, which is resolved in the theory of the unity and conflict of opposites, facilitates Lenin in comprehending phenomenon of complexity and interdependence of the world as interconnection with all particulars and different elements. "Contradiction is *the root of all movement and vitality,* and it is only insofar as it contains a Contradiction that anything *moves and has impulse and activity.*"[91]

In the reflection of contradiction, we are not allowed to attain the absolute finality, but truth content unveils itself only in working out the matter in the process of the resolution of contradictions. Universal aspect of reflection is closely bound up to practice of resolving social contradictions for the unity of opposites.[92]

However, Lenin fails to articulate the problem of contradiction through the conceptual position of creative power and non-violence principle, which finds its historical social embodiment in politics of mutual recognition and the difference. For Lenin,

---

[90] "Conspectus of Hegel's Science of Logic," in *Lenin Collected Works 38,* 180.
[91] Ibid., 139.
[92] Kolakowski, *Main Currents of Marxism* 2: 463-4.

negative dialectics remains only at the level of self-contradiction and serves as an instrument to attain political hegemony with violence, in other worlds, one party's totalitarian dictatorship over against the subaltern. Here, a dialectic between the dominant and the subordinated turns into political discourse of dictatorship, which reduces the position of hegemony to the most direct form of coercion and violence on the part of the vanguard party.

This device of the monster swallows up negative dialectics and the life of the subaltern into its bureaucratic governance, while assimilating civil society and morality into serving class struggle for state dictatorship. Socialist hegemony is expressed in the party's dictatorship and driven with ideological bureaucracy with repressive mechanism. Dictatorship, the most direct form of coercion, is exercised only except for destroying the state apparatuses, rather than the withering away of the state.

For example, a discourse of socialism (Soviet power plus electrification) underwent from capitalist economic system (N.E.P: 1921-1929) to collectivization (1929-1933). Here, the Marxist-Leninist type of hegemony is transformed into biopolitical dictatorship, resulting in death politics of terror in terms of deportation, enslavement, and concentration camps. One party dictatorship degenerates into central committee rule by a privileged caste, and it turns into a cult of personality with a dictator and politics of great terror and purges.[93] Here, 'man' turns into the enslavement to productive forces as treated in regard to labor power alone, while becoming most valuable capital. It is nothing more than a component of the productive forces (in the case of Stakhanovism).

Given this, direct democracy without a parliamentary system would degenerate into a disunified, economic–corporate system under bureaucratic domination of socialist party, or anarchist-

---

[93] Ibid., 489.

syndicalism.[94] It is worthwhile to take into account state integrative apparatuses. These may entail juridical-institutional regimes such as family, religious community, education, political parties, the trade union, the official network of mass media, and the cultural apparatus.[95]

An integrative approach to civil society and the state reacts against the binary assumption on state/bourgeoisie and the soviets/working class. It runs counter to capitalist authoritarian statism and socialist centralist statism, both of which are embedded with techno-bureaucratic statism of experts and hegemony.[96]

Moral position becomes crucial in the integrative relation between the state and civil society, in which the conscience and the sense of responsibility is articulated with political praxis and strategy for the social whole of moral society; it keeps in view recognition and creative freedom, organic solidarity, and no violence. It transcends limitation of tactics, class interests and consciousness, and ethics.[97]

Civil State and Popular Sovereignty

Our trajectory starts off with Hegel's conceptual dialectics of the dominant and the dominated toward recognition, freedom, and creativity. This epistemic stance leads to reexamination of a significant side of republican democracy in Rousseau's idea of popular sovereignty, in critical interrogation with Hegel. For the discussion of Hegel and Rousseau, first I take on Rousseau and Machiavelli, who sharpens Rousseau's' democratic position in regard to Hegel.

---

[94] Jessop, *The Capitalist State*, 180.
[95] Poulantzas, *State, Power, and Socialism*, 28.
[96] Ibid., 255.
[97] Lukacs, *Tactics and Ethics*, 9.

Rousseau and Machiavelli

Rousseau sees Machiavelli's profound political theory of democracy in *The Prince,* which offers great lessons to the people, although Machiavelli pretends to give lessons to the monarch. It is important to see difference and contrast between *The Prince* and his *Discourses on Titus Livy* and *History of Florence*.[98]

Niccolo Machiavelli (1469-1527) stands in the tradition of Renaissance humanism, and his position in *The Prince* focuses on a form of leadership which requires the prince's skill (or virtue) in order to gain power, glory, and security as conflicted with Christian morality.[99] In *The Prince*, he reinforces his view of a human being in terms of 'half man and half beast.'[100] To keep the faith in a prince, Machiavelli holds, "there are two ways of contending, one in accordance with the laws, the other by force; the first of which is proper to men, the second to beasts.

But since the first method is often ineffectual, it becomes necessary to resort to the second. A prince should, therefore, understand how to use well both the man and the beast.[101] Machiavelli does not hide his intention to express the significance of the people; "concerning the government of Princes," it is "in like manner to understand the People a man should be a Prince, and to have a clear notion of Princes he should belong to the People."[102]

For his political theory of hegemony Gramsci takes Machiavelli as a forerunner of the modern Jacobin and *The Prince* as the precursor of 'modern' communist party (Jacobin force). The

---

[98] Rousseau, *Social Contract,* "Genevan Manuscript," Book I. Ch. VI.
[99] "Machiavelli's Letter to Francesco Vettori," in *Classics of Moral and Political Theory*, 481.
[100] Machiavelli, *The Prince*, 45.
[101] Ibid.
[102] Ibid., viii.

state (the prince) is rooted in the people through coercion, consent, and moral (or charismatic) leadership.

For Hardt and Negri, *The Prince* can be regarded as "a revolutionary political manifesto," because people as the constituent power become a foundation of the government (the prince) in constitutional democracy.[103] The new concept of sovereignty is driven in the constitutive network of powers and counter powers through self-reforming process. This notion of the expansive power in networks is framed within republic democratic framework, which is linked up with a universal republic. Machiavelli's dialectics of republic lies in the relation between freedom and expansion, in which the empire becomes possible. There is an expansive concept of freedom in which corruption and destruction also would reside.[104]

Unlike the global theory of Empire, Rousseau draws attention to Machiavelli's *Discourses*, while investigating the Roman republic in which the interests of the community as a whole were pursued; "there is no doubt the public interest is never a guiding principle except in republics...The vast majority have interests that coincide with the public interest."[105]

Res publica (public affair in Latin translation of the Greek *politeia*) was translated among Renaissance scholars as the republic as a form of government in contrast to the monarchical or aristocratic state. In all three types of authority the republic had a fair share in power.[106]

For Machiavelli, the first founding principles of the Roman republic could be seen in its return to "the tribunes of the people,

---

[103] Hardt and Negri, *Empire*, 63.
[104] Ibid., 372.
[105] Machiavelli, "Discourses," Book 1. Ch. 2.
[106] Ibid.

the censors together with all those laws that were a barrier to the ambition and the insolence of men."[107]

A reform principle in the republic back to the founding principles makes the republic more capable of adapting itself flexibly to changing circumstances by virtue of citizens of differing characters than monarchy.[108] In effect, Machiavelli mediates the political conception of ancient Rome with that of the modern state (prince) toward political freedom and reform. "It is easy to understand how a people acquire such a love of political freedom, for we see by experience that city-states have never been successful, either in expanding their territory or in accumulating wealth, except when they have been free."[109]

Rousseau acknowledges that there is the significance of republican democracy and political freedom in Machiavelli, but Rousseau conceptualizes city state in accordance with popular sovereignty, general will, universal recognition, and economic justice. Its distinctive character is seen in Rousseau's critique of capitalist development, economic inequality, and colonial exploitation accorded with abusive, evil contract, which is stipulated in inequality and consolidated in privilege of the wealthy.

Rousseau's couplet of economic 'development' and 'social inequality' helps to circumvent the progressive significance of reforming progress and expansion of republic governance (Machiavelli), which is driven in subsequent development of industrial capitalism and the bourgeois 'civil society built upon evil contract.[110] This vantage point reexamines a critically renewed synthesis between Rousseau and Hegel. Rousseau's

---

[107] Machiavelli, "Discourses," Book III. Ch. 1.
[108] Machiavelli, "Discourses," Book III. Ch. 9.
[109] Machiavelli, "Discourses," Book II. Ch. 2.
[110] Colletti, *From Rousseau to Lenin*, 162.

civil state would not be far removed from Hegel's ethical state, which intervenes crisis and contradiction of economic society.

Rousseau and Hegel

For Rousseau, freedom is actualized and realized in and through society, which is founded upon a legislative system with a positive implication of freedom for all equality. Popular sovereignty aims at creating a new moral and social order, a just society in which a human being is denaturalized and transformed into the status of citizen for the common good and economic justice; it reacts against the 'invisible hand' (Adam Smith), competition struggle, and its government in the bourgeois society.

This position takes issue with the limitation of Hegel's critique of Rousseau. Hegel in his *Philosophy of Right* has an ambivalent attitude toward civil society in terms of morality-enhancing type as well as a detrimental type of pathology. If civil society leads inevitably to colonialism and war at the international level, Hegel requires the state as the rational actuality of ethical life and freedom. His understanding of the state in the concrete universality challenges Rousseau's civil state based on general will (proceeding from and even conflated with the individual will), because the latter does not regard universal will an absolutely rational element.

In Hegel's view, Rousseau reduces the union of individuals in the state to a social contract, which is based on arbitrary will, individual opinion, and capriciously given express consent. This perspective, Hegel argues, "destroy[s] the absolutely divine principle of the state, together with its majesty and absolute authority." (§ 258)

In the Rousseau's theory of social contract, Hegel observes the realization of social substance as formed and realized by the formation of the individual. All citizens constitute general will with majority through universal suffrage. In this argument, Hegel worries that Rousseau's civil state ended in the context of the French Revolution up to the maximum of frightfulness and terror.

This suspicion brings Hegel to identify his political compromise with the Prussian monarchy, in which his Cassandra-like warning appears against the July revolution in France (1830; replacing the constitutional monarchy with parliamentary monarchy) and the English reform bill (1831).[111] Hegel's self-consciousness still remains regressive at the universal-abstract level, which runs counter to his own sociology of externalization and conceptual principle underlying the union of the universal with the full freedom and welfare of the individual.

But Rousseau's limitation would be perhaps seen in his lack of conceptual clarity in dealing with the significance of differentiated role in a given society, to put it otherwise, incapable of recognizing the moral dimension of rationalized division of labor. Such blindness would be led to a terrible form of homogenizing tyranny, which appears to be insidiously in the Jacobins, although Rousseau is suspicious of any totalitarian form of Leviathan.

If Hegel seeks to conceptualize the anti-colonial notion of state in the rational actuality of ethical whole through freedom, universal recognition, and common good, he does not need to reject Rousseau's anti-colonial approach in terms of citizen as political, moral subject in which he defines his principle of participation and economic distributive justice.

As earlier noted, Hegel conceptualizes a democratic vision of mutual recognition and revolution in critique of political dominion an economic wealth, as seen the dialectics of discourse

---

[111] Habermas, *Theory and Practice*, 189.

between the noble and the base. This position is furthered in conceptual dialectics underlying recognition, perfect freedom with no violence, and creativity; this post-Marxist Hegel is not far removed from Rousseau's conception of the civil state, which has less to do with violence and terror in the Jacobin party.

Rather Rousseau's popular-legislative model under general will is based on people's consent and principle of economic justice (in preventing the free subject to enslavement to the capital) and universal recognition among equals. He takes issue with formal and representative democracy exposed to domination of Bourgeois political elitists. Such representative model should be renewed in terms of combined articulation between participatory or deliberate democracy and its judiciary controlling organ of central decision instances (such as governments, national and international multi-corporate enterprise).[112] Therefore, Charles Taylor asserts that "under the aegis of the general will, all virtuous citizens are to be equally honored. The age of dignity is born."[113]

In fact, Hegel follows in the footsteps of Rousseau to find the solution of struggle for recognition between master and slave only satisfactorily in a society of reciprocal recognition among equals, a democratic society with a common purpose, "in which there is a "'we' that is an 'I', and an 'I' that is a 'we'."[114]

In a like manner, Rousseau's contribution can be seen in his deliberation of public morals in the culture and society, by following a voice of nature within us against self-pride (*amour propre*), a source of evil. It features one's identity as cultural authenticity of moral being in which existence of moral sentiment is the source of joy and contentment. The underlying premise

---

[112] Fetscher, *Rousseau politische Philosophie*, 18, 26.
[113] Taylor, "The Politics of Recognition," in Taylor et al, *Multiculturalism*, 47.
[114] Ibid., 50.

here characterizes participatory democracy in its distinctive articulation of universal recognition in public festivals, which have no division between performer and spectator.[115] But he denounces a fateful moment to the degree that society takes a turn toward corruption, luxury, and injustice; thus, people feel desire for preferential esteem and honor.[116]

Conclusion

Our sociological reading of Hegel and Christian public theology has attempted to introduce postcolonial portrayal of Hegel, which has significance in post-Marxist age. I do not avert his critique of Christian religion, which is caught in inward piety and beautiful soul in the representational and pictorial language. When the gospel is no longer preached to the poor, the salt has become dumb. The idea of reconciliation is inherent in revelation of Christ.[117]

In his conservative leaning to Napoleon's state, Hegel defends an authoritarian system of the government and its disciplinary state in contrast to antagonism within modern civil society. In the politics of terror in the French Revolution, Hegel is recast upon a concept of rational, ethical state, which comes to terms with morality-enhancing side of civil society.

In the examination of the principle of recognition and concept, it is worth clarifying Hegel's relation between the state and civil society as constructed in accordance with the critical reason of emancipated individuals (seen in the dialectic of the dominant and the subordinated) toward an organic solidarity. In a sociological framework, the state is founded on social formation, which becomes the actual sites of various existences

---

[115] Ibid., 47.

[116] Ibid., 29. 35.

[117] Habermas, *Theory and Practice*, 190.

of civil institution and state non-repressive apparatuses. To put it otherwise, the state is conceptualized in terms of institutional ensemble of social systems imbued with moral communication according to ethically regulated consensus (freedom, recognition, difference, and common good). This perspective brings a positive significance of the state to the doublet of social division of labor, the individual personality, and organic solidarity.[118]

Crucial in the sociology of externalization is the critique of political power, economic wealth, social discourse of the flattery system, and imperial racism. This position is constructed in terms of recognition, freedom, and creativity in exclusion of violence and dictatorship. The state is not "a thing-instrument that may be taken away, nor a fortress that may be penetrated by means of a wooden horse, nor yet a safe that may be cracked by burglary: It is the heart of the exercise of political power."[119]

Social life is more and more organized through the institutions and associations of a free and democratic civil society along with administrative organic council. It reacts against the excessive power of the state with repressive apparatuses and economic privilege in industrial and commercial context. This social integrative model of meaningful work in critical synthesis of Rousseau and Hegel would be established as a public institution (with code of law) within a political system in mediation with civil society.

The couplet 'constitutional democracy and civil society' finds its significance in public theology to elaborate religious moral forces and communal councils for political, civil unit or the elementary division of the state. Civil society can be located as "a veritable sociological monstrosity"[120] in a vast system of national

---

[118] Durkheim, *The Division of Labor in Society*, xiii.
[119] Poulantzas, *State, Power, Socialism*, 258.
[120] Ibid., Liv.

or municipal corporations, and it is to be comprehended in terms of the diversity of social interests and their connections in democratic, pluralist context. Along the functional differentiation of the social systems, the well-spring of all moral activity can be seen in subordination of the particular, individual to the general, common interest.[121]

Excursus: Religion, Colonialism, and Slave

Our discussion of dialectic of master and slave, I find it critical to examine a prophetic figure of Bartolome de Las Casas (1484-1566), which is met with serious critique by the proponents of Empire. Postcolonial debate occurs around the legacy of Las Casas. It is argued that his solidarity with Amerindians can be seen only in light of the discussion of human rights instead of anti-colonialism.

In the wake of Christopher Columbus' discovery of America in 1492, the Council of Castile (established under Queen Isabella in 1480) met to pursue a colonialist project of a new crusade for gold.

The Genoese phase of historical capitalism paved the way for future participation in the trade between Seville and Castile's colonial empire. In February 1495 three hundred slaves arrived alive in Spain, and they were put up for sale in Seville by a churchman, Don Juan de Fonseca, the archdeacon of the town. In his report, they were as naked as the day they were born, having no more embarrassment than animals.[122]

The Genoese merchants converted the flow of silver from America to Seville by helping the king of Spain. Slaves became the main trading commodity in Europe's conquest and colonization

---

[121] Ibid., xliii.
[122] Konig, *Columbus*, 82.

of North and South America and the Caribbean islands from the fifteenth century onward. African laborers were deemed more fit than the indigenous people for sugar plantations in the tropical conditions in the New World.

Along with the double entry bookkeeping (widely used in Florence and Genoa by the end of the 15th century), mercantilism emerged in connection with imperialism, then such connection can be characterized in terms of settler colonialism, capitalist system of slavery, and nationalism.

Bartolome de Las Casas (1484-1566) wrote his account of the painful chapter in the history of *ecominenda* and colonialism in *The Devastation of the Indies: A Brief Account* (written in 1542). The colonial system of *encomienda* was a direct creation of the Spanish Crown and its ideological justification of Christianization. Land and Indians were assigned by the Spanish king to the conquerors for the sake of evangelization.

On the contrary, the chief function of the *encomienda* was to supply a labor force for the mines and cattle ranches. It depicts the barbarity of the conquistadores and colonialists particularly in the islands of La Hispaniola (present day Haiti and the Dominican Republic).

In this *ecomienda* type of settler colonialism, the indigenous were, in fact, more poorly treated than the slave. The bare life, or *homer sacer* began with colonialism and slavery. European capitalist world economy came to exist in the sixteenth century (1450-1640) drawing upon colonial exploitation, slavery, and biopolitical genocide.[123]

According to Hardt and Negri, Las Casas' concept of equality was based on the Christian idea of conversion, which is caught in a Eurocentric view of the Americas. Their argument becomes

---

[123] Wallerstein, *Modern World-System* 1: 94.

questionable and even controversial: "Las Casas is really not so far from the Inquisition."[124]

What do they mean by the standard of the Inquisition? The Spanish Inquisition was established in 1478 to promote enforced conversion with the public humiliation of penitents, particularly from Judaism and Islam at that time. Las Casas' position of authentic evangelization, which is based on persuasion and dialogue, must be seen in his recognition of God siding with the victims.

In his last will we read: "I testify that it was God in his goodness and mercy who chose me as his minster...on behalf of all those people out in what God calls the Indians...For almost fifty years I have done this work, back and forth between the Indies and Castile...All that the Spaniards perpetuated against those [Indian] peoples...was in violation of the holy and spotless law of Jesus Christ...such devastation, such genocide of populations, have been sins, monumental injustice!"[125]

This statement has little to do with subjugating or converting the Indians to European culture in the sense of Inquisition. In fact, the final judgment (Matt. 25:31-46) remains normative in the thought of Las Casas, who acknowledges the Indians as scourged christs.[126]

Las Casas was of post-Eurocentric character in his public debate with Juan Gines de Sepulveda (1490-1573), one of Spain's most important Renaissance humanists and theologians. In the Valladolid Controversy in front of a council of jurists and theologians (in the year of 1550-51, as organized by King Charles V), Sepulveda undertook the religious, intellectual justification for the Spanish right of colonial conquest.

---

[124] Hardt and Negri, *Empire*, 116.
[125] Las Casas, *Indian Freedom*, 9.
[126] Gutierrez, *Las Casas*, 95.

He synthesizes the Christian doctrine of just war with the Aristotelian logic of natural servitude (in Aristotle's Book I of *Politics*) for colonial logic of enslavement. Against this, Las Casas advocates for God of mercy and justice, in whom all humans were created equal according to the image of God. After he debated with Sepulveda, Las Casas maintains that the indigenous people were endowed by nature with Aristotle's principle of prudence—monastic, economic, and political.

The Indians were very prudent people who governed their republic justly and prosperously. The even surpassed the most prudent of all, the Greeks and Romans by looking at the rules of natural reason.[127]

Marx was keenly aware of the history of primitive accumulation in mercantile colonialism in connection with or articulation with industrial mode of production. Within a history of religion there is anthropological-prophetic problematic, which underlays the different forms of historical individuality and practices in different instances (economic, political, ideological, and technical).

This refers to a history of religious ethical practice, which is no longer reducible to the economic history of class struggle, but it is articulated or juxtaposed with other instances through peculiar prophetic reasoning as religious effect for human rights; this is seen in epistemological rupture with and struggle to Eurocentric Renaissance humanism. A biblical notion of the image of God cannot be implemented in abstract universality, but only in concrete universality in the specific life of those victimized.

Las Casas' limitation of African slavery does not go unnoticed, because of his unqualified substitution of the indigenous with African slave in plantation work, but his position is not racially biased. In his later stage he corrected his position and was committed to racial justice against the European colonial system.

---

[127] Las Casas, *Indian Freedom*, 226-7.

Las Casas' type of solidarity is patterned in terms of effective history standing for margins and from them. He is differentiated from Sepulveda's Eurocentric type of religion, colonialism and slavery, which was allied with the Inquisition.

A post-Eurocentric interpretation is concerned with clarifying Lacas' position in his own context rather than upholding the reader's presentism. But this reading strategy does not merely sidestep his limitation, but critically renews its problem in reference to today's pressing issue with racial justice. A critical reading of effective history finds its meaning in the concrete universal framework to uphold the recognition struggle and conceptual principle.

Chapter 4.

Prophetic Public Theology: Political and Emancipatory

This chapter is a study of public theology in the tradition of prophetic theology in the German Confessing Church. In the first two sections, I make an explication of Helmut Gollwitzer's theological position in taking on historical materialism, prophetic exegesis, critique of ideology, and politics of biblical eschatology, and class struggle. I also critically complement the biopolitical, sociological perspective in the discussion of other social scientists' arguments concerning ideological appellation, fascism, and military politics.

Then, it is important to take on the significance of liberation theology in Latin America, especially with focus on Clodovis Boff and Louis Althusser. Boff's theory of historical materialism can be critically assessed in reference to Althusser. A critical reading is undertaken in dealing with Althusser's theory of social formation and effective history in terms of dialectical theory.

Finally, I focus on the distinctive regime for public theology in explication of the relation between state, ideological apparatuses, bureaucracy, and civil society, while considering global governance of biopolitics, public health, and neocolonial structure of world system. It is significant to articulate biopolitics with multinational medical industrial complex, which becomes central in African public theology and its critique. A theory of late capitalism in world system facilitates transcending some limitations of dependence theory which allied with the liberation theology.

1. Political Theology and Public Theology

Moltmann distinguishes political theology from liberation theology by way of different political background; the former is imprinted with the reality of the poverty-stricken people of Latin America, born out of the North-South conflict, while the latter is grounded in the cold war of divided Europe within the East-West conflict. Political theology stands in prophetic inheritance of theology, religious socialism, and the Confessing Church against the Third Reich.

During the era of Allende in Chile, the movement of the Christians for Socialism held its conference in 1972 in Santiago de Chile. Liberation theology can be understood as the first form of the postcolonial theologies in challenging the century-long colonial exploitation and economic dependence on Europe and North America. Its motto is obviously seen in the preferential option for the poor, in which an economic theory of dependence plays a major role as a critical analysis of the unequal relations between the metropolis and the periphery.[1]

In the prophetic type of public theology, however, Moltmann characterizes Helmut Gollwitzer as the most important one, who deploys the significance between Christian Gospel and emancipation in commitment to society and the world. He was one of the best pupils of Karl Barth by standing in the tradition of the Confessing Church during the Third Reich. In solidarity

---

[1] Moltmann, *God for a Secular Society*, 50.

with the student group in the 1960s, Gollwitzer was confronted with the reality of the capitalist downfall of humanity and crimes against it, standing for the revolution of life.²

What is central in Gollwitzer is the Gospel about the Kingdom of God, which is imbued with the promise as the anticipation of the hope of the reality of God, as explained in the gospel narrative. Every traditional theme of theology is to be reemployed and contextualized in the horizon of world transformation, because "God the wholly Other demands the society to be completely different."³

Gollwitzer and Historical Materialism

Gollwitzer respects the differences of theological models and discourse between Barth and Tillich, while advancing his social question of meaning as a real question through a hermeneutical and social scientific framework. Following in footsteps of Barth, Gollwitzer integrates Paul Tillich's socialist principle and method of correlation into his public discourse of life questions as central religious and real questions. As Gollwitzer maintains, "Tillich rightly can rely on the situation of the today's human being and relates his interpretation of Christian message to the human situation."⁴

For Gollwitzer, Christ and Prometheus are not mutually exclusive, nor in contradiction. Prometheus was the saint and the martyr for the young Marx, so that Prometheus in the Marxist calendar is not necessarily denounced as anti-Christian.⁵ His public theology in the philosophical and social scientific framework is featured by his theory of correlation in taking on the

---

2   Ibid., 51.
3   Pangritz, *Der ganz andere Gott will eine ganz andere Gesellschaft*, 9.
4   Gollwitzer, *Krummes Holz-aufrechter Gang*, 33-4.
5   Ibid., 13.

path from the 'crooked timber' (Kant's description of a human being) toward an 'upright march' (Ernst Bloch's description of a human being).[6]

Gollwitzer seeks to elaborate the significance of the historical, materialist inquiry for his theology. He takes into account Engel's clarification of historical materialism (in Engel's letter to Joseph Bloch, September 21/22, 1890).

In this letter, Engels writes: "According to the materialist conception of history, the production and reproduction of real life constitutes *in the last instance* the determining factor of history. Neither Marx nor I ever have maintained more. Now when someone comes along and distorts this to mean that the economic factor is the *sole* determining factor, he is converting the former position into a meaningless, abstract and absurd phrase. The economic situation is the basis but the various factors of the superstructure...all these exercise an influence upon the course if historical struggles, and in many cases determine for the most part their *form*. There is a reciprocity between all these factors in which finally...the economic movement asserts itself as necessary."[7]

What counts in historical materialism is a social critical method in interrogating history and society. Social history is not to be reduced to a single determining causality as grounded in the mode of production. The spheres in the superstructure retain relative autonomy in terms of their specific histories, immanent causalities, developments, and controversies.

In view of change in the relation of production, the change in the superstructure runs slower and longer; it does not take

---

[6] Ibid., 9.
[7] "Historischer Materialismus und Theologie," in Gollwitzer, *Auch das Denken darf dienen* I: 75. English Citation from https://www.marxists.org/ history/etol/ newspape/ni/vol01/no03/engels.htm

place simultaneously at the same level as transformation of the economic base (infrastructure). The former is more conservative and delaying than change in economic production, which can be obviously seen in late capitalism. The transformation of economic production is less influential in the history of religion than political history.[8]

Based on the reciprocity principle, Gollwitzer modifies or better articulates Marx's sentence in the *German Ideology*: "Morality, religion, metaphysics, all the rest of ideology and their corresponding forms of consciousness, thus no longer retain the semblance of independence. They have no history, no development; but men, developing their material production and their material intercourse, alter with this their real existence, their thinking and the products of their thinking. Life is not determined by consciousness, but consciousness by life."[9]

Seen in mutual influence or determination, Gollwitzer argues, intellectual, religious, or ideological spheres can unfold their course in accordance with economic intercourse and development. What is at issue in history is that the human spirit or intellectual mind becomes the central transferring factor. The human creative mind makes nature available to the productive force and uses it for the human being through labor. It refers to the objective spirit in the social cultural realm. There is a creative human response to the external challenge (natural environment). Marx's dialectical method is framed with the relation between human response and external challenge.[10]

A mutual determining aspect is expressed in Marx's own statement of the aesthetical dimension in ancient Greek culture:

---

[8] Ibid., 76.
[9] "The German Ideology," in *Karl Marx Selected Writings*, 164.
[10] "Bermerkungen zur Materialistichen Bibellektűre," in Gollwitzer, *Umkehr und Revolution* 1: 250-1.

"The difficulty we are confronted with is not, however, that of understanding how Greek art and epic poetry are associated with certain forms of development. The difficulty is they still give us aesthetic pleasure and are in certain respects regarded as a standard and unattainable ideal."[11]

To the degree that human consciousness, or the artist's products and epic poetry is determined by life and created within the social material condition, they still transcend their given social condition, working cross-culturally in effecting human life in different times and places. It implies a reality of the 'constant' in the intellectual sphere such as an art, religion, or language, which are not merely produced in the social economic basis nor reduced in the mode of production. Instead, it performs itself throughout the social change and historical development.[12]

Primacy is ascribed to creative human mind in the superstructure in interaction with economic infrastructure and social formation. The human mind still cuts across the environment of social cultural system, which evolves along with the process of rationalization in historical course and produces functional differentiations of social subsystems.

Accordingly, Barth comes to a brief concluding remark: "Yet it [historical materialism] is so only *per accidens* and not *per essentiam*."[13] Barth's interpretation implies that historical materialism has less to do with economic reductionism or necessity in an essential sense, because it interacts with intellectual spheres, which are influential in organizing economic system in a rational,

---

[11] Cited in Lukacs, *The Young Hegel*, 510.
[12] "Bemerkungen zur Materialistichen Bibellektűre," in Gollwitzer, *Umkehr und Revolution*, 247.
[13] Barth, *Church Dogmatics*, III/2: 387.

functional, differential manner. Economic forces are relative and even accidental in regard to power of intellectual spheres.

Such a position finds its significance in Gollwitzer, who utilizes Engel's statement: "According to the materialist conception of history, the production and reproduction of real life constitute *in the last instance* the determining factor of history."

The production of real life and its social regulation in the relations of production are, in the last instance, taken as the driving force among other factors. The economic interest of the individual is not the essentially determining factor in the last instance, but the economic development in rationalization, specialization, and differentiation should be the ground force of history in interaction with intellectual spheres of superstructure.[14]

Economic system communicates itself with other spheres of social system correlating with the economic development through structural coupling and articulation. This structural position features Marx as a critical thinker of social formation and differentiation in terms of a dialectic between human response and external challenge.

Social Formation and Technological Rationality

Marx elaborates a historical materialist method in the Preface to *A Critique of Political Economy,* and he argues that relations of production correspond to a definite stage of development of the material productive forces. The sum total of this correlation (mode of production) constitutes the economic structure of

---

[14] "Historischer Materialismus und Theologie," in Gollwitzer, *Auch das Denken darf dienen*, 82.

society, in other words, foundation of the society of political economy.

Intellectual spheres, such as a legal or political sphere, arise and are specialized in correspondence to definite forms of social consciousness. The social, political, and intellectual life process in general is conditioned by the mode of production of material life. In the developed forms of the productive forces through *natural science, or technological advance*, a conflict would occur in its relationship with the existing relations of production at the rational level in administration, rational organization, and distribution. When such conflict turns into fetters, an epoch of social revolution begins.[15]

At this point, there is priority of natural science, which changes and transforms the mode of production. Natural science along with technological innovation is bound to the politico-legal sphere and the ideological practice, by influencing social existence, while entering into corresponding forms of the human consciousness. A development in the womb of bourgeois society creates the material conditions for the dissolution of the antagonism. This affirms Marx's thesis of historical materialism: "It is not the consciousness of men that determines their being, but, on the contrary, their social being that determines their consciousness."[16]

Social system communicates itself in human cognition through technological innovation, the correlation of which characterizes Marx as a critical, systemic thinker in dealing with social formation, risk, and transformation.

However, this stance does not necessarily discard the operative autonomy of the intellectual aesthetic sphere in transcending the

---

[15] "Preface to *A Critique of Political Economy*," in *Karl Marx Selected Writings*, 389.
[16] Ibid.

given social economic condition in its cross-cultural effect. Rather it entails a space of the intellectual sphere in fighting against the conflict and contradiction brought by the transformation of productive forces through technological progress and innovation in natural science.

Technological rationality finds also significance in Weber's theory of rationalization and his concept of purpose (or instrumental) rationality, which is utilized to clarify the phenomenon of reification in the area of legal system, administration, and social spheres. Concurring with Weber, Lukacs observes that "there arises a rational systematization of all statues regulating life."[17] "The specific type of bureaucratic consciousness"[18] appears to be one of the major sources in which human life is threatened in multiple forms of alienation and inequality.

In the reified and hierarchical relations of social stratification, the principle of rational mechanization, calculability, and domination, together with symbolic violence, penetrates and conditions every aspect of life. The phenomenon of social reification perpetrates and infiltrates into all realms of society, culture, and nature along with functional differentiation.

In his critique of Feuerbach, Marx writes: "But the human essence is no abstraction inherent in each single individual. In its reality it is the ensemble of the social relations."[19] If the human being is conceptualized in terms of the ensemble of the social relations, this implies the significance of the reciprocity between intellectual spheres and economic relations in influencing and determining social existence. In Marx's definition of 'the ensemble of the social relations' we read: "A cotton-spinning jenny is a

---

[17] Lukacs, *History and Class Consciousness*, 96.
[18] Ibid., 99.
[19] "Theses on Feuerbach" VI, in *Karl Marx Selected Writings*, 157.

machine for spinning cotton. Only in certain circumstances does it become capital. Torn from those circumstances it is no more capital than gold is money or sugar the price of sugar."[20]

The historical, materialist inquiry can become a social scientific method in grasping the dynamism of historical context and social change of human life. It conceptualizes epistemic theory of social formation with diverse instances or spheres in rationalization, stratification, and reification. The social totality or formation is advanced through scientific-technological rationality in organizing and regulating economic production, social relations, biopolitics, public health, and institutions for need of human life. In fact, social formation is no longer a harmonizing concept, but it entails conflict, brokenness, and contradiction along with functional differentiation. A systemic theory of society focuses on class domination and social stratification replete with class struggle, risk, and structural coupling and transformation.

For Gollwitzer, the historical materialist approach has a particular moment of truth in which human consciousness must be transformed into coping with social life and existence. In his view, religion is allied with the power of the state (alliance between throne and altar) underwriting the economic system and mechanism for the powerful. But religion has its own autonomy in retaining the critical, emancipatory role regarding the status quo.[21]

Remarkable in Gollwitzer is his focus on capitalism and ecological threat. In the global stage of capitalism humankind has entered into ecological pressure and catastrophe, which press all people and nation states into global interdependence. He takes issue with particularistic thought which is attached

---

[20] Cited in Lukacs, *History and Class Consciousness*, 13.
[21] "Historischer Materialismus und Theologie," in Gollwitzer, *Auch das Denken darf dienen*, 86.

to domination and material security. It pursues privilege and violence, affirming that the history of humanity is one of class struggles. It runs counter to common good and universal value such as human dignity, economic justice, and ecological sustainability. Threatened by ecological catastrophe, we are all in the same boat facing up to environmental problem.[22]

Ecological regime under technological domination becomes one of the most distinguished problems in underwriting the significance of moral communication for survival of life and alternative system of economics and social change. This ethical stance runs counter to capitalist system in the network of particular thought, privilege, and financial interests.

Gollwitzer's heuristic position focuses on technological rationality and its dominion, which becomes crucial in the pressing issue of global warming, dangerous climate change, and pollution, requiring moral commitment to the common good and the survival of our civilization at stake.

Critical Renewal: Idea and Interest

Gollwitzer attempts to renew and reinterpret the historical materialist theory by way of complementation and critique. Here, he draws special attention to the relation between the idea and interest (as formulated in Marx in his *Holy Family*).[23] "The idea always disgraced itself, insofar as it differed from the interest."[24]

Marx's formulation is bound to the reality of the French Revolution. The interest of the bourgeoisie in the 1789 won and had effective success. The interest is so powerful in its practical realization of the political idea, but the real conditions of the

---

[22] Gollwitzer, *Die kapitalistische Revolution*, 35.
[23] "Historischer Materialismus und Theologie," 87.
[24] "Bemerkungen zur Materialistichen Bibellektűre," 253.

masses for emancipation were substantially different from the bourgeoisie. It remains a disgrace or failure, because the mass did not find its real interest in the political idea of revolution.[25]

The reality of discrepancy can be sought in the failed relation between discourse and collective interest. If Marxist theory is deviated from its own concern and interest and becomes the discourse of hegemony in justifying violence and privilege, it also profanes itself. This aspect of discrepancy reinforces the immanent critique which remains crucial in Gollwitzer. A religious discourse should be distinguished in terms of the immanent critique from the source. It problematizes the disgrace effect of the discourse in representing the status quo of epistemic systems and power relations, while reinterpreting the source of discourse for solidarity and emancipation.

Indeed, Tillich is concerned with the position of the young Marx, who contrasts with the cause-effect relation in predicting the economic realm. Economic activity must be examined in connection with all aspects of the human being. A human being, when apart from social consciousness, would be a meaningless and empty concept. A materialist inquiry seeks to unveil the extent to which a specific false consciousness, or ideological factor would emerge in particular social situations affecting social existence; a discrepancy arises in certain relations of inherited concepts and symbols to a new historical reality.

If a symbolic world becomes ideological, the concepts and symbols are employed in serving status quo of social order; it provides an ideological function in obscuring the actual situation of human life. Various aspects of superstructure or social fields are interwoven, interacting with human process of self-creation; creative praxis is embedded with social historical situations. Apart

---

[25] "The Holy Family," in *Karl Marx Selected Writings*, 141.

from this connection, scientific theory or discourse remains in discrepancy in the sense of false consciousness or ideology.[26]

In the history of ideas, compromise or accommodation takes place in regard to social cultural forces, but it can be recast in a historical materialist frame of reference and through the emancipatory interpretation. There are conflicting interests of the biblical world in social circumstances. The prophetic hermeneutic seeks to analyzes the extent to which biblical statements or discourse would be stamped and conditioned in their critique of, or accommodation to the social forces and privilege.

Historical materialism counts as a critical inquiry, and it does not necessarily announce that the Gospel would be merely a human product. The Gospel as the idea should not be ineffective by disgracing itself. Rather, in Marx's own view, the disgrace of the idea takes place when differentiated from the interest and its practical realization. An individual stands before options, whether to follow its own material interest or follows the idea of the Gospel.[27]

Gollwitzer seeks to cut across limitations of historical criticism through the materialist lens; the former focuses on sociological condition of religious ideas within universal history of religion. Here, compromise or accommodation tends to undermine the significance of religious source as immanent critique regarding historical stream in ideological tainting.

A critical dialectic between idea and interest features the significance of immanent critique by qualifying historical, materialist analysis of social formation and functional differentiation at the social cultural level, especially in terms of the mutually influential interplay between infrastructure and

---

[26] Tillich, *The Socialist Decision*, 117.
[27] "Bemerkungen zur Materialistichen Bibellektűre," 257.

intellectual instances. Technological rationality in the progress of natural science plays a major role in shaping social structure and diverse social fields; it involves rational organization, specialization, regulation, and epistemic practice in dealing with elective affinity between religious ideas and material interests.

A bureaucratic governance is established in terms of political ruling system with ideological apparatuses in civil society. This systemic function makes human practical attitude more urgent to create an alternative to the prevailing status quo than ever.

Idea and Masses in Discourse and Power

Gollwitzer draws attention to Marx's statement: "Theory becomes a material force when it grips the masses."[28] Marx observes that the victory of the idea should be expressed to the point of where it is no longer differentiated from the collective material interest of the masses. In connection with interest of the masses, such alliance implies optimism residing in the historical, materialist theory. It also entails attitude of suspicion toward the victory of the idea in the whole development of history when distracted from the collective interests of the masses.[29]

Marx may imply the significance of the discourse in its practical dimension and power relations, because the discourse has performance in influencing and grasping the heart of the masses. It is relevant to undertake a critical analysis of power-ridden discourse and the channel of human practice. Language correlates with consciousness, and the combined aspect is bound up to actual life process in public intercourse. It may have double function; expression of interconnection between ideas

---

[28] Cited in Lukacs, *History and Class Consciousness*, 2.
[29] Gollwitzer, "Bemerkungen zur Materialistichen Bibellektűre," 258.

and material interests or distortion of such relationship by false consciousness.[30]

This stance helps me to construct Gollwitzer's insight into the twofold sense of class struggle along with Marx's significance of discourse and power. This sociological articulation of discourse-power and class struggle describes Foucault's genealogy of discourse of hegemony (focusing on biopolitical strategy from above); the sociological articulation is undertaken in dealing with multiple factors in social stratification.

The reciprocal relation between ideas and material interests can be examined in light of the immanent critique, which is concerned with accommodation, compromise, and distortion in the network of power relations in history and society. It is bound to reality of class/status struggle again reality of impersonal forces. Whenever material interest assumes the form of idea, it presents itself as a general interest.

This sociological insight into articulation remains decisive in exposing the extent to which discourse would be allied with material interests and power relations. There is regime of disgrace (privilege, domination, and power), which can be sustained in political dominion of human life, nature, and bureaucratic apparatuses.

Language and Religion

Gollwitzer's thesis of ideas and material interests safeguards the importance of language in his critical and emancipatory exegesis of the Scripture. For him, language is not merely reduced to ideological superstructure, nor is it part of the economic basis. Language is a relatively independent phenomenon located between economic basis and the intellectual sphere. In theological

---

[30] "The German Ideology," in *Karl Marx Selected Writings*, 164.

deliberation of revelation as speech event, theology of the living, emancipatory word of God cuts across limitations of the Marxist version of language as class ideology.

Discourse-power interplay appears to ally cultural hegemony with a universal thought-language even in the former Soviet regime. Thought correlates with language, thus material base consists of relations of production, while the superstructure serves the base as its instrument. Here, language (not bound up with particular classes) is directly linked with creative forces and belongs to the flattering system in serving power mechanism and ideological interpellation. Language as matter of class ideology disappears and is solidified in an ethnic–racial sense in which the Russian is ideologically elevated as a universal thought-language (Russian chauvinism).[31]

By contrast, the word of God as constant is explicated in hermeneutical frame and through prophetic exegesis from below. A heuristic method of the social historical hermeneutic is integrated into deepening the meaning of the gospel. Individual, seen in the ensemble of social relations, is comprehended within the social material existence. The prophetic language in the Hebrew Bible is bound to the social predicament, and Jesus' discourse of the kingdom of God is in solidarity with public sinners and tax collectors.

Prophetic Exegesis and Scripture Hermeneutics

Religion has a double standard; it is both an opium of the people and the expression of real suffering along with a protest against it. If religion expresses real suffering and protest, it is no longer determined according to the economic basis. It retains a

---

[31] Kolakowski, *Main Currents of Marxism* 3: 141-2. 158.

more independent role with its prophetic moral. Religion does not die out.

It is Max Horkheimer who paves a path to religion as a longing for the Wholly Other (*totaliter aliter*), which plays a critical role in changing the status quo. Religion retains a significance in constructing the social cultural reality in accordance with prophetic rationality engaged in God the Wholly Other.[32]

This perspective finds significance in Marx's position of religion as social protest against oppression and predicament. We read a dimension of categorical imperative in the young Marx: "The criticism of religion ends with the doctrine that man is the highest being for man, that is, with the categorical imperative to overthrow all circumstances in which man is humiliated, enslaved, abandoned, and despised, circumstances..."[33]

Likewise, Gollwitzer maintains that the categorical imperative in Marx's moral impulse finds its place and revolutionary impulse in prophets' confrontation with social problems and also in Jesus' solidarity with the impoverished (Lk 4:18). Jesus' proclamation does not merely include apocalyptic judgment, but a joyous message (glad tiding) in conversion (*metanoia*) to the coming kingdom of God in solidarity with public sinners and tax collectors.

Metanoia in the biblical sense must be radical and it implies revolutionary character in political, social sense.[34] For Gollwitzer, a theological view is dialectically driven and conditioned by the move from above to below; here, the 'above' does not mean the upper class in social relation from above.

---

[32] Ott, *Max Horkheimer's Critical Theory of Religion*, 103.
[33] "Towards a Critique of *Hegel's Philosophy of Right*: Introduction," in *Karl Marx Selected Writings*, 69.
[34] Gollwitzer, *Die kapitalistische Revolution*, 130. 113.

Instead, it refers to God above, adopting the standpoint of the living Word of God. To the degree that people hear the Word of God and are grasped by it, to what do they orient themselves along with the Word of God?

A theological reflection begins with the relation between faith and the Word of God, asking what people undertake with religion or Gospel. What response or answer do they make concerning the challenge of the Gospel? In the theological context, it is significant to adopt a hermeneutical suspicion of power relations in explicating the extent to which the religious idea of the Gospel would be accommodated to serve those in power.

Thus, suspicion is associated with social critical analysis of discourse in the political, social, and religious sphere in order to unveil its interplay with power relations and its domination. The material interest can be disgraced by the idea as the source of the immanent critique concerning the history of the church. The historical Christendom is reformism as bound to a system of domination; it should be overcome in terms of the Gospel about the kingdom of God and social reform and revolution.[35]

Ideological function (disgrace effect) aside, religious language retains an emancipatory effect in actualizing the relation between ideas and material interests for practical realization. Listening attentively to the Word of God and undertaking deliberate exegetical work, Gollwitzer focuses on the prophetic dimension of Scripture, in which the responsibility is expressed in "not similar things, but the same thing."[36]

God continues to perform 'the same thing' of solidarity and emancipation in the prophetic message to us in the present. This aspect emphasizes metanoia in the biblical sense, which must be radical; it means transformative and revolutionary in

---

[35] Ibid., 106. 96.
[36] Gollwitzer, *An Introduction to Protestant Theology*, 59.

political, social and cultural realms. The church in the sense of a permanent revolution moves in approximate manner toward the concrete utopia. "Thy will be done on earth as it is in heaven."[37]

God and Ideological Interpellation

Gollwitzer's position contrasts with a theory of 'ideological' interpellation in the structure of all ideologies in general. Althusser argues that an ideology interpellates individuals as subjects in the name of a Unique and Absolute Subject (God). In relationship between God and faithful individuals, God occupies the unique place of the Centre and interpellates individuals as subjects. God will recognize God's own in the individuals, who in return recognize God and themselves in God.

This mutual recognition is caught in the triple effect: subjection, universal recognition, and absolute guarantee. Thus, the subjects go, recognizing that 'it's really true', or 'this is the way it is.' Their obedience to God is true to the priest, the boss, and the engineer, while loving their neighbor.[38]

At this point, Althusser takes into account Hegel as a theorist of universal recognition, or ideology. In Althusser's argument, religious ideology exists in the religious Ideological State Apparatus within the capitalist social formations, and its functioning and structure hold for all other ideologies in which other ideological apparatuses play a more important role. But their convergent effect always has the same objective in justifying the daily, uninterrupted reproduction of the relations of production in the human consciousness; the latter refers to "the material comportment of the agents of the various functions of capitalist social production."[39]

---

[37] Ibid., 153.
[38] Althusser, *On the Reproduction of Capitalism*, 197.
[39] Ibid., 198.

Althusser's theory of ideological interpellation is mistaken, because he misrepresents the relationship between God and Moses. God's promise materialized in Torah does not necessarily mean the assimilation of the covenant partner to the world of the idol. On the contrary, God's promise dethrones it. God's Name is not the Absolute Subject of ideological interpellation, but transcends it, because prophetic consciousness confronts reality of evil and interpellation of fascism in impersonal forces.

This aspect is also circumvented still in Hegel's theory of universal recognition in which he takes issue with a theological language of divine reconciliation back to the pure inwardness and beautiful soul. A prophetic hermeneutics entails a parrhesiatic critique of ideological interpellation coming from capitalist commodity fetishism and its power mechanism. Biblical exegesis focuses on the source of the Scripture principle and undertakes a critique of the historical streams through the source; the source of the immanent critique is the Hebrew scripture, Jesus, and Jesus-witness in primitive Christianity.

Creation and Grace

In Gollwitzer's view, the biblical account of creation affirms God's announcement of its good. All creatures are good according to divine affirmation. The possibility of the world is grounded only in God's gracious will, which reacts against the self-deification of the world and the human self-autonomy. A human being is determined to be an image of God to stay and live in creation, and divine love reflects in his/her life as God's partner in gracious covenant.[40] Creation as grace points to a healing of the relation to nature, which is tainted in a ruthless exploitation. Good life includes creaturely life and ecological integrity, which

---

[40] Gollwitzer, *Krummes Holz-aufrechter Gang*, 227.

can be improved by the transformation of the capitalist system of production.

God's grace is opposed to Marx's thesis of the self-creation of human being through labor. According to the young Marx in his *Paris Manuscript* (1844), "the creation is therefore a conception very hard to expel from the popular consciousness. The independent status of nature and of man is inconceivable to it, because it contradicts all the tangible evidence of practical life."[41]

Gollwitzer acknowledges that Marx stands in the tradition of the modern rebellion against Church's teaching of God's grace. This extends from Renaissance humanism through Enlightenment to the modern contemporary ideology, which is relevant to Marxist theory.[42] An antithesis between autonomous freedom and heteronomous dependence has always been in the theological tradition of grace and human free will, as seen in Augustine's controversy with Pelagius or Luther against Erasmus.

For Gollwitzer, a theology of grace is not separated from a theology of human freedom. A genuine freedom is born from God's grace, that is, divine overflowing love. Creation is the merciful love, because *Amor Dei non invenit, sed creat suum diligibile* (God's love does not discover its object but creates it—Martin Luther).[43]

Creation and evolution do not exclude each other, and the last as the telos is already proclaimed in the beginning. The light of the Future of God shines upon the beginning (Rev. 22:5). The last corresponds to the beginning, while the consummation (glorious) to the creation (good). There is no biblical story of

---

[41] Cited in Gollwitzer, *An Introduction to Theology*, 156.
[42] Ibid., 157.
[43] Gollwitzer, *Krummes Holz-aufrechter Gang*, 225.

creation without eschatology, and vice versa.⁴⁴ In this proleptic correlation, Gollwitzer holds, creation as grace "is not yet complete, but is on the way to still greater glory; it is a fight against all obstacles to salvation, reservation, and consummation of the creature in the kingdom of God."⁴⁵

There are so many diverse times and places in the historical streams, thus in expressions of these. Ideological critique implies a point of convergence with the biblical sources for humanitarian vision and praxis relevance in contrast to conformism and accommodation, as seen in ideological interpellation and its assimilation.

In apprehending the source as the critique of the stream, "most sources are not in agreement with the course of the river."⁴⁶ Return to the source of the biblical text means swimming against the stream to arrive at the source. The most sources are not in agreement with the diverse streams in the course of river, even in pollution. Being radical means returning to the root.

Gollwitzer incorporates a dimension of the immanent critique into biblical exegesis. The intention of the biblical text is clarified in terms of dialectical relation between idea and material interests; social location, political interest, and power structure can be investigated—with precision of critique of ideology, in other words, the immanent critique under the principle of the grace as the source.⁴⁷

---

44 Gollwitzer, *An Introduction to Protestant Theology*, 223.
45 Ibid., 145.
46 Ibid., 109.
47 "Historischer Materialismus und Theologie," 79.

2. Class Struggle, Politics of Eschatology, and Civil State

In his book *Capitalist Revolution* (1973), Gollwitzer seeks to clarify global stage of capitalism in the neocolonial condition, while articulating critical theory of social formation with world economic system. In challenging capitalism with a fascist face, a critical analysis of class struggle and global economic system is required to summon church for responsibility, solidarity, and emancipation.[48]

He uncovers the standpoint from above as idealism, self-deception of upper strata, which perpetuates its class struggle from above; it is determined and defined by interest of the dominant class for their public welfare and privilege against the underclass.[49] This perspective cuts through limitations of Marx's theory of class struggle: "The history of all hitherto existing society is the history of class struggles."[50]

Class Dominion from Above, Fascism, and Military Politics

In Gollwitzer's account, "there is class struggle, where there is the class society. ...it is an inevitable characteristic of relation in a class society...*The class struggle is always and primary class struggle from above*. Class struggle from below is answer, reaction, and counter force."[51]

---

[48] "Andreas Pangritz's Introduction," in Gollwitzer, *Die kapitalistische Revolution*, 8-9.
[49] Gollwitzer, "Bemerkungen zur Materialistichen Bibellektűre," 254.
[50] "The Communist Manifesto," in *Karl Marx Selected Writings*, 222.
[51] Gollwitzer, *Die kapitalistische Revolution*, 85.

Struggle is expressed in the development of popular movements and citizen initiatives, in which democratic organs mushroom at the base and self-management occurs in elimination of class privilege and dominion. It shifts to modification and transformation of relations of forces within the state in terms of democratic road to social justice; it has little to do with centralization of political power on the hands of Soviet council and the workers by smashing or destroying the representative democracy or state apparatuses.[52]

Gollwitzer's democratic socialist position implies an aspect of state power or hegemony (force and consent), which is characterized as the class struggle as hegemony and bureaucracy in relation to the class struggle from below (trade union) and across (citizen initiative and student movement).

In dealing with social totality, it is substantial to form counter discourse from below in protest to the class struggle from above – the system of domination through state power, hegemony, and bureaucracy. In emphasizing the class dominion and ideological struggle in the superstructure, it is difficult to underpin a model of binary opposition between the exploiter and the exploited; alliance among class and status between citizen initiative, students, and the subaltern comes into critical focus.

In the discussion of class struggle and military politics, Gollwitzer argues that capitalism in its damaged stage of contradiction leads to and grasps fascism. It demonstrates its self-destructive face of barbarism, when the situation is dangerous for it and damaged by crisis.

The liberal democracy has the face of the possessive class, but if it has fear, its face shows fascism. In the election of parliamentary democracy, whether (leading to socialism) and fascist dictator, the latter was chosen.

---

[52] Poulantzas, *State, Power, Socialism*, 260.

In dealing with the neocolonial reality of structural violence, Gollwitzer argues, we stand in alternative to 'socialism or barbarism (Rosa Luxemburg).'[53] In a like manner, Tillich also insists that "the future of Western civilization can be either socialism or barbarism." "The salvation of European society from a return to barbarism lies in the hands of socialism."[54]

Since capitalist dominion is understood as the system grounded in a specific mode of production, Gollwitzer concurs with Max Horkheimer's statement: "Anyone who speaks of capitalism must also speak of fascism."[55] Of special significance in Horkheimer is the critical analysis of the convergence between liberal and totalitarian ideologies. These have emerged in the aftermath of monopolization of economic life by reducing reason to technological rationality within the authoritarian structure of capitalist society.

In the conjuncture between the development of capitalist monopoly, authoritarian ideologies, and institutions of liberal capitalism, the whole social structure could be easily deformed. The deformed social formation incorporates the working class and its organization into the authoritarian institutions of late capitalism.[56] The complicated structure of authority has reached its climax under liberalism, while it provides a key to understanding the human pattern of reaction in the period of the totalitarian state. "Relations of dependence in the economy, which are fundamental to social life, may be fully derived in theory from the State...which should be unconditionally accepted by the masses..."[57]

---

[53] Gollwitzer, *Die kapitalistische Revolution*, 66.
[54] Tillich, *The Socialist Decision*, 161-2.
[55] Gollwitzer, *Die kapitalistische Revolution*, 71.
[56] *Critical Theory: Selected Essays Max Horkheimer*, xviii-xix.
[57] Horkheimer, "Authority and The Family," ibid., 89.

The totalitarian state and its social roots could remain still intact in the wake of failure of the totalitarian regime in Germany. Along with Horkheimer, Gollwitzer accentuates action and reaction of the class, which is split into many fractions, yet it is united through a common interest; it is comprehended more through class instinct than class consciousness. Its individual demand should be perceived with respect to its different consequence and strength.

In the period of the totalitarian state there occurs the ultima ratio in elimination of parliamentary democracy. In the damage of capitalist interest, a fascist government can be observed in the case of Greece, Turkey, and Chile. Here, fascist dictators become tolerable conditions for the capitalist background and environment, even they are wished in many ways.[58]

Gollwitzer radicalizes Horkheimer's thesis in a way that capitalism leads necessarily to fascism. If people have elections to choose between parliamentary democracy (in peaceful path toward socialism) and fascist dictatorship (against socialism), they choose fascism, which utilizes a crisis of economic development for the seizure of political power. There is a true parallel between today's political situation of military dictatorship and German experience of National Socialism of 1933.[59] Fascism rises to political power imbued with strong restoration of a strong state power in its emphasis on nationalism; it attacks the trade union and working class party as well as reacts against capitalists of foreign countries. The nationalist form of capitalism in Germany was preserved except for Jewish capitalists who were expropriated.

In the Nazi's model of 'a steered economy' the individual capitalist is subordinated to a unified national policy concerned with elimination of the contradictions of capitalism; the

---

[58] Gollwitzer, *Die kapitalistische Revolution*, 72.
[59] "Lehrstück in Chile," ibid., 132-3.

latter consists in 'economic stagnation, relatively low levels of production, and mass unemployment.'⁶⁰ The organs of monopoly capital are increasingly absorbed into the state apparatus with its authority, which might be aptly described as 'state capitalism' in 'a highly centralized, state-directed economy,'⁶¹ which retains the state's full assistance and protection.

The ruling classes with economic and political power in a parliamentary democracy are merged into one under fascism. The expanding economic functions of the state with ruling oligarchy come to terms with the centralization of capital, which might be called 'a formal marriage between the state and monopoly capital.'⁶²

This political economic analysis of fascism complements the judiciary-institutional model and biopolitical approach by relocating its combination within the capitalist framework for major economic reason. What remains crucial in fascism is seen in stagnation and mass unemployment. In its inability to solve these problems, it requires militarism and imperialist war of redivision in violence and bloodshed to unveil the deep-seated reality within contradiction of capitalism.⁶³

In Gollwitzer's view, the capitalist state is vulnerable to military fascism, as seen in the case of Chile. In his reflection of the political lesson in Chile's armed forces against the government of President Salvador Allende (1973), he argues for the thesis of radical side of capitalism, which undergirds fascist coup and military dictatorship.⁶⁴

Allende was a socialist politician to be elected president in a liberal democracy in Chile. With support of the US government,

---

⁶⁰ Sweezy, *The Theory of Capitalist Development*, 343.
⁶¹ Ibid., 341. 344.
⁶² Ibid., 340.
⁶³ Ibid., 344.
⁶⁴ "Lehrstück Chile," in Gollwitzer, *Die kapitalistische Revolution*, 132-37.

the Chilean air force bombarded the Moneda (the seat of the Chilean government). Ironically, the democratically elected Allende was regarded as a threat to democracy by the Nixon administration and was murdered in the presidential palace; at last, he was succeeded by the brutal dictator General Augusto Pinochet, who ruled over Chile by a military junta for the next seventeen years.

In the phase of late capitalism, an extreme form of military dictatorship would emerge in exceptional cases and situations, engendering fascist states like the Spanish or Chilean military system.[65] The democratic form of socialism was blocked in Chile, while a form of neo-liberalism was introduced with the aid of Milton Friedman at the Chicago School of Economics. Gollwitzer reacts against this barbaric and brutal act as an example of class struggle from above, the privileged in abolition of democracy and in military act of massacre.

A critical notion of class struggle from above reinforces and characterizes the governing reality of disciplinary system, along with military intervention; it becomes "the fundamental motor of the economic and political transformation of postcolonial countries and subordinated regions."[66]

Eschatological Politics: Reform and Revolution

Marx himself was not doctrinaire in assessment of the transition from the capitalist society to socialist society. In the appraisal of the Paris Commune (1871), he appreciates the form of popular government, featuring responsible and revocable election of councilors at short terms through universal suffrage;

---

[65] Mandel, *Late Capitalism*, 497-8.
[66] Hardt and Negri, *Empire*, 246.

it accentuates maximal public participation in governance, resembling a direct form of democracy.

Marx's interpretation of the Paris Commune is differentiated from leading French leftists such as Pierre-Joseph Proudhon and Auguste Blanqui. Followers of Proudhon in majority, together with Jacobinism and Marxists took initiative in directing the revolt by calling for municipal authority and social reform under the socialist, democratic republican government. The Communards were consisted of petite bourgeoisie (shopkeepers, white-collar workers and artisans included).[67]

The French socialists' political ideologies were so complex, that they cannot be reduced to a Marxist position, which was blended with a political ideology in Lenin's view of the state and revolution on behalf of the dictatorship of the party.[68] The communards were the successors of the *sanculottes* of 1789 (artisans, small business-people and producers), and they called for a better democracy and more public policies with social justice and universal recognition. They were not neatly classified into the working class of Marxist theory or a proto-Soviet workers and soldiers.[69]

But Marx's political conviction is seen in centralization of all instruments in the hands of the state. It means the proletariat organized as the ruling class by means of despotic inroads,[70] in other words, a form of despotic socialism for a short time. Marx fails to articulate his ethical reasoning and significance in conceptualizing the struggle of liberation with the realm of necessity (alienation/social reification in a society) toward the freedom from the necessity of exchange value (a utopian society).

---

[67] Tombs, *The Paris Commune, 1871*, 1-2.
[68] Schulkind, ed. *The Paris Commune of 1871*.
[69] Coman, "Vive la Commune?"
[70] "The Communist Manifesto," in *Karl Marx Selected Writings*, 237.

In his later stage, however, Marx allows for an approximation to the ultimate telos with eschatological proviso. Utopian praxis for a socialist society would be thwarted with eschatological seriousness.

The realm of freedom or total liberation is heading and only approaching. Freedom in the associated producers under collective control always remains in the realm of necessity, because the true realm of freedom begins beyond such control. A socialist society is not equated with the reality of freedom, in other words, an association of free human beings in solidarity. Indeed, a socialist society only flourishes within the realm of necessity as the basis of freedom which is only approachable.[71]

This perspective would not contradict a political theory of alliance between reform and revolution. The decentralized form of democratic government would be projected into the reform movement in civil society by influencing the party's policy through universal suffrage, participation, and citizen initiative movement. This position finds a parallel with a democratic road to socialism, or democratic socialism, in which representative democracy and popular social movements remain crucial in transformation of the relationship of forces within the state toward decentralized self-management networks and institutions.[72]

In the strategic relational approach to the democratic socialism, there are *forms of articulation* of the double processes: combining state (together with transformed representative democracy) with development of direct, rank-and-file democracy (together with) the social movement for decentralized self-management.[73]

Representative democracy is not capable of avoiding capitalist authoritarian statism, without social movement

---

[71] Marx, *Capital* III: 959.
[72] Poulantzas, *State, Power, Socialism*, 262.
[73] Ibid., 264.

of direct democracy; the latter tends to be captured in the socialist Leviathan (dictatorship of the proletariat or the party's dictatorship) without representative democracy (based on universal suffrage).

A democratic road to socialism requires complementarity between reform politics and revolution, in which Marx's concept of dictatorship of the proletariat is versed into democratic, social republic sense. This perspective finds parallel with Gollwitzer's eschatological politics, in which he synthesizes reform with revolution, considering a new role of the state as the greater directive and crisis manager.

A dependence of the economics upon the state has occurred. It appears to tame anarchistic increasing of capital interest and subordinate to the common welfare. The opportunity of the state is also taken seriously by the socialist movement, because in the phase of late capitalism there is no other choice remaining than effecting its democratic endeavor at least partly within the capitalist state.

This exhibits itself as reformist within every responsible group, because reform and revolution are no longer in mutual exclusion. Gollwitzer's thesis reads: "Reform *or* revolution—it is no alternative for socialists. Reform *instead of* revolution—it is a delight for capitalists. Reform *and* revolution – it is a socialist solution."[74]

In fact, Gollwitzer does not identify socialism with a Marxist version, but socialists may employ historical materialist theory as a theoretical instrument or a social scientific frame of reference in order to analyze the situation in the public spheres as well as on the globe; it is wielded as a social scientific inquiry to develop a practical strategy in taking issue with the neocolonial reality of structural violence, injustice, and inequality. He seeks

---

[74] Gollwitzer, *Die kapitalistische Revolution*, 82.

to comprehend the objective of democratic socialist society by fulfilling the original goal of the French revolution (liberty, equality, fraternity) to cut across class dominion and privilege; democracy cannot be realized without socialism, which should perfect the incomplete legacy of democracy.[75]

The alternative 'reform or revolution' has become abstract after the collapse of ex-Soviet Union. Reformist thesis (Bernstein) reacts against the Marxist theory of the breakdown of capitalism, while convinced of gradual and peaceful elimination of the problems of capitalism; it is integrated into reformist capitalism resulting in the resignation of socialist revolution.

A socialist distance goal can be seen in Kautsky's notion of an ultra-imperialist phase, which would predict a complete internationalization of the world economy. It sees a gradual weakening of imperialist contradictions which leads to the phase of ultra-imperialism. A new peaceful phase of capitalism is united as a single world trust (an ultra-imperialist phase), and it will progress to the international cooperation among various national financial capitals.

However, such view becomes meaningless in its lack of influence upon the present strategy and tactic. It negates the problem of the present in the contradiction of imperialism and competition of nation states in the phase of neo-colonialism. Gollwitzer's politics of eschatology strives to take on the relationship between civil society and political society. Civil consciousness and its critical moral (in the sense of citoyen) must not necessarily be discarded as a form of bourgeois, but on the threshold toward democratic socialist principle.

Civil consciousness and virtue are based on popular sovereignty, co-decision of citizen in the community, and universal suffrage,

---

[75] Gollwitzer, "Why Am I, as a Christian, a Socialist? Theses," in McMaken, *Our God Loves Justice*, 187.

and they react against the bourgeois consciousness and its egotistic private interest. "The socialist development is also the decision for the continuity of civil revolution through the socialist one... Social revolution always a long way and carries out in nucleus, evolutionary in many ways of reform. Therefore, contradiction between reform and revolution is only temporal."[76]

At issue is how to further the relaton between democratic state and civil society by upholding politics of solidarity between citizen initiative, church, and those committed to social justice, recognition and common good. The politics of solidarity remains crucial in connecting the reform to social transformation. Socialist position is not necessarily identical with a Marxist one.

Democratic State and Civil Sovereignty

Theological reflection of democratic state and civil society remains crucial in Gollwitzer's eschatological politics. He incorporates Barth's political theology and a theory of civil society in Rousseau for solidarity and emancipation into his social critical framework.

He concurs with Barth's position as expressed in "Christian Community and the Civil Community." "The church must stand for social justice in the social sphere. And in choosing between the various socialist possibilities (social liberalism? co-operativism? syndicalism? interest-free economy? moderate or radical Marxism?), it will always choose the movement from which it can expect the greatest measure of economic justice."[77]

According to Gollwitzer, a Marxist theory leaves individual rights behind for social justice. It argues that the formation of

---

[76] "Citoyen oder Bourgeois," in Gollwitzer, *dass Gerechtigkeit und Friede sich küssen*, ed., Pangritz, 217-8.

[77] Cited in Gollwitzer, "Must a Christian Be a Socialist?" in McMaken, *Our God Loves Justice*, 177.

individual rights is made in the interest of the bourgeoisie, which secures private egoism in the capitalist economic context. A dualism is expressed in the separation of the individual being from life of human species.

In this split of the human being into the public and private realm, the bourgeoisie triumphs over citoyen, such that the private interest is prioritized in opposition to the interest of the common good. However, Marx remains constrained to comprehend the dialectic of individual rights and citizen, in which a theory of civil society (conflated with bourgeois society) seeks a way of controlling every domination of human being over against human being.[78]

Unlike Marx, Gollwitzer is concerned with the synthesis of alliance between civil initiative and democratic socialist principle, in which he deals with a theory of reciprocity between the political, intellectual superstructure and material base in accordance with the relation between reform and revolution.

He takes into account the dialectical relation between state, economic expansion, process of rationalization, and scientific technology, which are bound up to the development of natural science and its scientific-technological organization and investment in bringing profound change in class/status consciousness between citizen and laborer. Gollwitzer's social scientific approach to state power, fascism, and war in late capitalism is conceptualized in a neocolonial frame, while emphasizing an integrative role of the state and civil society through citizen initiative in alliance with the subaltern.

Civil society is taken as an adequate point of mediation and resistance to the colonizing system of the power mechanism with technological, discretionary rationality. It defends the realm

---

[78] "Der Kampf für Menschenrechte—Heute noch zeitgemäß?, in Gollwitzer, *Umkehr und Revolution*, 182.

of civil society from the hypertrophy of the late capitalist state with the bureaucratic administration, which is embedded with monopolies proper, pressure groups, employer's organizations, and lobbies.[79]

In Gollwitzer's view, the liberal, democratic state has a reforming force, which reformulates capitalist organization and makes it possible to run such a social economic system in a humanitarian direction. The state, which stands over the party and class, is equipped with the formal equality, human rights, and universal suffrage. The democratic state in its capacity of social welfare is the guard of the common good, or the greatest contracting authority, patron, and conductor of scientific research and crisis manager.[80]

Gollwitzer takes into account priority of civil society over against the state, striving for political power in the parliamentary democratic system through balance of the common good against the capital interest. For the democratic socialist direction, he considers the codified laws in terms of *suum cuique* (the distribution of what is due to each person), in which fairness is a decisive criterion for all the members of society.

The state has the task to secure law, freedom, and peace. More freedom is feasible with equality of rights, which includes no damage to the community, and no injury to life of other people. It is significant to combine the two aspects of law: the *suum cuique* and the defense of freedom.[81]

This constitutional, judiciary position is based on the sovereignty of the people, in which law and order are established to remove more privilege and promote more co-humanity and solidarity. The constitution should secure the sovereignty of the

---

[79] Mandel, *Late Capitalism*, 490.
[80] Gollwitzer, *Die kapitalistische Revolution*, 81.
[81] Gollwitzer, *An Introduction to Protestant Theology*, 200.

people in the sense of "the free codetermination and cooperation of all in the process of decision in society."[82] The sovereignty of the people should be kept in terms of the co-determination and cooperation of all members in society for mutual recognition, distributive justice, and peace. "The chance of the state is to be taken seriously in the socialist movement,"[83] where there is no other alternative left, by looking at combination between reform and revolution.

3. Liberation Theology and Postcolonial Significance

In the discussion of Gollwitzer and historical materialism, it is relevant to deal with liberation theology, which takes the people's praxis as the starting point; historical praxis is interpreted through social analysis and then scrutinized in light of the kingdom of God. Ethics is seen as participation in the struggle for the liberation of the oppressed.[84]

The principle 'preferential option for the poor' characterizes the privileged status of epistemology of liberation theology, which seeks to analyze and interpret social reality through the eyes of the poor and the Scripture, theological sources, and church tradition. The category of the poor refers to "indigenous peoples, peasants, manual laborers, marginalized urban dwellers... The women are doubly oppressed and marginalized."[85]

Liberation theology is characterized as the first ranked anticolonial theology with strong emphasis on the reality of under-

---

[82] Ibid., 203.
[83] Gollwitzer, *Die kapitalistische Revolution*, 82.
[84] Gutierrez, *A Theology of Liberation*, 116.
[85] Gutierrez, *The Power of the Poor in History*, 137.

modernity and economic justice. It is sharply differentiated from public theology, which focuses on the incomplete project of modernity, civil society, and legitimacy of late capitalism.

Historical Materialism and Social Scientific Theory

In our discussion of liberation theology, it is critical to examine Clodovis Boff's theory of historical materialism in its hermeneutical blending. Boff elaborates a liberative-ethical epistemology in which he focuses on the significance of a theoretical model in dealing with raw materials historically given. The real object (or raw material) is completely different from the object of knowledge (idea or conception), because the first is concrete-real, while the second is concrete-ideal.[86]

Theoretical generalities are differentiated in three instances of generalities. What is at issue is to comprehend the process of scientific knowledge as emerging from general abstract or ideological ideal. There is in no way the direct identity between the initial state of knowledge (the first naiveté) and the final state (the second naiveté in the postcritical sense). A science of interpretation works on given concepts as raw materials by transforming them into another concrete knowledge system.

The final result through this epistemological procedure is the synthesized knowledge which is mediated and transformed through interpretation or theoretical practice. A real transformation or paradigm shift is called an epistemological break.[87]

Boff's liberative epistemology is indebted to Louis Althusser's position of theoretical practice, which is involved in producing

---

[86] Boff, *Theologie und Praxis*, 135.
[87] Ibid.

knowledge through the operation of transformation.⁸⁸ It is an essential realization and performance of the world in human cognition and thought, in other words, a critical self-production.

Boff concurs with Althusser and maintains that the process of the theoretical practice has three moments: Generalities I (initial abstraction, or part of production condition of the knowledge), Generalities II (theoretical medium of production or building of conception; theoretical concept), Generalities III (scientific products of the knowledge process, or concrete generalities; empirical concept). "*The theoretical practice produces all Generalities III through the working of Generalities II upon the Generalities I.*"⁸⁹ Generalities III is engendered and acquired through theoretical practice in epistemological break or rupture with Generalities I.

Accordingly, Boff moves on to a theory of correspondence of relations (Paul Ricoeur), in which Jesus of Nazareth in his own life context in regard to Christ and the church in early life context of the church. As church tradition is seen in terms of its historical and social context, so our contemporary theology is in relations of correspondence to our own context. Boff's liberation epistemology is of hermeneutical character, because his model of correspondence takes on a dialectical encounter between the text and context in which scripture, church tradition and our life setting are taken up in a dialectical, context-sensitive manner.⁹⁰

However, questions can be raised about the extent to which Boff would mediate Althusser's empirical theory of knowledge with hermeneutical practice within the framework of correspondence. According to Althusser, the interpretation or theoretical practice is conditioned in the process of abstraction

---

[88] Ibid., 133.
[89] Ibid., 136.
[90] Ibid., 242.

and reconstruction. They elaborate the empiricist conception of knowledge, which presents a process taking place between the subject and the object as given; "the whole empiricist process of knowledge lies in fact in an operation of the subject called *abstraction*."[91]

In the empiricist theory of knowledge, knowing means the subject of abstracting of its essence from the real object. "Empiricist abstraction, which abstracts from the given *real* object its essence, is a *real abstraction*, leaving the subject in possession of the *real* essence."[92] To the degree that knowledge abstracts the essence from the real object through a process, it is already really present in the real object which retains the essence.

An empiricist mode of representation maintains that the knowledge is inscribed in the structure of the real object, which awaits the discovery of the agent. This empiricist mode of discourse is caught to specter of natural-analytical attitude, which emphasizes the theoretical appropriation of reality on the part of the agent in terms of process of abstraction. A theoretical practice can partly grasp the object or essence of knowledge.

The active intellectualist reproduction of reality refers to a process of theoretical practice, in which the abstract and the concrete, the universal and the particular are integrated. "[The empiricist theory of knowledge] gives the real presence of the pure naked essence, knowledge of which is then merely sight."[93]

However, this empiricist theory of knowledge runs into the danger of underpinning idealist dualism, because a theory of knowledge abstracts the essence from the real object through a process. The essence is already really present in the real object. Essence in the structure of the real object waits for the agent

---

[91] Althusser and Balibar, *Reading Capital*, 35.
[92] Ibid., 36.
[93] Ibid., 37.

to discover. This perspective establishes real-concrete objects of knowledge for his theoretical practice, which sidesteps a transcendental reality of life-world (history, tradition, language, and culture), which underlays the real-concrete object as socially given.

It is important to analyze the real-concrete object (socially given) through dialectical articulation of diverse factors in terms of negativity, mediation, and sublation. The socially given is to be clarified at a higher level in concrete universal manner, rather than taking it for granted. However, a major problem, which plagues Althusser's theoretical practice, can be seen in his conceptual insufficiency in synthesizing symptomatic reading with empiricist theory of knowledge. If a symptomatic reading discerns "the lacunae, blanks and failure of rigor," it seeks to see "interrupted and governed by the threatened irruption of a repressive discourse."[94]

This epistemological and critical reading runs counter to Ricoueur's theory of correspondence, which is grounded in hermeneutical frame. Althusser's theoretical practice is concerned with region of effective history (subjugated) in contrast to history of correspondence.

For the articulation between epistemic practice and symptomatic reading, it is worth taking into account the social given as a complex reality of synthesizing diverse particulars into a social whole. It can be analyzed and described through conceptual problematic, which has an epistemic practice (contradiction, mediation, sublated social whole) in connection with the world of signification (in history, culture, tradition, and religion).

---

[94] Ibid., 143.

Theory of Articulation and Problematic Unity

To critically complement Boff's position, I examine Althusser's theory of articulation in dealing with different practices or discourses. Sociological theory of articulation finds its significance in Foucault's theory of problematization. The absence of problems and their presence within the problematic requires a symptomatic reading (Althusser) of what is repressed in the text. It searches for underlying contradiction or absence by which to unveil what cannot be said in the text.

Such problematic-deconstructive reading or theoretical practice comes to terms with archeological reading of the discourse as hegemony invested in rationalization (or normalization) and power relations. In Althusser's account, Foucault provides substantial insight into epistemological break or rupture in his study of cultural formation in different historical times. "There is nothing in true history which allows it to be read in the ideological continuum of a linear time that need only be punctuated and divided."[95]

A historical break does not produce a 'present' within a structure of contemporaneity. There is no correspondence within diverse spheres or instances (the economic, the ideological, the aesthetic, the philosophical or the scientific), because they "live in different times and know other breaks and other punctuations."[96] The co-existence of a presence and absence, or articulation of two moments can be regarded simply as "the effect of the structure of the whole in its articulated decentricity."[97]

---

[95] Ibid., 103.
[96] Ibid., 104.
[97] Ibid.

In the structured whole of society, social formation is articulated as a system of an organic hierarchized whole with rank and influence, which are embedded within different levels or instances of the social structure. Each level is assigned a peculiar time and practice with peculiar rhythm, specificity, and punctuations (development, revolution, breaks, and rupture).

Every instance is relatively autonomous and independent and grounded in a certain type of articulation in the whole. It articulates "relations of relative effectivity" within the whole, even in guiding and stimulating economic development.[98] In the type of articulation, displacement, rupture, transformation, and torsion, social scientific inquiry can be undertaken in a diachronic sense in dealing with different histories (political history, history of religions or ideologies, a history of philosophy or science, etc.) in their relative independence in the specific dependence.

This features a reality of correlation or intersection in the social historical context in terms of articulating relations of differentials with their respective operation. The backwardness, forwardness, survivals, and unevenness co-exist in the structure of the real historical present, in other words, the present of the conjuncture or combination of events.[99]

This perspective cuts through limitation of correspondence, or empiricist theory of knowledge, and it requires an archeological analysis of the subjugated discourse or episteme. Such epistemic stance features effective history (centered on break, decentricity, and difference), which reacts against the marching history of progress and technological rationality tainted with colonial power in the west. The effective history helps buttress a postcolonial stance in seeking to measure and appraise the dislocation of colonial histories and cultures against the line of a single

---

[98] Ibid., 100.
[99] Ibid., 106.

continuous reference time. The latter regards the dislocation as backwardness or forwardness in terms of its ideological reference time.

A scientific theory of social formation with a plurality of instances is featured in its approach to effective history, which focuses on articulation of diverse social fields and practices as dislocated and absent. This reality is built in social stratification, while taking issue with the historical reference to linear march and progress (Eurocentric position). Thus, it is critical to incorporate a scientific theory of effective history into anamnestic reasoning of those marginalized and subjugated in history, culture, and society. This sociological articulation reinterprets social formation in accordance with ideological struggle in superstructure in dealing with the mode of production through technological rationality and innovation.

Economic infrastructure in the index of effectivity is also a determinant in the last instance (in a narrow sense); yet the mode of production includes the instances of the superstructure for reality of social formation (in the comprehensive sense).[100]

A dialectical theory of social formation as a problematic whole (contradiction, exploitation, and commodity fetishism) calls into question what is taken for granted as socially given in examination of class affiliation, functional differentiation, social stratification, job opportunity, and hierarchical relations of authority. The dialectical theory of social formation does not necessary conflict with Althusser, but cuts through his epistemic limitation.

---

[100] Althusser, *On the Reproduction of Capitalism*, 22.

Critical Summary

A relational whole in social formation is juxtaposed with problematic unity between economy, culture, and the state. An epistemic theory of effective history seeks to problematize and explicate the way the social formation and its ideological apparatuses are organized and operative in social institutions and practices through commodity fetishism, functional differentiation, and ideological interpellation.

Seen in the structure of the whole, a theory of dislocation deconstructs the Eurocentric concept, because "the concept dog cannot bark."[101] A reality of dislocation in colonial order of things and postcolonial time has its own history, rhythm, and interaction with life-world in the constellations.

An epistemic genealogy of social formation and effective history in plurality of instances cannot be neatly clarified by theoretical practice, but an archeological interpretation of ideological apparatuses and practices goes through conceptual problematic, critical distance (symptomatic reading), discourse clarification, and semantic reconstruction for recognition, solidarity, and emancipation. It must be deciphered in an archeological-anamnestic frame of reference to rewriting the history of vivid present for reparative justice and postcolonial recognition and difference.

Sociological theory of articulation requires discourse clarification in dealing with the regime of historical, social effectiveness, in which I critically complement limitation of theoretical practice and naïve empiricism through phenomenology of dialectics. Although the concept 'dog' does not bark, without the conceptual problematic, we do not classify what the dog is like.

---

[101] Althusser and Balibar, *Reading Capital*, 105.

In *The Poverty of Philosophy* (1847), according to Marx, "with the water-mill, you have feudalism; with the steam engine, you have capitalism."[102] As the productive forces come in line with their level of development, they endow themselves with their relations of production, in which every revolution in the productive forces "leads to non-correspondence with the old relations of production."

They "precipitate a revolution in the relations of production that puts the new relations of production in new (and adequate) correspondence with the new productive forces."[103] In Marx's historical materialist theory, there is no explicit emphasis on class struggle in connection with state ideology and its bureaucratic apparatuses.

A notion of correspondence is of Hegelian dialectical conception in which its play game comes into subsequent contradiction between content (the productive forces) and form (the relations of production) according to duplet 'externalization and alienation,' which deifies commodity as fetishism or mystification. It is also a notion of problematic relation which is crucial in social articulation of diverse instances, or structural coupling.

A reality of commodity fetishism at the level of relation of production appears to be the source of alienation in the life of laborer and their body (already biopolitically exploited in the technological process of productive forces and scientific management). A historical mode of production is driven and conceptualized in dialectical procedure of self-contradiction, negativity, practical mediation, transformation, and a relational whole of totality (idea of universal and mutual recognition among equals).

---

[102] Althusser, *On the Reproduction of Capitalism*, 210.
[103] Ibid.

The social being determines its individual and social consciousness, which is to be explained *from the contradictions of material life* in the dialectical process of antagonism, crisis, and transformation through technological innovation. Thus, "with the steam engine, you have capitalism." Primacy must be credited to scientific, technological rationality, which is transposed upon state power.

Marx goes beyond Hegel, with precision of natural scientific achievement, industrial civilization, and world market. Marx's logic of *Capital* consists in creating a world after its own image through its scientific, technological revolution, as penetrating into empire in the phase of late capitalism.

This aspect is a missing in Althusser's interpretation of historical materialism, which is excessively attached to the scientific side of ensemble of social relations of production. He undermines biopolitical reality of alienation, public health, diverse fields of social stratification, and role of natural scientific development, which remains a driving force in characterizing the mode of production and ideological interpellation.

Although Marxist theory is made to underpin the epistemological rupture in the sociological articulation of effective history, it must not be identified with Althusser's anti-historicism and anti-humanism.[104]

A sociological theory of articulation is concerned with diverse instances and practices, requiring an archeological analysis of social discourse, ideological interpellation, material interests, and power relations in dealing with rationalization, specialization, and bureaucratic administration in social stratification with reference to effective history.

'Man' as an ideological animal in self-evident fact is a dialectical animal in conceptual regime (contradiction, mediation,

---

[104] Althusser and Balibar, *Reading Capital*, 119.

meaningful discourse, and transformation). But ideology in general is not entirely conflated with life-world, meaning, and justice. Ethics of life-world remains a source of interpretation, recognition struggle, and common good.

4. Public Theology and Critical Epistemology

State, Ideological Apparatuses, Bureaucracy

In the discussion of public theology and critical epistemology, it is significant to appropriate Althusser and Weber in a critical, comparative manner, while engaging in state, ideology, and bureaucracy. A juridico-political model concerns the question of what legitimizes power through the laws; it is also connected with an institutional model concerning what the state is.

Althusser's contribution can be seen in his theory of legal-political superstructure, especially in his distinction of the state power from the state apparatuses. He takes into account Ideological State Apparatuses (ISAs accorded to a system of institutions, organizations, practices, or legal-moral ideology in civil society, or systems of functional differentiation), which runs beyond the Marxist idea of the state as a repressive force of execution and intervention (transitional descriptive theory of repressive state apparatus). A specific system or sphere is distinct and determinate from other ISAs, with no recourse to physical violence.[105]

In a like manner, Weber is concerned with the administrative mechanisms, which are involved in the formation of modern sovereignty. He defines the state in terms of *"the monopoly of the legitimate use of physical force,"* in which politics strives to

---

[105] Althusser, *On the Reproduction of Capitalism*, 78.

influence the distribution of power within a state or among states.[106]

A modern state retains several regimes: (1) an administrative and legal order under legislation; (2) an administrative apparatus in performing official business in accordance with legislative regulation; (3) authority binding over all persons (citizens) in the area of the jurisdiction; (4) the legitimate use of physical force and coercion as prescribed in the legally constituted government. In sum, "legal order, bureaucracy, compulsory jurisdiction over a territory and monopolization of the legitimate use of force are the essential characteristics of the modern state."[107]

If Weber focuses on the repressive side of state power, Althusser argues that primary ideological formations are realized in institutions or organizations, in which discourse formation is undertaken and materialized in each social field or apparatus in terms of rationalization, specialization, and institutional support. This institutional support later becomes the basis of disciplinary technology.

If a human being is defined by nature as an ideological animal, ideology functions like unconsciousness. This definition stands closer to sociological theory of ideology as collective representations, which are combined with life-world. It reacts against a non-dialectical position of the absolute (Shelling) that Hegel cuts across. If all cows are grey in the night, it is difficult to acknowledge the symbolic-material representations of ideologies or their material existence in multiple apparatuses or fields. A human being as an ideological animal acts in material practices according to his/her ideas. 'Kneel down, move your lips in prayer, and you will believe.'[108]

---

[106] "Politics as a Vocation," *From Marx Weber*, 78.
[107] Bendix, *Max Weber*, 418.
[108] Althusser, *On the Reproduction of Capitalism*, 186.

In the inversion of order of things, ideology already entails a practical dimension in struggle with other ideological forms. It has double reference to individuals as ideological animals in terms of interpellation as well as constitution of them.[109] Theory and practice are united and embodied in ideological discourse and its material practice (or rituals). A primary ideology (first naiveté) is realized in the ritual practice, while generating the second ideology (second naiveté) in the enriched practice in the process of reproduction. "There is no practice whatsoever except by and under an ideology." "There is no ideology except by the subject and for subjects."[110]

Althusser's position of ideology-practice-agency is worth considering for the way in which he focuses on a problematic relation between epistemic structure and human agency; he has a vista for dialogue with sociological theory of state and civil society. Systemic theory of communication in different fields is influenced and guided in the network of social ideology or episteme, which is rationalized along with functional differentiation and codified by the power of the state. 'Man' is constructed as an ideological animal under the bureaucratic administration in the network of discourse, communication, rationalization, and power.

If the class/status struggle occurs in diverse fields of civil society for recognition and power, it has ideological effects within ISAs. The (bourgeois) holders of state power exercise their class power through the various specialized apparatuses within the state ideology. This ideological governance is executed and penetrated into social body through the political system of bureaucracy, but the bureaucratic governance remains a lack of conceptual clarity in Althusser.

---

[109] Ibid., 188.
[110] Ibid., 187.

At this point, it is worth considering the way in which Weber approaches to legal domination and bureaucracy; there is the significance of the relation between political leadership (leader) and the performance of the official in the administrative work. A political concept of democracy prevents the development of a closed status group of officials by shortening the term of office by election. Democracy comes into conflict with bureaucratic rule.[111]

Once established, bureaucracy is "an instrument for societalizing relations of power," because it is "a power instrument of the first order" for those in control of the bureaucratic apparatus.[112] A governmental bureaucracy is affected and buttressed by the rule of the law as well as by experts with professional qualification. The officials are given the authority to complement their assigned functions, while the idea of calculability under legal dominion is like a vending machine, whose function is central in the bureaucracy.

This governmental bureaucracy becomes necessarily functioning government per se. As Weber maintains, "[the calculability of decision-making] and with it its appropriateness for capitalism…[is] the more fully realized the more bureaucracy "depersonalizes" itself…In the place of the old-type ruler who is moved by sympathy, favor, grace, and gratitude, modern culture requires for its sustaining external apparatus the emotionally detached, and hence rigorously "professional," expert."[113] Thus, bureaucratic organizations are undertaken "according to *calculable rules* and 'without regard for person'"[114]

---

[111] Bendix, *Max Weber*, 226.
[112] Ibid., 228.
[113] Cited in Bendix, *Max Weber*, 427.
[114] "Bureaucracy," *From Marx Weber*, 215.

The specific nature of bureaucracy fits into the modern capitalist enterprise and its rational character. It operates efficiently like a machine through depersonalizing the execution of official tasks. An administrative impersonality would cause a negative effect by subsuming under calculation of means and ends (purpose or instrumental rationality).

In the transition to constitutional government, Weber holds, the concentration of the power of the central bureaucracy occurs in one head, such that officialdom is placed under the prime minister.[115] The impersonal dominion of the bureaucracy has its second attribute in terms of "the concentration of the means of administration," while taking place in the development of capitalist enterprises (Marx). It is also seen in public organizations of government, the army, political parties, and universities, among others.[116]

If Marx treats the bureaucracy embedded within the civil society purely in a negative manner, Althusser's scientific theory of social formation is not superseded by or absorbed into economic infrastructure. Remarkable in Althusser's scientific theory is his approach to the ideological role of the state.

He facilitates a better comprehension of relation between state (repressive ideology apparatuses) and civil society (integrative ideological apparatuses) in dealing with rationalization, legitimacy, functional specialization, and bureaucracy.

ISAs retain a significant social cultural function in reproducing the capitalist mode of production and strengthening complex reality of reification and its commodity fetishism in social formation. But he remains constrained to the elaborate relation between division of labor and moral development, or civil society, culture, bureaucratic rule, and parliamentary democracy.

---

[115] Ibid., 234.
[116] Ibid., 221.

It is worthy to examine Weber's position in this regard. Bureaucracy implies the rational structure of domination based on a type of the professional expert. It underpins a rationalist way of life, economic advantage, and the creation of educational certification.

On the other hand, it seeks expert knowledge "in the impersonal and functional routinization of administration."[117] It keeps professional knowledge and intentions secret by becoming an administration of secret sessions. The concept of the official secret is specifically invented by the interest of the bureaucracy.[118]

The educational ideal of a bureaucratic age refers to the expert with impersonal authority and power. In company with the rationalization of education, "the educational patent is turned to economic advantage," while the certificate of education forms "a privileged stratum in bureaus and in offices."[119]

In Weber's analysis, democracy reacts against the status character of bureaucracy by putting the election of officials for short terms. But it promotes bureaucratization in an unintended manner, because it benefits the interest of capitalist organization and functional differentiation and specialization. The bureaucracy has its consequence as "a crypto-plutocratic distribution of power."[120]

If Althusser helps to distinguish ideological realms of civil society from state repressive apparatuses, Weber focuses on sociological analysis of political governance in terms of bureaucracy and social stratification. Weber has not sufficiently managed to conceptualize the significance of civil society in his theory of the state.

---

[117] Ibid., 237.
[118] Ibid., 233.
[119] Ibid., 241.
[120] Ibid., 230.

Critique of Bureaucracy and Civil Society

Weber's stance runs counter to Bismarck's real politics under the slogan of monarchical government, which prevented a genuine parliamentary regime through one man's creative leadership.[121]

In a political Ideological State Apparatus the Prussian Junkers (landed aristocrats symbolized by Otto von Bismarck), their army, and their police provided a shield and leading personnel. A unified Germany after Prussia's victories in wars with Austria (1866) and France (1871) was formalized in the Palace of Versailles (1871).

Germany had a parliament, a monarchy (the Hohenzollern), and a chancellor (Bismarck). Its nationalism was spelled out in the political ideology that was very national and very socialist (with several progressive social and economic reforms). But it had particularly no democratic political apparatus. Such historical legacy continued to be embodied in Nazism.[122]

In dealing with state and ideological apparatuses, power is exercised by the dominant class over against the subordinated. It implies an ideological governmentality by state apparatuses, which are executed and administered by bureaucracy over the entirety of social body.

This refers to a theory of ideology in general, which functions eternally like unconsciousness. The structure, the site of constitution of the subject, has reactive action and its ideological interpellation upon human individual and its social formation, thus its apparatus exercises power of ideology which exists in the apparatus rather than false consciousness.

---

[121] Bendix, *Max Weber*, 444.
[122] Althusser, *On the Reproduction of Capitalism*, 144.

If Marx argues that ideology in the sense of false consciousness has no history of its own, epistemic structure would be a site of generating its social functionality and effect (ideological class struggle within the superstructure in non-homogeneous effective history). The state apparatus is in no way traversed by the class struggle, because it is an apparatus of domination in its entirety. Thus, class struggle is differentiated and specialized into ideological, cultural, pedagogical, and social spheres for the problematic unity rather than reducible merely to economic sphere.

Deplete 'ideology and interpellation' is constitutive of humanity and displays diverse historical forms in which subjectivity is constituted, for example in the modern theory of social contract, liberty of the individual, and commodity exchange. It runs a different course from theory of hegemony and historic bloc of mass movement.[123]

What remains a barrier in the transformation of ISAs to a new mode of production is a complex reality of ISAs, which is caught up to social cultural reification. A phenomenology of agency-habitus deep-seated in the ISAs is not easily to be overcome by class consciousness of the proletariat or even in post-revolutionary phase.

This complex reality starts off with deliberation of social formation and rule of commodity fetishism, while discussing the relation between parliamentary democracy and civil society. However, Althusser runs short off at this point. In his analysis of political problems in Germany, Weber defends an effective parliamentary regime as a bulwark against mob rule, while arguing against monarchical and bureaucratic absolutism.

When the bureaucratic absolutism encroaches upon the political process and political leaders, "the pathology of legal

---

[123] Ibid., XV.

domination" would occur in usurping the rule-making political powers through the process of legislative powers.[124] However, the efficiency of Caesarism (an authoritarian or autocratic political principle induced by Julius Caesar) is often grown out of republic democracy, and it resets upon the position of the Caesar which is comprehended "as a free trustee of the masses (of the army or of the citizenry)."[125]

Rationalization of political democracy in civil society is exposed to vulnerability, as seen in pathology of ideological apparatuses inscribed to political despotism. We observe a historical repetition of Caesar (the individual name) to caesar-title (the Roman emperor). The murder of Caesar, historical person, is not complete, but continues to embody its power struggle in the political installation of caesarism within the parliamentary charismatic leadership.

In the disenchantment of rationality from the magic of the world, a resurgence of impersonal forces from graves would be seen in the historical repetition in Caesar-person as caesar-title in our present. Mass democracy has potentially dictatorial or "caesarist" elements in charismatic appeal of the political leader (a plebiscitary leader) to the mass through universal suffrage. This authoritarian populism, which is based on people's consent, evolves toward the authoritarian statism or fascism of capitalist state.

According to Poulantzas, Weber defines the capitalist state in terms of holding a monopoly of legitimate violence, and he establishes the legitimacy of its concentration of state force in terms of a rational-legal legitimacy, which is based on law and bureaucracy.[126] However, the democratic parliamentary model in

---

[124] Bendix, *Max Weber*, 451.
[125] Ibid., 202.
[126] Poulantzas, *State, Power, Socialism*, 80.

citizen participation is not necessarily identified with a totalitarian assumption of charismatic political leadership, in which Carl Schmitt is seen as an heir of Weber's theory of the state.

Against this plebiscitary form, Weber maintains that parliamentary democracy retains a greater advantage in allocating responsibility for political decision in legislative control over a bureaucratic government and its administration. Two types of political leadership (plebiscitary and parliamentary) are indispensable under legal domination.[127] Indeed, Weber buttresses this democratic direction.

"Yet, the highly developed system of committee work in the English Parliament makes it possible and compelling for every politician who counts on a share in leadership to cooperate in committee work…The practice of committee reports and public criticism of these deliberations is a condition for training, for really selecting leaders and eliminating mere demagogues."[128]

Like Althusser, the role of the state is not restricted to an instrumental conception of the state as class dominion or dictatorship, because it cuts across the couplet repression plus ideology (the repressive state apparatuses: the government, the administration, the army, the police, the courts, and the prison among others). Parliamentary democracy is of special significance along with popular struggle, because the institutions and liberties of representative democracy must be preserved in a plurality of parties alongside the developing organs of direct rank–and–file democracy.

A parliamentary forum entails different interests in diverse social movements (feminism, racial justice, ecological movements), which find a place in the parties. The latter has a

---

[127] Bendix, *Max Weber*, 457.
[128] "Politics as a Vocation," *From Max Weber*, 107.

certain irreducible tension with working–class parties.¹²⁹ On the other hand, the dominant ideology comes to organize other repressive apparatuses (army, police, juridical system, prisons, state bureaucratic administration), whose primary task is to exercise legitimate physical forces and violence over the human body as political institution.¹³⁰

This refers to an exceptional state in the elimination of a plural party system and through physical repression, which leads to open war against the dominated. Against this despotic direction, democratic civil society is rationalized, specialized, and differentiated along with administrative organic establishment.

It remains a site of resistance against the excessive power of the state with repressive apparatuses (power mechanism), which is stratified in social economic and political cultural privilege in social formation. Privilege and inequality are driven in ideological interpellation and justified through mass media and network of information to control society.

However, in the political tradition of liberalism, the parliamentary form of democracy constitutes a type of critical reflection on state power and its ideological function in problematizing the extent to which power relations (executive, legislature, judiciary) should be brought to balance. A distinction can be made between state and civil society in a form of schematization, because it is "characteristic of a particular technology of government."¹³¹ Civil society and its democratic initiative become sites of resistance and struggle by cross-cutting the logic of capital accumulation, national-popular hegemony from above, and its colonization of civil society and life-world.

---

[129] Jessop, *The Capitalist State*, 180.
[130] Bendix, *Max Weber*, 29.
[131] "The Birth of Biopolitics," in *The Essential Foucault*, 204.

Sociological Articulation and Biopolitics

A biopolitical type of state apparatuses is combined with a theory of discourse in power relations. It is realized and materialized in terms of rationalization, functional specialization, and bureaucratic administration in centralization of all spheres of public life, which underwrites the pathology of reification in capitalist society.

A theory of 'power-knowledge relations' entails many epistemic effects in determining the forms and domain of knowledge and ideological apparatuses in the historical rupture, transformation, and difference. Coupled with epistemic effect, the reality of biopolitics is seen in the realm of a productive force in the technical division of labor, alienation, discipline, and surveillance; 'the mechanical force of labor' is heightened, or 'the social productive power of labor' reinforced.[132]

Surveillance is made a decisive economic operator in the internal part of the production machinery as well as in the disciplinary power. It is reorganized, specified, and integrated into the diverse fields (education, penal system, army, and so on) of society.[133] A biopolitical type of rationality and discipline in Weber's sense is differentiated and specialized into diverse spheres in capitalist society along with bureaucratic governance. In the factory as well as in the bureaucratic state machine, it "parallels the centralization of the material implements of organization in the discretionary power of the overlord."[134]

Weber's sociological analysis of discipline and bureaucracy can be enhanced in terms of articulation between the individual (political subject in the judiciary-institutional regime) and

---

[132] Foucault, *Discipline and Punish*, 163.
[133] Ibid., 175-6.
[134] Ibid., 262.

commodity relation, in which the human body is seen as an appendage of the machine and regulated as a political institution through scientific management (Taylorism). A capitalist state is materialized in the intersection between judicial political ideology and body politics (alienation and exploitation) plus social reification.

Bureaucratic administration co-ordinates with production line in its despotic system of Taylorism (technical division of labor). The state enters into normalization of economic relations of production and legalizing labor contract in the sense of laissez faire capitalism, which takes root in this institutional materiality.[135]

In a sociological analysis of synthesis of multiple determinations, actual events cannot be reduced to a single principle of explanation, but seen as the resultant of the interaction of various causal chains and elements in the network of correlation, power, and structural coupling of different systems. This 'relational' character at the level of articulation facilitate many important concepts and instances in giving account of state theory,[136] which can be classified in terms of diverse types (repressive, interventionist, technological, bureaucratic, biopolitical, integrative, and public moral).

In fact, there is an aspect of organic solidarity which thwarts the technical division of labor in terms of agreement and consensus on the common foundation of the social organization. It has judiciary dimension of contractual relationship, which is legally established in protection of the poor and the weak against the tyranny of the rich and their privilege.[137]

---

[135] Poulantzas, *State, Power, Socialism*, 65.
[136] Jessop, *The Capitalist State*, 252.
[137] "Discourse on Political Economy," in Rousseau, *On the Social Contract*, 221.

Sociological clarification of economic justice and moral solidarity or defense of life-world against power mechanism can be enhanced in a broader material spectrum by critically renewing Foucault's descriptive-functionalist understanding of power relations, which dispense with legislative protection and initiative of agency.

Health Empire and Biopolitics

Biopolitical sociology is effective in allocating social division of labor and fabricating discourse in the management of public health and medical apparatus. A social division of labor is established as the first order for premising genealogy of knowledge-power upon discourse; "where there is power, there is resistance," which does in no way exist 'in a position of exteriority in relation to power.'[138]

In the second order of epistemological discourse, power and knowledge are joined together. The discourse in multiplicity of discursive elements "can come into play in various strategies." Thus "the discourse can be both an instrument and an effect of power, but also a hindrance, a stumbling block, a point of resistance and a starting point for an opposing strategy."[139]

The discourse clarification remains an undercurrent in examining diverse forms of communication in different structures (politics, economic, culture, education, religion, and public health among others), which are invented in the network of economic rationalization, episteme, bureaucratic governance, and power relations.

Capitalism in its historical genesis and development was started by socializing the body, and it was politically constructed

---

[138] Foucault, *The History of Sexuality* I: 95.
[139] Ibid., 101.

and socially organized in terms of a productive force and labor power. The medical apparatus and public health system are a part of neocolonial condition in the phase of late capitalism.

Society's control over body of individuals and population is characteristic of capitalist society, in which the body is a biopolitical reality, while medicine is its strategy.[140] The postcolonial condition is characterized in the neocolonial structure of domination and violence within the system of capitalist world economy underlying complex relations between metropolis, semi-periphery, and periphery.

In the neocolonial biopolitics, a structural violence can be seen in the powerful combination of 'exploitation, splitting, and infiltration,' which is materialized in medical industry complex, the international expansion of multinational healthcare corporations, racial stratification, and ideological propaganda.

A multinational corporation is established and has a growing role in public health care systems by moving from one region into global markets. It distributes production to the semi-periphery or periphery countries and enables the metropolis countries to undertake academic research, finance, global capital, and administration. The production of the periphery works for the former master of colonialism.[141] This world systems perspective characterizes the phenomenon of neocolonialism in the imperialistic stage of late capitalism, which reinforces the competition, rivalry, and conflict among inter-imperialist nation states.[142]

There are many diverse forms of exploitative relations in the technological recipient, in terms of trade, public health care

---

[140] "The Birth of Social Medicine," ibid., 321.
[141] Gollwitzer, *Die kapitalistische Revolution*, 43.
[142] Ibid., 45.

systems, credit guarantee with interest reflux, the enmeshing of bank and currency systems.

According to McCarthy, the free-market game is schemed in favor of the most powerful players in the metropolis (in their domination of international associations, agencies and agreements through the IMF, the World Bank, and World Trade Organization). In the contemporary forms of liberal internationalism new means of global exploitation is articulated in underdevelopment and dependency and continues its neoimperialist logic. It serves the interest of the metropolis countries, multinational corporations, and local elites by worsening structural dependency.[143]

A medical idea of governmentality gives the account of the third capitalism, which is driven through power, self-interest, and pursuit of profit. Manufactures of medical devices have economic power to fund medical education programs and hospitals, who adopt to use their device. A global health empire is on the rise to influence on and control public policy of the health care system.[144] Medicine and public health systems belong to the important regime of biopolitical governance in which an issue is "how to raise the level of health of the social body as a whole."[145] It has little to do with "offering support to a particularly fragile, troubled, and troublesome margin of the population."[146]

A medico-administrative knowledge undertakes medical inquiries into the public health and hygiene, while the medical doctor is granted social power in dealing with health and sickness of the population.[147] The biopolitical functions are not reducible to that ideology as such, but serve it as a material support,

---

[143] McCarthy, *Race, Empire, and the Idea of Human Development*, 198.
[144] Ehrenreich, *Third Wave Capitalism*.
[145] "The Politics of Health in the Eighteenth Century," ibid., 341.
[146] Ibid.
[147] Ibid., 346.

continuity, and reproduction through technological-medical division of labor and innovation.

In the global context, a neoliberal framework of biomedical reasoning prevails in Latin America and other developing countries, favoring commercialization, corporatization, and privatization of public health and social welfare services. The U.S. model of managed care is exported as a tangible model to the periphery countries (Latin America, Africa, and Asia), which are imposed to accept for a neoliberal principle of privatization of the health and social security systems.

This reality characterizes the industrial-medical complex in its regulation of international marketplaces in which legal limitations are established to access diverse healthcare service. Managed care organizations (MCOs) are touted by many experts for efficiency and cost-effectiveness, as found in the World Bank, multilateral lending agencies, and multinational corporations, and various associations of academia. However, such a model exacerbates the existing system of inequalities that underlays health care in the U.S.

"As public health systems are dismantled and privatized under the auspices of managed care, multinational corporations predictably will enter the field, reap vast profits, and exist within several years. Then developing countries will face the awesome prospect of reconstructing their public systems."[148]

Higher health care costs have brought higher surplus requirements, whereas increasing the number of uninsured citizens and lower profits. African public theology addresses the public significance of church's responsibility and theological clarification of social discourse, public health in HIV/AIDS, and power relations in every walk of life. It articulates African identity,

---

[148] Waitzkin and Iriart, "How the United States Exports Managed Care to Developing Countries." *International Journal of Health Services* 3, 489.

human dignity, biomedical justice, and cultural authenticity, and ecological integrity in society, culture, and nature. In the biopolitical time of the pandemic, it is critical to correlate health systems with social cultural effects in dealing with economic inequality, gender-based violence, and child protection issues in African societies.

Insofar as African public theology focuses on God's mandate in creation of all humans as living equally in community in terms of responsibility, common good, and care. It provides a biblical-hermeneutical vision for Africans and the globe by describing biblical narratives and their enriched semantics in their own life setting. It features a public leadership and moral integrity to build the future in terms of collective stewardship and servant attitude which counter a reality of corruption and egotism.[149]

In the Sub-Saharan context, African public theology finds it significant to articulate the relation between theology and public health, which implies the particular significance in most African context for rights to health and democratic governance.

A sociological analysis of religious construction of public sphere takes into account institutional practices, which are explicated in terms of elaborating ethical norm of public health, common good, and religious, cultural integrity in the African societies. In the ethical tradition of the Christian faith tradition, biomedical justice and public health become a central issue for the public theology in its self-understanding of the Christian churches and their identity as public religion in the society and world.[150]

Inequality of medical care and health service is differentiated and stratified in society in the medical-industrial complex in the

---

[149] Agang et al *African Public Theology*.
[150] Azétsop and Ochieng, "The right to health, health systems development and public health policy challenges in Chad."

network of corporations, which supply health care services and turns a profit; it discriminates and excludes the body of the poor and the uninsurable. Their life is shortened by unequal access to medicine and health care.

The income of physicians, health care organization, hospital, or the stockholder would be benefited from maximization of their interest in terms of biopolitical administration of medical service.[151]

The medical-industrial complex is governed by profit-seeking companies in health care as significant stakeholders, aiming to generate profit while decreasing the creativity and innovation in medical research. A resistance is concerned with common good, distributive justice, and integrity of life-world, while reacting against the dominant system of medical industry complex.

In the latter the materialization of ideology resides and is effective in the process of discourse formation and reproduction through the bureaucratic-rational mechanism under the state, government, and administration of public health. So is the end result a critique and change of the biopolitical governmentality of the dominant system of the medical industry complex.

Neocolonial Logics and Late Capitalism

Our analysis of the neocolonial aspect in the dominant system of medical apparatus and its inequality considers Gollwitzer's structural theory of imperialism, which runs counter to the basic, yet hasty thesis of postmodern Empire: "*The United States does not, and indeed no nation-state can today, from the center of an imperialist project*. Imperialism is over. No nation will be world leader in the way modern European nations were."[152]

---

[151] Farmer, *Pathologies of Power*, 175.
[152] Hardt and Negri, *Empire*, xiv.

On the contrary, imperialism is still alive in its neocolonial condition. There is no longer a tenable distinction between inside and outside, because the capitalist revolution integrates every different boundary, nation-state, and culture by dominating the public spheres within social stratification. Core zones are fused into semi-periphery society and periphery society in terms of division of labor in vertical and horizontal sense, exploitation, splitting, and infiltration. The metropolis is transferred to the periphery in the form of stock exchange, transnational or multinational corporations, in which the boundaries among nation-states are fluid and mobile.

An international reality of exploitation is bound to a concept of the vertical division of labor, which implies that the periphery serves as the provider of raw material and offers inexpensive labor forces and market to the metropolis. The existence of semi-periphery as the exploiter and the exploited implies that the upper stratum of the core runs a capitalist world economy in a smooth manner. Surplus of the whole world economy is appropriated in the operation of unequal exchange by the metropolis. Unequal exchange in its structure of exploitation is the key to the underdevelopment in the periphery. The lower wages are a consequence of underdevelopment according to a function of different organic compositions of capital between the metropolis, the semi-periphery, and periphery in the worldwide process of capital accumulation.

In Marx's analysis of capitalist economy, C (constant capital) + V (variable capital) + S (surplus value) equals total value (K*). All capital is divided into means of production (called the value composition) and living labor power (called the technical composition of capital); the combination refers to the organic composition of capital.[153]

---

[153] Marx, *Capital* I: 762.

The different allocation of organic composition of capital facilitates a social scientific clarification of unequal development between metropolis countries and periphery countries under the system of structural violence. It is also bound to political hegemony in allocating the capital flow through bilateral agreement, as seen in vertical line of division of labor and horizontal life of alliance between the political elites between the metropolis countries and the periphery countries. The reality of inequality is seen in multinational companies, the export of machines, equipment and vehicles reinforcing the trend of unequal development; the main flow of capital exports also takes place between the metropolitan countries, not merely from the metropolis to periphery in unilateral manner.[154]

Multinational corporations are in search of cheap resources and bring out pollution and climate change. They foist harmful industrial plants (auto, oil, mining) and destroy nature in the periphery (genetically engineered food), which become pollution havens. The destruction of nature in the periphery cuts down the rain forest and brings about the pollution of the seas. In the end, it strikes back at the metropolis with disastrous effects such as climate change. Regulations are required for companies to keep the ecological sustainability.[155]

Political system of hegemony and recalcitrance has perpetuate structural violence of economic system that contributes to global warming, climate change, pollution, and our planet's loss of fecundity in the ecosystem. Economic poverty pollutes the planetary life in our world systems in terms of the uneven distribution of access to economic wealth and wellbeing; the

---

[154] Mandel, *Late Capitalism*, 351.
[155] Moghaddam and Zare, "Responsibilities of Multinational Corporations on Environmental Issues," *Journal of Politics and Law*, 77-84.

ethical implication of distributive justice belongs to ecological sustainability.

Climate change presents the most profound challenge of the ecojustice, confronting social, political, and economic systems. Understanding of the trends in nature (pollution and extinction) and risks in our planetary society helps us how to interpret what is going on in a prudential way; then we move on to make response and moral decision about what is to be done in responsible and effective manner. Ecojustice belongs to ethics of life-world.

On the other hand, the ruling elite of the peripheries is politically bound to the center through economic interest, cultural influence, education, and military support. The particularistic interest of the elite in the periphery implies a horizontal line of the power system, which accords with the interest of the power elite of the metropolis. A delicate type of structural imperialism with its violence is 'the feature of imperialist relations.'[156] The working class in the metropolis has been consolidated into strata of middle class or integrated into the status quo of the existing society; this refers to foundation for splitting or dividing strategy of the elite in the center.[157]

The workers at the center take part in surplus value of unequal exchange with the periphery. In the structure of world trade the center shapes and adjusts the periphery to the interests and needs of the center. Marx's prophecy—that capitalism will create inevitably its grave digger—has proven to be wrong. The global reality does not produce a powerful proletariat as the grave digger of capitalism, but a theory of impoverishment can be visible and object in the periphery countries.[158]

---

[156] Gollwitzer, *Die kapitalistische Revolution*, 46. Footnote 1.
[157] Ibid., 44.
[158] Ibid., 76.

The strategy of infiltration or penetration takes place through the economic and cultural enterprise of the metropolis in relationship with the periphery. In the infiltration of the educational system, a binding of the elite of the peripheries with the elite of the metropolis is established. The accommodation of lifestyle to the culture of the metropolis alienates the indigenous tradition from the masses of the country. Equal status and equal rights remain an illusion.[159]

The double binding reality (the vertical and the horizontal) characterizes a global reality of infiltration in the networks of world system; metropolis, semi-metropolis (or semi-periphery), and periphery. The metropolis is in periphery, while semi-periphery takes part in increasing profit. It implies structural transformation of civil society and public spheres in social stratification and reification.

This postcolonial condition is not easily reduced into binary opposition simply through structural underdevelopment, as the dependence theory argues. Frank's dependent theory argues that the problem is structurally underdeveloped rather than the economic surplus. The system of contradiction and historical polarization was established between metropolis and satellite. It has been structured throughout the history of its persistence, expansion, and recreation of the capitalist contradictions.

The economic surplus of the satellite has been appropriated, contributing to economic development in the metropolis.[160] The term 'structural underdevelopment' is the key concept in characterizing the dependent theory in terms of external and internal contradiction. The external underdevelopment was generated by the metropolis' expropriation and appropriation of the economic surplus on the part of the satellite. The internal

---

[159] Ibid., 45.
[160] Frank, *Capitalism and Underdevelopment in Latin America*, 10.

one was generated in a chain-like fashion penetrating the underdeveloped world as a whole.[161]

However, the dependency theory fails to comprehend the dynamic relation of the world economy systems, which entail a periphery problem in core zones, and domination of the cores in semi-periphery or periphery. The role of semi-periphery becomes crucial in the international division of labor and in the world-systems along with functional differentiation and complexity.

The middle stratum is both exploited as well as exploiter in regard to the upper stratum of the center and the lower stratum of the periphery.[162] The type of infiltration integrates postcolonial mode of production in terms of informational accumulation and 'a global quasi state of the disciplinary regime.'[163]

In this process of infiltration, political power in the periphery has come into alliance with the power elite in the metropolis, which retain supreme authority, though sovereignty has taken a new form. Unequal exchange can be sought in the product of the indirect exploitation under free trade, because wages are low in the periphery countries. These countries are compelled to sell their goods at prices below their value in exchange for high-priced products of the metropolis countries.

They should purchase goods from the metropolis above their value. The metropolis protects the high-wage levels by virtue of tariffs, which leads to increase in wages. Thus, in unequal exchange the periphery countries are disadvantaged in decreasing their value of labor power. It gives new impetus to all other mechanisms of exploitation.[164]

---

[161] Ibid., xxi.
[162] Wallerstein, *The Capitalist World-Economy*, 23.
[163] Hardt and Negri, *Empire*, 255.
[164] Arghiri, *Unequal Exchange*, 130-31.

Marx's theory of exploitation (the law of the falling tendency of the rate of profit) is thwarted, even replaced by the law of rising surplus through absorption; it refers to transfer of the surplus value under the conditions of monopoly capitalism in international economic relation and division of labor.[165] There is no possibility of de-coupling national economies of periphery.

New centers appear in some regions of China and India and some other regions of eastern Asia, yet integrate into the globalization by exploiting it. The capitalist archipelago has emerged in Southeast Asia in which several islands (Japan, Singapore, Hong Kong, Taiwan and South Korea) have arisen above horizontal exchanges among local and world markets.[166] Semi-periphery archipelago subordinates' independent development to the world market whereas seeking a reality of "development through dependency."[167]

Critical Conclusion

In this chapter I have treated the relation between political theology and liberation theology in the discussion of several important theological positions for public theology, which is framed in the biopolitical formation. Biopolitical approach to neocolonial condition has come to take issue with dependence theory.

According to Leonardo and Clodovis Boff, "For example, in 1964 the Brazilian economy ranked 46th in the world in 1984 it ranked 8th. The last twenty years have seen undeniable technological and industrial progress, but at the same time there has been a considerable worsening of social conditions for

---

[165] Baran and Sweezy, *Monopoly Capital*, 8.
[166] Cumings, "The Political Economy of the Pacific Rim," in R. A, Palat, ed., *Pacific-Asia and the Future of the World-System*, 21-37.
[167] Duchrow and Hinkelammert, *Property for People, not for Profit*, 141.

the poor, with exploitation, destitution, and hunger on a scale previously unknown in Brazilian history."[168]

If this evaluation of economic development in Brazil is empirically grounded, a dependence theory can be proven wrong, because of its basic assumption of underdevelopment of the periphery. Military rule began in 1964 and came to an end in 1985. A new constitution was introduced in 1988, and it reestablishes social, civil and political rights and improves the democracy and economic development gradually. Civil society can be advanced with democratic consciousness of the citizen, while improving social capital and citizen's participation in policy making and social welfare system. If the economic situation of the impoverished becomes worse than ever in this context, regardless of technological and industrial progress, it is attributed to "the price paid by the poor for this type of elitist, exploitative, and exclusivist development."[169]

Does this poor refer to the working-class people? Wouldn't the economic development transform the entire social system as such by bringing a profound change in the public spheres such as education, job opportunity, public health care, and welfare system in more accessible and reliable manner than ever?

Brazil faces a huge gap and inequality between the rich and the poor, the reason for which can be found in the domestic system of social stratification in terms of monopoly, unequal distribution of schooling, income inequality, and privilege, and ethnic or racial discrimination of the non-white.

The problems such as ethnicity, racial justice, education opportunity, gender, and sexuality appear to be challenging issues for liberation theology to take into account the significance of civil society and its stratified form of social cultural formation.

---

[168] Boff and Boff, *Introducing Liberation Theology*, 5.
[169] Ibid.

This social cultural change calls into question a justification of counter violence against institutionalized system of violence. There is "ambiguous yet possible use of violence as a means of social change" in the context of liberation theology.[170]

What is an issue for public theology is the political significance of restorative justice, reconciliation, and common good in a post-apartheid South Africa in the 1990s. Requirement of creative non-retributive justice becomes decisive in the Kairos Document (1985), which seeks to eliminate the tyrants and establish a just government for the common good.

---

[170] Nessan, *Orthopraxis or Heresy*, 119.

Chapter 5.

Biopolitical Sociology: Late Capitalism and Global Empire

Gollwitzer's thesis of capitalist revolution remains crucial in featuring his public theology in social scientific framework, as well as in postcolonial condition. This chapter is a study of the world system, late capitalism, and empire, examining Gollwitzer's critical analysis of the capitalist system in terms of scientific, technological innovation, exploitation, and ecology. It is relevant to integrate Marx and Weber by explicating the way in which religious discourse would play a significant part in shaping economic ethics through elective affinity. An aspect of capitalism as religion can be analyzed in dealing with abstinence and commodity fetishism, because this aspect remains insufficient in Gollwitzer's analysis of capital accumulation with reference to biopolitical power and bureaucratic rationalization.

Then, conceptual clarity can be furthered in elaborating biopolitical genealogy and sociological analysis of state apparatuses, capital accumulation, and disciplinary system of body. Social scientific clarification of late capitalism and political hegemony of the state become decisive in explicating the extent to which the capitalist civilization would be bound up with world systems in a long century. This biopolitical sociology comes into a critical dialogue with postmodern theory of global empire, while relocating such global sovereignty with the world system of late capitalism.

Third, Gollwitzer's position implies post-Eurocentric significance, in which it is critical to examine comparative study of world systems in dealing with commercial revolution, Renaissance, and Christian philosophy of Eurocentric history. His structural theory of imperialism cuts across the Leninist position of imperialism and monopoly capital, but it provides a new vista to analyzing a structure of imperialism in neocolonial world system according to a Norwegian sociologist, Johan Galtung in the field of peace and conflict studies.

Fourth, a sociological position seeks to articulate a theory of elective affinity of discourse with material interests and power relations in the world systems, in which local wars would take place in mass ideological concentration and bureaucratic rule of disciplinary society. A sociology of war is explored in connection with world systems and military-complex industry in terms of ideological interpellation and biopolitical bureaucracy of coercion and military discipline. At last, biopolitical sociology is concerned with death politics of state and racial violence, while Gollwitzer's theology is brought to solidarity with American Black theology.

1. Capitalist Revolution: Scientific Technology and Ecology

In the discussion of the global stage of humanity Gollwitzer draws attention to the contemporary ecological crisis, which is bound to the explosion of population and hunger catastrophe. Global interdependence in its networks of positive and negative factors must be brought to universal responsibility, which takes issue with particularistic system of thought in threatening humanity and nature.

"Such [particularistic] thought is an isolated, cutout, after all, negligent self-satisfying thought...Today's crisis is...the increase of murderous collision of the particularistic interest into the self-murderous."[1]

Gollwitzer argues that particularistic thought implies domination, which is comprehended as security of material privilege with an instrument of symbolic and intellectual violence (limited wars included).

For Gollwitzer, capitalist revolution is the locomotive of world history, but an emergency brake is required to control the revolution. The capitalist revolution must be under control, because we live in a society imprinted with class dominion and struggle.[2] The urge for growth is necessitated by way of competition and in terms of expansion and accumulation of the capital for gaining extra profit; it utilizes production methods and seeks more effort to investment. "Growth is the characteristic feature of capitalism."[3]

Research in the natural sciences receives material sponsorship through the state, industry, and institutions, and it results in the exploitation of nature which is necessary for industry. To the degree that steam and machinery in the development of natural science have revolutionized industrial production, they expand the technological progress in "the exploitation of world-market given a cosmopolitan character to production and consumption in every country."[4]

---

[1] Gollwitzer, *Die kapitalistische Revolution*, 34. Footnote 1.
[2] Ibid., 14.
[3] Ibid., 55.
[4] "The Communist Manifesto," in *Karl Marx Selected Writings*, 224.

The expansion of trade and a new world market made an overwhelming impact in undertaking the transition from the feudal to the capitalist mode of production. Industry constantly revolutionizes trade, not vice versa. The machine is driven by steam to the degree that large-scale industry is indebted to the technical development. "The industrial capitalist is constantly faced with the world market."[5]

This position finds its climax in Marx's own statement: "The bourgeoisie, by the rapid improvement of all instruments of production, by the immensely facilitated means of communication, draws all, even the most barbarian, nations into civilization…; it compels them [all nation] to introduce what it calls civilization into their midst, i.e., to become bourgeois themselves. In one world, it creates a world after its own image."[6]

Given this, Gollwitzer expresses capitalism as the greatest revolution and revolutionary force that human history has seen thus far.[7] Capitalism as revolution implies its consequent secularization or economic rationality, in which natural science is the principle of capitalist economy for the sake of the universality of exchange principle in global world system. The correspondence between natural science and capitalism enables the industry to take natural science into service. An ecological crisis is bound to the market economic system through industry. The exploitation of nature becomes necessary through industry, in other words, "an exact, calculating, objectifying investigation of the nature."[8]

Every progress of capitalist agriculture is not only progress in skill and the worker, but also it is the progress in the skill to deprive the ground. In other words, it is progress in the ruin of lasting

---

[5] Marx, *Capital* III: 455. 453.
[6] "The Communist Manifesto," in *Karl Marx Selected Writings*, 225.
[7] Gollwitzer, *Die kapitalistische Revolution*, 57.
[8] Ibid., 59.

sources of fertility. The capitalist system implies the process of destruction through scientific technology and its combination with the social production process. It erodes and undermines the foundational source of all wealth: earth and the worker.[9]

Ecological concern remains central in Gollwitzer's analysis of capitalist system and global development, because we have entered into the phase of ecological survival with its catastrophe. With the combination between ecological problems and secularization, Gollwitzer does not completely reject Weber's thesis of inner-worldly ascetic and capitalist spirit in its significance in early capitalism, but the inner-worldly waste becomes survival condition of capitalism.[10]

Capitalism as Religion: Abstinence and Fetishism

It is true that Marx also anticipated Weber's thesis in the context of capital accumulation through the abstinence theory. The capitalist in this classic type brands individual consumption as a sin against accumulating, in which "the modernized capitalist is capable of viewing accumulation as 'renunciation of pleasure'."[11]

It is of special significance to clarify Marx's theory of abstinence in regard to Weber's Protestant ethic and capitalist spirit; this is not fully explicated in Gollwitzer's position. This sociological clarification helps us to renew Gollwitzer's approach to capitalist revolution and world economy through correlation between science and technology, which strengthens ideological powers and bureaucratic administration.

---

[9] Ibid., 66.
[10] Ibid., 53.
[11] Marx, *Capital* I: 740-1.

In Weber's account, European cities were taken as the seedbeds of political capitalism in competition for mobile capital and perpetual struggle for power, which was to expand capitalism in early modern world system.[12] This vantage point characterizes the political side of capitalism, which is differentiated from the rational side of economic capitalism. But he fails to systematize a sociological articulation between rational organizational side of capitalism and its political-imperialist side among nation-states.

In fact, the theory of abstinence in the Protestant ethic and its capitalist spirit is obviously seen in Marx's critique of Christian character of accumulation in the context of European colonialism. Marx denounces the history of Dutch colonial administration under control of the Calvinists in the Dutch West Indian Company (1621) as 'one of the most extraordinary relations of treachery, bribery, massacre, and meanness.'[13]

Capital accumulation is related to the abstinence theory in Marx's critique of Judeo-Christian ethos and Puritan entrepreneurship. 'Accumulate, accumulate! That is Moses and the prophets! 'Industry furnishes the material which saving accumulates.'[14] Marx's wholesale critique of the Judeo-Christian ethos is embodied in its mercantilist practice of colonial injustice and slave in the international affairs underlying plunder, pillage, and murderer.

The lust for gold awakens, and the hoarder sacrifices the lusts of the flesh for gold, taking seriously the 'gospel' of abstinence. Columbus' 'discovery' of America, the slave trade, colonization of America, the Dutch West Indian Company, the English East Indian Company, British rule in India, and Chinese markets in

---

[12] Arrighi, *The Long Twentieth Century*, 12.
[13] Marx, *Capital* I: 916.
[14] Ibid., 742.

the shape of the Opium wars[15] – these all fashioned a world according to their own image through the capitalist revolution as well as imperial militarism.

In Marx's theory of abstinence (Chapter 24.3 of *Capital* I), private consumption or expenditure of the capitalist in double-entry book-keeping is regarded to be a robbery, which is committed against the accumulation in conquering the world of social wealth. Original sin can be seen in the 'unfortunate' capitalist, who feels a human warmth toward his/her own Adam in eating the fruit of knowledge of good and evil (Gen. 2:17).[16]

However, the classic type of capitalist at the historical dawn of capitalism brands individual consumption as a sin against the function of the capitalist as a personification of capital, which is predominant through avarice and the drive for self-enrichment. It implies abstinence from consumption for accumulating in the first stage of historical capitalism.

For example, merchant's capital or commercial capital appears in the specific function of mercantile wealth, "in the period when feudal production was first overthrown."[17] This refers to the initial stage of industrial capitalism as dominated by commerce and trade. Merchant capitalists are agents of industrial capital, or real capitalist, making "the greater part of the surplus value." Along with creation of a new world market in the sixteenth and partly the seventeenth century, "the sudden expansion of trade...happened in reverse on the basis of the capitalist mode of production."[18]

Commercial mode of production, consistent with 'the non-subjection of production to capital,' can be seen in the history

---

[15] Ibid., 915.
[16] Ibis., 740.
[17] Marx, *Capital* III: 455.
[18] Ibid., 451. 453.

of trade as conducted in the Venetians, Genoeans, Portuguese, and Dutch.[19] Every development in commercial capital provides production with a character of orientation to exchange-value, while becoming "precondition for the concentration of monetary wealth." In the fifteenth century the merchant becomes an industrialist in the trade relationship between Italy and Constantinople.[20]

The phase of commercial capitalism would partially correspond to Weber's notion of European city states as the seedbeds of political capitalism.[21] Accordingly, the term 'commercial capitalism' refers to "the agile, already modern and indisputably effective form taken by economic life in the sixteenth century." "The imperatives of large-scale, long-distance commerce, its accumulation of capital, acted as driving forces. It was in the space defined by a commercial economy that industrial activity was kindled at Genoa, Florence, Venice, and Milan, particularly in the new and revolutionary textile industries, cotton and silk."[22]

However, in the modern context, Marx sees accumulation as renunciation of pleasure, along with the capitalist development and its progressive accumulation. Its progress of capitalist production takes place 'in the form of speculation and the credit system,' which is 'a thousand sources of sudden enrichment.' At a certain stage of historical development, a conventional degree of prodigality has so reached that "luxury enters into capitals' expenses of representation."[23]

A degree of prodigality "becomes a business necessity to the 'unfortunate' capitalist." The modern type of capitalist, unlike the

---

[19] Ibid., 445.
[20] Ibid., 444-54.
[21] Arrighi, *The Long Twentieth Century*, 12.
[22] Braudel, *The Mediterranean* 1: 319.
[23] Marx, *Capital* I: 741.

miser, a classic type of capitalist, squeezes out labor power from workers, while enjoining them 'to renounce all the enjoyment of life.' A Faustian conflict occurs between passion for avarice and the desire for enjoyment; in other words, accumulation accompanies the phenomenon of expanding consumption.[24]

The 'unfortunate' capitalist becomes painful in his/her abstinence from consumption for the sake of desire to accumulate. But to accumulate capital has a positive end with pleasure attached to it, which appears as much as consumption does. Thus, in a Hegelian fashion, Marx finds it logical to regard consumption as abstinence from accumulation. (*determinatio est negatio*).[25]

But the capitalist's expenditure and prodigality are "always restrained by the sordid avarice and anxious calculation lurking in the background." It "nevertheless grows with his accumulation, without the one necessarily restricting the other"[26] This Faustian type of conflict occurs in the breast of the capitalist.

In fact, Marx's theory of abstinence denounces capitalist rationality as one of the major reasons involved in slave trade, brutality, and colonialism. It is no longer an ideal type of capitalism, but a Eurocentric colonialist type of capitalist exploitation that makes the underdeveloped into waste and slave.

At this point, Marx comes to terms with Luther's prophetic critique of merchants and their practice of usury, which is bound to the love of power in the desire to get rich. In Luther's critique of mammon, Marx quotes, a usurer is a double-eyed thief, murderer, money-glutton, and 'a great huge monster,' who "wants to be God over all men."[27]

---

[24] Ibid.
[25] Sweezy, *The Theory of Capitalist Development*, 81-2.
[26] Marx, *Capital* I: 741.
[27] Ibid., 740. Footnote 22.

In Hegel's logic, Marx holds, 'quantitative differences pass over by a dialectical inversion into qualitative distinctions.'[28] A capitalist change occurs with different stages of development of capitalist production, according to their special technical conditions to the point of formation of trading companies, the forerunners of the modern joint stock companies.' These are characterized by Luther as pure monopolies or 'the Company Monopolia.'[29]

They worked as powerful levers for the concentration of capital, in which the colonies provided a market for the European country to make a vast increase in accumulation and monopoly of the market.[30] According to Marx, "Commercial capital, when it holds a dominant position, is thus in all cases a system of plunder, just as its development in the trading peoples of both ancient and modern times is directly bound up with violent plunder, piracy, the taking of slaves and subjugation of colonies; as in Carthage and Rome, and later with the Venetians, Portuguese, Dutch, etc."[31]

Holland was the model of the capitalist nation in the seventeenth century, and it "stood at the zenith of its commercial greatness in 1648" in its "almost excessive possession of the East Indian trade and the commerce between the south-east and the north-west of Europe."[32] The 'strange God' "perched himself side by side with the old divinities of Europe on the altar." 'The making of profit' is "proclaimed as the ultimate and the sole purpose of mankind."[33]

---

[28] Ibid., 423.
[29] Ibid., 424.
[30] Ibid., 918.
[31] Marx, *Capital* III: 448-9.
[32] Marx, *Capital* I: 916.
[33] Ibid., 918.

It is difficult to understand Marx's abstinence theory about Puritan entrepreneurship without his notion of primitive accumulation as original sin in the political economy.[34] In the genesis of the industrial capitalist (Chapter 31 of *Capital* I), Marx sharply denounces "the Christian character of primitive accumulation"[35] embedded in the Christian colonial system, which is obviously seen in Spain in the discovery of gold and silver in America; such colonial enterprise of accumulation was furthered in Portugal, the Netherlands, France, and England.

Elective Affinity: Religion and Fetishism

The classic-modern type of abstinence becomes a driving force in Marx's analysis of articulation in dealing with accumulation as renunciation of pleasure as well as exploitation. This double reference can be seen in Weber's ideal typological research of the 'strange God' and Puritan idea of double predestination; religious idea is bound to material interests in terms of elective affinity, in which an ideal type of capitalism and its ideological legitimacy are imbued with its purpose (or instrumental) rationality; thus inner-worldly asceticism is materialized in capitalist system but trapped into an iron cage through legal-bureaucratic administration.

A sociological clarification of elective affinity helps to describe the way in which subject matter (religious idea) and truth content (ethical cultural manifestation) are historically connected and culturally constructed through material interests and established in the network of ideological legitimacy and power relations; elective affinity can be explored in a wider relationship of reciprocal influence and meaningful action in the agency of religious carriers.

---

[34] Ibid., 873.
[35] Ibid., 917.

Elective affinity can be elaborated not only in historical causal adequacy, but also in sociological theory of articulation in terms of immanent critique (based on the subject matter and truth content), historical analysis of instrumental or utilitarian system of rationality (episteme), power relations in status/class group in social cultural stratification. The subject matter and truth content function as source of immanent critique in analyzing disgrace effect of religious discourse and its pathological consequence in the sense of iron cage.

By doing so, Weber's analysis of capitalist rationalization and its resultant reality of the iron cage can be discerned in Marx's critique of commodity fetishism and its secret (Chapter 1. 4 of *Capital* 1). Commodity, when emerging, changes into a thing transcending sensuousness. Capitalist social order turns into religious alchemy and mystification, which functions as a hidden rule or structure by eliciting irreconcilable contradiction.

It stands on its head with the mystical character of the commodity and through its exchange value with power of representation in relation to all other commodities. Hence, the social relation of the producers exists as suprasensible, objective, and social, in other words, "the fantastic form of a relation between things"[36] apart from and outside the producers.

A phenomenon of fetishism or reification is analogously characterized in terms of "the misty realm of religion"[37] in its social character – mammon or idol worship, which occurs in 'material relations between persons and social relations between things.'[38] A capitalist logic of effective affinity creates desire, transgression, greed, and blame, while complementing a dialectical logic of struggle and recognition between the

---

[36] Ibid., 165.
[37] Ibid.
[38] Ibid., 166.

dominant and the dominated in the social order. The religious character of capitalism can be seen in its pure cult of mammon with utilitarian mooring, while perpetuating its cult of fetishism and blaming the victims.

As Walter Benjamin writes, "God's transcendence has fallen, but he is not dead. He is drawn into the fate of man." Thus, the God of capitalism "must become concealed and may only be spoken of in the zenith of his culpability. The cult becomes celebrated before an immature deity, [while] every image, every idea of it injures the secret of its maturity."[39]

Of special significance in historical materialist exposition is a vantage position to scrutinize the social phenomenon of reification from a dialectical standpoint of integrating the isolated facts of social life into a totality, which requires critical scientific method.[40]

In Lukacs' account, the fetishistic character of isolated parts in the reification of all human relations should be investigated in terms of methodological primacy of the totality in historical understanding of social relations.[41] If the method of totality is involved in examining a dynamic dialectical relationship with the different, various elements, it is concerned with a mutual interaction in every organic body of social formation.[42]

Biopolitical Power and Bureaucratic Rationalization

In dealing with objective reality as a social process, there is significance for sociological clarification of the process of rationalization, calculation, specialization, and mechanization.

---

[39] *The Frankfurt School on Religion*, ed. Mendieta, 260.
[40] Lukacs, *History and Class Consciousness*, 8.
[41] Ibid., 9.
[42] Ibid., 13.

The dominant transforms the political and institutional structures in terms of scientific management and economic technology for the bourgeoisie, as seen in the development of the factory system (Taylorism and Fordism) in the 1920s and 30s in the US.

This is called passive revolution (Gramsci) undertaken by the dominant social forces to preserve the relative weakness of the rival progressive force. It implies that the dominant class intervenes in the realm of civil society to preserve its own hegemony in the interest of war of position. It requires the political leadership of the party. It is distinguished from reinforcement of the hegemonic positions of the dominant in intervention and control of every realm of political, cultural and administrative among others.[43]

In the technical, specialized division of labor, Marx observes that the worker in the factory is "crippled to the point of abnormality."[44] The passive revolution in this regard is defined in terms of biopolitical increase of the power in rate of exploitation. Marx's scientific method implies that "the principle of rational mechanization and calculability must embrace every aspect of life."[45]

In the 'enchanted, perverted, topsy-turvy world' of fetishistic reification, a dialectical method of totality as a whole mediates Weber's sociological explication of rational calculation and the strictly rational organization of labor underlying rational technology; it gives account of the modern capitalist concern.[46]

---

[43] SPN, 222. 239. Gramsci finds the war of position more appropriate in an advanced Western State than the war of movement (or war of maneuver), which would occur in the seizure of State power, but within the strategic context of a war of position. Sassoon, *Gramsci's Politics*, 198.
[44] Lukacs, *History and Class Consciousness*, 99.
[45] Ibid., 91.
[46] Ibid., 95-6.

This sociological articulation characterizes a notion of passive revolution in terms of the colonization of life-world generating phenomenon of social reification. A rational systematization of all statutes regulates life in the bureaucratic state with the legal system for prediction and calculation. Bureaucratic activity pertains to the social phenomenon of reification by adjusting "one's way of life, mode of work and hence of consciousness, to the general socio-economic premises of the capitalist economy."[47]

Along with critical theory of social formation, Gollwitzer takes into account the relation between capitalist revolution and world economy, which is based on a structural theory of imperialism in a global context. He argues that technological rationality plays a major role in undergirding capital accumulation and expansion, in which a theory of abstinence may find its significance contributing to the survival and growth of capitalism through religious legitimacy. Trade and commercial capital have developed, providing a new impulse and orientation toward exchange-value, while it "expands its scope, diversifies it and renders it cosmopolitan…"[48]

On the other hand, the capitalist revolution has brought rationalization and emancipation, improving the life standard, care of the people, removal of famine, control of pandemics, general promotion of the health situation; many welfare programs are the result of organizing and mobilizing to demand better treatment under capitalism. In short, they are the welfare society which apologetics of capitalism defend.

This refers to capitalist contribution to the great civilizing influence of capital, which brings "even the most barbarian nations into civilization."[49] This vantage point relocates the

---

[47] Ibid., 98.
[48] Marx, *Capital* III: 449.
[49] "The Communist Manifesto," in *Karl Marx Selected Writings*, 225.

notion of passive revolution within the active side of capital civilization by resisting its force from below.

2. Biopolitical Sociology: State Apparatuses and Capital Accumulation

In the discussion of capitalism and technological rationality, it is substantial to integrate abstinence with political control of the body, while effective division of labor is rationally organized. Biopower is seen in Marx's analysis of alienated labor and the bodily life of the laborer. Its strategy is exercised in many forms and modes of application, which drives the capitalist development through legal-bureaucratic administration, technological management, discipline, and control of society.

Accordingly, Foucault holds, "the biopower was without question an indispensable element in the development of capitalism."[50] This perspective forms the second stage bound up to the development of capitalism in regard to the first stage of an ascetic morality or abstinence. Disciplinary society and the society of control are appropriated through the biopolitical strategy and hierarchy of administrative bureaucracy. If Foucault considers the political power over the human body and its specific mechanism into the realm of explicit calculations, the knowledge-power method at the epistemological level is made an agent of transformation of human life in terms of discourse, governance, and administration.[51]

The concept of apparatus bridged relations between life and politics. The judicial institution is increasingly incorporated into a

---

[50] Foucault, *The History of Sexuality* 1: 140-1.
[51] Ibid., 143.

continuum of apparatuses (medical, administrative, institutional, and so on), which aims at regulating life with reference to norms and from the strategic necessity of life for politics. The concept of "apparatus" implies "a thoroughly heterogeneous ensemble" of elements such as institutions, architectural forms, regulatory decisions, administrative measures, and laws.

State apparatus belongs to a social administrative formation which responds strategically to social cultural problem with a political urgency. This is why apparatus enjoys a dominant strategic function. It is also "a set of strategies of the relations of force supporting, and supported by, certain types of knowledge."[52]

In a like manner, Weber's analysis of discipline reinforces an administrative side of the ideological state apparatuses. The content of discipline and its quality are methodically trained and exactly execute the received order for submission under the disciplinary code; its obedience is rationally uniform.[53]

The military discipline is the fountain of all discipline, and it is the ideal model for the modern capitalist factory and rational organization in terms of calculation, profitability, and work performance, as seen in the American system of scientific management.[54] This biopolitical sociology is grounded in the whole process of rationalization and social apparatuses, in which discipline of human body and control take place in the factory as well as in the bureaucratic state machine. It "parallels the centralization of the material implements of organization in the discretionary power of the overlord."[55]

---

[52] Foucault, "Confessions of the Flesh," in *Power/Knowledge*, 194–96.
[53] "The Meaning of Discipline," *From Max Weber*, 253.
[54] Ibid., 262.
[55] Ibid.

Given this, a method of elective affinity focuses on the correlation of religious discourse and material interests in terms of power relations, in which biopolitical technology along with ideological apparatuses is scrutinized at diverse levels with respect to role and strata of the agency. This sociological approach to biopolitical-discretionary power can also be seen in Marx's view of alienated labor (biopolitical) and technological rationality (discretionary).

A reality of commodity fetishism reifies the entire social body and penetrates into human consciousness, turning the exchange value into mediating or representing value in the network of information. Exchange value of the commodity is not merely exchanging, but it has a representing and governing value inscribed into human life. Commodity decides on one's value, dignity, and position.

Commodity has a religious function in ruling the society, individuals, and the world through money. In the dialectical model of the employer and the employee, the commodity-in-representation appears to be a deified form through money and its representing value, in which society and culture are more and more commodified or reified by biopolitical mechanism with social apparatuses.

In our discussion of social formation in commodity fetishism, ideological struggle is bound up with natural scientific revolution, which becomes one of the major features for mechanism of production in ushering into an epoch of social-cultural revolution. In dealing with a relation between the structural whole of social formation, natural science becomes a driving force to economic development and technological rationality in the intellectual sphere, which is generally induced through state power, bureaucratic administration, and economic-institutional support.

This power mechanism from above in superstructure stratifies diverse social fields and agents, while bringing the agents into struggle for multiple forms of capital and power (symbolic, cultural, social or religious). Natural scientific progress occurs in the intellectual sphere, reinforcing biopolitical control in the capital accumulation and expansion through social rationalization, functional specialization, and bureaucratic regulation in social cultural apparatuses; the modern world is created according to the image of the capital and commodity fetishism along with rationalization and scientific technology. It hinders the metabolic process between human being and the earth by ruining the fountain of all wealth, the earth and worker.

The development of the productive power of labor (in the production of iron, coal, and machinery) is connected with progress in the field of intellectual production, especially, natural science and its practical, technological application. State apparatuses are ideologically created, and human individuals are exposed to ideological interpellation, which is a part of biopolitical governmentality. This sociological clarification facilitates a genealogical position in analyzing the discourse of capitalist revolution and its global civilizing mission in the worldwide network of power relations and information within a long century.

Debate: Capitalism in A Long Century

Why is capitalism prevailing in a long century? Capitalism has devoured the Marxist-Leninist State, not vice versa. It is important to examine the postponement of the change, or the long century of capitalist revolution. Marx includes several reasons as counteracting causes to crisis; (1) cheapening of the elements of constant capital in the organic composition of capital; (2) raising the intensity of exploitation of labor; (3) relative surplus overpopulation (the reserve army), (4) foreign trade, and (5) the increase in share capital.[56]

These counteracting elements defend Marx against the theory of breakdown of capitalism in terms of historical inevitability. Rather, the countervailing elements perpetuate the logic of capital accumulation in connection with domestic exploitation, as well as with the world market and colonialism. It would be ready for the imperialist stage of monopoly capitalism, which is accelerated by this generation and absorption of the surplus. This perspective cuts across the automatic inevitability of the collapse of capitalism, which would be framed within the falling rate of profit.[57]

Marx acknowledges that there is the inner necessity of the capitalist mode of production with its resultant overproduction toward an ever extended market, because capital invested in foreign trade can produce a higher rate of profit according to rate of competition of commodities with those of less developed countries.[58]

It implies a law of rising surplus in the metropolis in regard to the periphery, which is characterized by neocolonial logic of exploitation, splitting, and infiltration. The expansion of foreign trade along with the creation of a new work market had tremendous impact on the rise of the capitalist mode of production. This clarification helps to comprehend Marx's theory of primitive accumulation (Chapter XXIV of *Capital* I) in reference to the expanded scheme of reproduction and capital accumulation (Chapter 21 of *Capital* II).

---

[56] Marx, *Capital* III: 339-48.
[57] Baran and Sweezy, *Monopoly Capital*, 72.
[58] Marx, *Capital* III: 345.

In fact, Marx maintains that genuine capitalist production, accumulation of capital cannot exist without foreign trade,[59] in which overproduction of commodities and its crisis are transposed to a colonial market for sale and exploitation. In the process of expanded reproduction, a historical materialist explanation is given onto capital accumulation in the phase of colonialism.

Thus, the world market becomes indispensable in dealing with the domination of a capitalist mode of production in connection with state hegemony, colonialism, and advance of natural science. Capitalist logic of commodity fetishism finds its culmination in its representing value for unequal exchange with the periphery, while capitalist totality becomes worldwide by making the world according to the image of capital through technological innovation and political hegemony.

This capitalist social formation is bound up with complex realities under ideological apparatuses. Biopolitical power relations in state apparatuses remain crucial in undertaking capital accumulation in historical systemic cycle through world market (imperialism) and technological rationality and scientific management. The capitalist mechanism perpetuates social formation into multiple realities in stratification, functional differentiation, and inequality under commodity fetishism, while governing the society and culture with ideological interpellation in degrading integrity of ecological life.

Taken all together, biopolitical sociology provides a genealogical framework to clarify the state hegemony with colonial appendages, as operative in world-economy system. It is concerned with a theory of capital accumulation in the long century rather than preparing the collapse of capitalism at the disposal of a non-capitalist market.

---

[59] Marx, *Capital* II: 546.

However, Rosa Luxemburg takes issue with Marx's model of simple reproduction in the two departments of social production (production of means of production and that of means of consumption) in terms of organic composition of capital (constant capital, variable capital and surplus value are total value).[60]

In Luxemburg's view, accumulation in the development of capitalist production "cannot in general be fitted into a schematic relation between pure capitalist concerns at all."[61] She takes issue with Marx's model of simple or expanded reproduction which refers to a 'pure' capitalist system with equilibrium instead of an accumulation.

In her basic argument we read: "Marx's analysis of accumulation was developed at a time when imperialism had not yet entered on to the world stage. The final and absolute rule of capital over the world...entails the a priori exclusion of the process of imperialism."[62] In the capitalist expansion, Luxemburg argues, the backward nations and their strata of population are incorporated into the orbit of capitalism, in which its surplus value is accumulated and realized through the exchange relationship with the non-capitalist milieu. In this hunting for accumulation the advanced countries in their raid "turn into a chain of economic and political catastrophe: world crisis, wars, revolution."[63]

Such a position entails a significant insight into imperialism, and it may serve as an ideological weapon against imperialism, while provoking the international working class to rebel.[64] In Lukacs' account, Luxemburg was "to take up the thread where

---

[60] Luxemburg, *The Accumulation of Capital*, 69.
[61] Ibid., 69.
[62] Ibid., 145.
[63] Ibid., 60.
[64] Ibid. Sweezy, *The Theory of Capitalist Development*, 206.

Marx left off and to solve the problem in his spirit"[65] in reference to Marx's so-called primitive accumulation.

However, Luxemburg's theory of accumulation bound to the collapse of capitalism disregards periodic crises of capitalism, importance of the role of the power of the state in its regulation of distributive investment resources, enhancement of internal market, armament industry, and welfare system.

More than that, foreign trade acquires raw materials and necessities of life more cheaply than at home. It cheapens elements of constant capital and raises the rate of profit. World market is an integral part in Marx's analysis of crisis and business cycle in which crisis and depression are seen as restorative forces necessarily in the long run.[66]

In effect, Luxemburg's thesis of the connection between imperialism and capital accumulation can be incorporated into a legal-bureaucratic framework, in which a reality of compound reproduction with its surplus value occurs inside the biopolitical sphere of capitalist production (in the social formation reified through commodity fetishism), bureaucratic administration in terms of discipline and coercion in social cultural apparatuses; this capitalist logic transposed its contradiction and crisis upon its outside through trade value of the commodity, capital export, and military power in backward countries.

This genealogical model of capitalist mode of production in social stratification, world market, and colonialism (or imperialism) gives an account of historical and contemporary capitalism in its long century as the world-system through the systemic cycle of capital accumulation; a Genoese cycle (from the fifteenth to the early seventeenth century), a Dutch cycle (from the late sixteenth century through most of the eighteenth

---

[65] Lukacs, *History and Class Consciousness*, 31.
[66] Sweezy, *The Theory of Capitalist Development*, 155.

century), a British cycle (from the latter half of the eighteenth century through the early twentieth century), and a U.S. cycle (beginning in the late nineteenth century and continuing into the current phase of financial expansion).[67]

The State in Late Capitalism and the World Market

In fact, the genesis of capitalism is based on exchange, circulation, and trade while production implies division of labor, forcing human beings to exchange goods for surplus value. "The market spells liberation, openness, access to another world." To the extent that society becomes a generalized market society, however, "there is no simple linear history of the development of markets." Multiple articulations of markets are seen as juxtaposition between the traditional, the archaic and the modern or ultra-modern, even up to today.[68]

Of special importance is the hegemony of the state in this process of accumulation along with scientific-technological advance, which propels the capitalist revolution and its globalizing civilization; it fashions world market and global society according to the image of capital and biopolitical system of sovereignty. The era of colonialism begins with free trade, in fact, for exploitation and profit in religious and political mantel which "has substituted naked, shameless, direct, brutal exploitation."[69]

Expanding the market over the whole surface of the globe is a capitalist way of exploiting the world market which is "given a cosmopolitan character to production and consumption in every country."[70] In the drive to growth and accumulation,

---

[67] Arrighi, *The Long Twentieth Century*, 7.
[68] Braudel, *Civilization and Capitalism* II: 26.
[69] "The Communist Manifesto," in *Karl Marx Selected Writings*, 223.
[70] Ibid., 224.

biopolitical-discretionary strategy is imbued with scientific rationality and bureaucratic administration, and it continues to fashion the world system according to the dialectic between overproduction and world market in cosmopolitan relation through its neoliberal governmentality.

According to Hardt and Negri, there are missing volumes of *Capital*, because Marx's various notes on the state and the world market are fragmentary and insufficient. They acknowledge that Marx has difficulty in linking the state with the world market in a fundamental and integrative sense. A Marxian theory of the state would become complete, only when the full realization of the relationship between the state and capital would bring the nation-states to decline in a profound sense.[71]

Hardt and Negri formulate a postmodern theory of Empire, while incorporating the neoliberal principle of economics into a global imperial sovereignty. The modern concept of sovereignty is centralized in the will and person of the prince; but it comes in conflict with capitalist sovereignty, which shapes global governmentality; it is "expressed through a decentralized economy of rule and management of goods and population."[72]

Along with the process of decolonization, a global factory society and a global Fordism have reigned, and finally a global quasi-state of the disciplinary regime emerges.[73] This understood, it is relevant to examine Weber's theory of the state and its bureaucratic domination.

Weber makes essential features of modern state in terms of legal order, bureaucracy, compulsory jurisdiction, and legitimate use of force. Weber's parliamentary democracy or constitutional democracy is not far removed from the principle of social

---

[71] Hardt and Negri, *Empire*, 236.
[72] Ibid., 328.
[73] Ibid., 255.

contract. "The state is not allowed to interfere with life, liberty, or property without the consent of the people or their duly elected representatives."[74]

More than that, Weber is concerned with an essential element of bureaucracy in its discretionary power with the biopolitical apparatuses, which are completely undermined in the political tradition of social contract and civil society.

On the other hand, Marx was interested in elaborating connections between the capitalist mode of production and the world market, in which his critique of colonialism implies biopolitical governance of the state. His genuine concern is with the withering away of the state, after revolution in the advance via the proletarian dictatorship in the form of social republic.

On the contrary, Lenin's idea of the state does not lead to the withering away of the state, but it is caught to the "hypertrophy of bureaucracy," which emerges out of "the lack of socialist democracy on political level, the lack of worker's self-management on the economic plane, [and] the lack of freedom to create on the cultural plane."[75]

As Weber argues, "the Soviets have preserved, or rather reintroduced, the highly paid enterpriser, the group wage, the Taylor system, military and workshop discipline, and a search for foreign capital. Hence, in a word, the Soviets have had to accept again absolutely *all* the things that Bolshevism had been fighting as bourgeois class institutions."[76]

Specific factors of alienation, discipline, and injustice in public spheres of socialist society result from bureaucratic distortion in intensifying social coercion and inequality, while degenerating into the party's dictatorship, politics of terror,

---

[74] Bendix, *Max Weber*, 422.
[75] Mandel, *The Formation of the Economic Thought of Karl Marx*, 194.
[76] "Politics as a Vocation," *From Max Weber*, 100.

and collectivization; or otherwise, a populist type of collective cannibalism is driven by a deified personality and power war, which is also seen in the Cultural Revolution (1966-1976) in China.

A social scientific analysis of the transitional historical stage is required in dealing with worker's self-management, democratic-central planning, liberating role of scientific technology and progress, higher education, lessening of working day, and creative realization of human subject and activity among others.[77]

However, such position turns out to be illusionary, because the global reality of neoliberal economy invalidates democratic socialist enterprise and self-management through the authority and power in final decision on the part of the big shareholders, their mangers, and representatives.

In fact, the era of late capitalism is featured in a further development of monopoly capitalist epoch in entering a qualitative change through the concentration and centralization of capital, while underpinning the neoliberal principle. A significant role in late capitalism is given onto economic function of state intervention in the sense of state-regulated capitalism.

This structure of late capitalism has surpassed competitive capitalism because of its monopoly, regulation, and state intervention. The advanced stage of the accumulation unfolds along with economic concentration of companies in the rise of national and multinational corporations. A possibility of postmodern society can be explored within the phase of late capitalism in a current historical era.[78]

The state has a political function in cutting through difficulties in the valorization of capital (over-capitalization or over-accumulation). It creates social welfare systems and offers

---

[77] Mandel, *The Formation of the Economic Thought of Karl Marx*, 199.
[78] Habermas, *Legitimation Crisis*, 17. 33.

opportunities for guaranteeing profitable investments of this capital in the armament industry, the environment industry, overseas aid, and infrastructural works. This characterizes a social function of crisis management in the last capitalist state,[79] pace self-regulating market in neoliberal context.

According to Habermas, late capitalism is characterized by the crisis tendencies, which are explored in the economic crisis (from the economic system), rationality and legitimation crisis (from the political system), and motivation crisis (from the socio-cultural system).[80] A critical, theoretical analysis of modernity integrates the whole of modern life down to three different spheres: the economic (market), the political (state), and the sociocultural (sociological theory of the civil society). Capitalist economy finds its significance in the sphere of circulation, trade, and marketing in connection with the state and civil society.

This epistemic position can be complemented by biopolitical sociology in clarifying discourse in the network of power relations and global mode of information. Indeed, it is difficult to affirm that there is an autonomous development of capitalist economy, with detachment from the state, its imperialist politics, and market. The affairs of the state and of capitalism are inextricably bound together with scientific-technological development, ideological interpellation, and military power.

In the strategy of balance of power among nation-states, a regional war would occur in a neo-realistic structure of international politics for hegemony, the logic of which is caught in rivalry, security competition, arms race, and anarchy. In the outbreak of war there is no higher ruling body or centralized authority in the international system to enforce and punish

---

[79] Mandel, *Late Capitalism*, 485.
[80] Habermas, *Legitimation Crisis*, 45.

perpetrator. In an anarchic structure of global politics, in fact, we have no "government over government."[81]

This complex reality in multiple articulations is considerably over-determined upon each aspect and development, shaping the historical totality and organizing world systems in the phase of late capitalism according to core-semi-periphery-periphery relations. Current nation-states are so embedded with the world market that any true democracy would be threatened. Such countries policies further capital, while placing more and more power and privilege into the hands of corporations; it turns CEOs into oligarchs.

3. Eurocentric Position: World System and Structure of Imperialism

It is Samir Amin that conceptualizes a tributary world-system divided into core and peripheral areas. The world has gone through a long transition under political power from primitive communism to the community stage, the tributary stage (pre-capitalist societies), and finally capitalism as the world-system.

In fact, Amin reacts against the Marxist periodization of world history (Asiatic, slavery, feudalism, capitalism, socialism).[82] All tributary cultures are based upon the preeminence of the metaphysical and religious aspiration in the search for absolute truth. In the historical course, tributary ideology was already present in the accomplishments of ancient Egypt. Hellenistic, Eastern Christian, Islamic, and Western Christian constituted the ideology of the tributary mode of production.[83]

---

[81] Mearsheimer, *The Tragedy of Great Power Politics*, 30.
[82] Amin, *Eurocentrism*, 221.
[83] Ibid., 100. 111.

Given this economic system, it is out of the question for Amin to establish any opposition between Greek thought and 'Oriental' thought, because the latter does not exclude Greece. It is difficult to establish a logic of binary opposition within the world systems, thus discarding the opposition between Greece (the West) and Egypt, Mesopotamia, and Persia (the East) as Eurocentric artificial construction of the world order.

World System, Black Death, and Renaissance

For post-Eurocentric direction, it is important to critically renew Amin's tributary system in terms of European commercial revolution. The earlier phase in the vigorously monetary development would be embedded within the two centuries from 1250-1350 (commercial world system) preceding the modern capitalist world-system (1450-1640). The commercial capitalism can be seen in post-Eurocentric comparison with the Afro-Eurasian world system against feudalist interpretation of medieval history.[84]

Europe's economic expansion can be seen in terms of commercial revolution and was connected with the crusades (1095-1291), Byzantine Empire, Muslim world, Mongol Empire (1206-1368) and Hanseatic League (1356); these established the linkage of medieval period to modern capitalism through a thousand years of virtually uninterrupted medieval growth.[85]

Commercial modes of production cannot be subsumed into the tributary system or the feudal mode of production, which is based on the aristocracy in the control of arable land, in social

---

[84] Abu-Lughod, *Before European Hegemony: The World System A.D. 1250-1350.*
[85] Lopez, *The Commercial Revolution*, Vii.

hierarchies from top to bottom, or deep-seated inequality of power, privilege, and wealth. According to Marx, "the modern mode of production in its first period, that of manufacture, developed only where the conditions for it had been created in the Middle Ages."[86] The first sporadic traces of or attempts at capitalist production were found in the fifteenth century in certain Italian city-states of the Mediterranean.

This perspective would imply a structural rupture of the commercial capital associated with merchant banking, textile industry, and world trade. Already in the thirteenth century we observe "efflorescence of cultural and artistic achievement," together with economic integration in many parts of the world.[87] A capitalist world economy can be seen in the thirteenth century Italy. The modern capitalist form in the sphere of high finance is attributed to a Florentine invention based on the networks of banking, and it was founded on its wool industry and the trade expansion (in the late thirteenth century).

But Genoa in mid-fifteenth century can be regarded to the forerunner of modern finance capitalism through alliance with the new crusade of emerging Portugal and Spain for the New World. The colonial empires helped to reinforce Genoese systemic cycle of capital accumulation until the late sixteenth century.[88]

By doing so, it would be fair to locate the capitalist era within the thirteenth century in world systems rather than in the beginning of industrial area in the sixteenth century.[89] This argument can be more clarified in dealing with the Black Death (known as the bubonic plague, 1347-1352). Boccaccio's *Decameron* narrates in

---

[86] Marx, *Capital* III: 450.
[87] Abu-Lughod, *Before European Hegemony*, 4.
[88] Arrighi, *The Long Twentieth Century*, 118-9.
[89] Marx, *Capital* I: 876. Braudel, *Civilization and Capitalism* II: 239.

a series of conversations about the changed reality brought about by the Black Death (1348) in a villa near Florence.

The Black Death has come to restructuring of medieval economic structure. This pandemic, together with successive outbreaks of endemic diseases, has piecemeal destroyed the social economic system of feudalism, changing social status quo and causing social mobility; no longer was a person's status or destiny fixed or determined by birth. Because of loss of population, the nobility found themselves in serious financial difficulties and obliged to sell their serfs and land to wealthy merchants.[90]

Wealthy merchants such as the family of Medici sought to patronize arts and architecture to win the public's esteem, compensating their lack of traditional authority and humble origins. The Florentine wool industry was rapidly expanded in the late thirteenth century, and its high finance was embedded with the networks of the wool trade.

The turmoil in the market by the Black Death in its subsequent endemics (from 1348) engendered a background for the political struggle culminated in the revolt of the Ciompi (1378). The oligarchical rule by the city's wealth merchant families (1434) was replaced with the establishment of monarchical rule by the Medici, who fused his high finance with the expansion of the Florentine State.[91]

Nonetheless, Florence experienced 111 years of people's hunger, and only sixteen very good harvests were recorded between 1371 and 1791.[92] Actually, the Italy-Byzantine eastern Mediterranean had extended to the Italian city-states, and Renaissance was propelled by Greek scholars in the aftermath of Byzantine Empire (1453). The merchant capitalism assumed the

---

[90] Huppert, *After the Black Death*.
[91] Arrighi, *The Long Twentieth Century*, 96, 101, 104.
[92] Braudel, *Civilization and Capitalism* I: 74.

modern character already during the High Renaissance Florence with the house of Medici, and the textbook of double-entry book-keeping (1494) was published.

Dominating nation states (with the Peace of Westphalia of 1648) should play significant role in hierarchical relationship with the dominated in politico-military competition and according to unequal exchange and maximization of profit.[93]

If commercial world system based on exchange, banking system, and trade is taken as the first phase of capitalist system, such a financial system was also prevailing in Abbasid caliphate (Baghdad), Song/Ming China, Mamluk Egypt or Muslim Spain.

This comparative study in global history of commercial capitalism does not necessarily acknowledge progress of technology or its Eurocentric modernity erected on the pillar of linearity and colonialism. In the comparative study of world economies, it is more relevant to seek diverse, alternative interpretations of modernity and capitalism or world systems as an ensemble of social cultural relations and political governance in the post-Eurocentric sense.

The European world economy in the twelfth and thirteenth centuries would not be conceived of without the long distance trade system, which was stretching through the Mediterranean into the Red Sea and Persian Gulf and into Indian Ocean and finally reaching China.[94]

---

[93] Skocpol, *Social Revolutions in the Modern World*, 55–71.
[94] Abu-Lughod, *Before European Hegemony*, 12.

Eurocentric Progress, Christian Philosophy, and Imperialism

Gollwitzer is convinced of a scientific theory of articulating capitalism with colonialism and world market, but he does not share in the Marxist belief in historical progress in a unilateral manner. Gollwitzer is suspicious of Marxist faith in progress, because we are faced with the ruin of the natural foundation of life and destruction of people in the military mass murder of 20th century. His fundamental thesis reads: We strive for progress without having a faith in it, because we believe in God.[95]

Crucial in Gollwitzer is the social scientific inquiry into the articulation between social totality under society fetishism and world market, such that he investigates capitalist revolution and imperialism, implying a critique of Eurocentric neocolonialism. He observes that Marxist faith in progress and freedom would be in parallel with Augustine's philosophy of history in *De civitate Dei*. The historical philosophical conception of progress implies secularization of Christian eschatology. Through Hegel's philosophy of the Spirit the process of history is conceptualized in dialectical movement to realize freedom. It finds its impulse through economic development and scientific-technical progress underlying Marx's utopian notion of classless society, the kingdom of God without God.[96]

Against the Marxist faith in progress, Gollwitzer reemploys historical, materialist inquiry not as the doctrinaire way of prediction about historical progress through calculation. Instead, it is qualified as the social scientific inquiry of exploring social totality through interaction between intellectual sphere and material production. Capitalist logic is articulated with capitalist

---

[95] Gollwitzer, *Krummes Holz-aufrechter Gang*, 143.
[96] Ibid., 126.

revolution at the worldwide level in connection with structural theory of imperialism.

This perspective accounts for Gollwitzer's critical appropriation of historical materialist theory for capitalist system of world economy, in which he extends its insight to call into question Christian character of capital accumulation and its Eurocentric theology of history.

For Gollwitzer, European colonialism has not ended yet, but has changed its forms. Decolonization allowed the previously colonized countries to gain political independence and formal equality. It has continued in the ideology of developmental aid, however, the class struggle on the global scale is carried on and has become the phenomenon of neocolonialism or imperialism. The decolonization has not put an end to Euro-American imperialism, but only modified it in a specious manner. European colonialism and its effective exploitation over great parts of the world is still the decisive factor of the modern history in the postcolonial context.[97]

Structural Theory of Imperialism

Gollwitzer's model of imperialism can be seen in postcolonial approach to neo-imperialism in differentiation from Lenin's model before World War I. The latter is concerned with monopoly capital and export of capital in the form of monopolies. The financial capital of an oligarchy is combined with international monopoly, dividing up the world. Finally, the superpowers completed the territorial division of the world.[98]

Capitalist imperialism is defined only at the highest or last stage of its development in its qualitative change in terms of

---

[97] Amin, *Eurocentrism*, 41.
[98] Sweezy, *The Theory of Capitalist Development*, 307.

monopolies or the financial capital and its export. This type of explanation is mainly based on finance capital, international monopolies, and territorial division of the world.

But it has become obsolete, no longer tenable to the point of clarification of complexity of the neocolonial reality between the metropolis, semi-periphery, and the periphery, according to global, domestic stratification and hierarchy. The periphery like archipelago is scattered within the core, while the core is formed and stratified in the diverse social fields within the periphery.

The global drive to a collision between capitalist and pre-capitalist mode of production in Asia, Africa, and America results in violence, war, and revolution by using militarism. The primitive accumulation should be seen in reference to capitalist expansion in its imperialist phase bound to colonial conquests and world wars.[99]

Accumulation must be seen in the relation of the world system, which is organized in vertical division of labor according to relation between the metropolis, the semi-periphery and the periphery. In the horizontal division of labor, neocolonial reality is conditioned and established in phenomena of archipelago in each zone.

Given the neocolonial condition, Gollwitzer undertakes sociological clarification of the structural theory of imperialism (Johan Galtung) by his critical, creative reading of Marx's economic theory. He is suspicious of Lenin's thesis: "socialism is Soviet system plus electrification,"[100] because direct democracy was not realized in the ex-Soviet Union and former socialist countries in Eastern Europe. Rather, electrification, or industrialization was dependent upon and driven by Western technology.

---

[99] Luxemburg, *The Accumulation of Capital*, 147.
[100] Gollwitzer, *Die kapitalistische Revolution*, 78.

In his definition of socialism as Soviet power plus electrification, Lenin favored state capitalism in Germany and Western culture through dictatorial methods. In NEP (the New Economic Policy) the kulak was to be rehabilitated and encouraged by sacrificing the poorer peasants.[101] The Russian worker has to be schooled in the culture of capitalism and its pattern of modernization in order to become a skilled technician and disciplined worker. Lenin's patronage of the Taylorist system is a well-known fact, in which the American engineer F.W. Taylor's idea of scientific management is praised for a mechanized collectivism.[102]

In the Soviet bureaucracy direct responsibility is assumed for the activities in "sending down its most loyal and trusted comrades to take command of it [the local apparatus] in military style."[103] It refers to the crux of a dictatorship of the bureaucracy which replaces a dictatorship of the proletariat.

In effect, the decolonization (world market), rationalization of production (Taylorism and Fordism), and disciplinary principle are three mechanisms in driving an American form of modernity along with Keynesianism in the New Deal. The latter creates the function of the state as disciplinary government in regulating economic system and development by liberal planning.[104]

Sweezy finds it necessary to renew the insufficiency of Lenin's theory of imperialism in terms of nationalism, militarism, and racism. Nationalism expresses the aspiration of the rising middle class for glorification of one's nation, economic unity, cultural freedom, and armaments; militarism and expansion of armies become the inevitable means to fulfilling this end.

---

[101] Carr, *The Bolshevik Revolution* 2: 291.
[102] Figes, *A People's Tragedy*, 744.
[103] Ibid., 687.
[104] Hardt and Negri, *Empire*, 242-8.

A theory of racial superiority is associated with the combination between nationalism and militarism, as seen in the ideology of 'white man's burden' or in the Third Reich in Germany. The working class in the metropolis takes part in the profits through imperialist foreign policy, improving their standard of living. In the intensification of imperialist rivalries, a process takes place by leading to war in which the working class loses much.[105]

In the imperialist policy the power of the state has augmented in uniting the working class through repression (by force to guarantee law and order) and concession (in the extension of social legislation for worker's compensation, unemployment insurance, and benefit payments). There is the connection between monopoly and state intervention.[106]

This perspective may find significance in Gollwitzer's position of European imperialism, which extends stratification of white domination all over the great parts of the world. The decolonization has only modified the Euro-American imperialism, not ended it. It features a structural theory of imperialism in the world system.

4. Globalization, Neocolonial Condition, and Biopolitical Sociology

In a systemic theory of capital accumulation, the state plays the major role in accumulating the capital and its expansion toward international realm and more markets on the globe. There is the contradiction between such international tendency and the national setting, which is characteristic of the modern capitalism. A multinational company remains crucial as an

---

[105] Sweezy, *The Theory of Capitalist Development*, 315-6.
[106] Ibid., 317-8.

example in its function operative in branches or companies in several countries.[107]

Gollwitzer acknowledges this aspect of capital accumulation in Marx's thesis of "the great civilizing influence of capital," which refers to capitalist revolution.[108] "Scientific-technical projection, higher living standard, economic, cultural and ideological binding of other countries, military instrument of control – these all together form the unique structural power, which the white world center has acquired through the colonial and the capitalist revolution; the maintenance of the power serves its politics.

It is the particularistic interest, which seeks to equate itself with universal interest. It has always been the ideological interest of legitimacy of the dominant. Johan Galtung has described the method of maintenance of such power with the conception: exploitation, division, and infiltration.[109]

The principle of neocolonialism is exposed in terms of exploitation, splitting, and infiltration between the metropolis and the periphery in which the power prestige of nationalism is bound to cultural mission in the supremacy and racism. The capitalist revolution in neocolonial regime has entered to the stage of economic globalization by precipitating the neocolonial condition and its Euro-American superiority in transition from Western modernization to global modernization.

According to Thomas McCarthy, in a shift from modernization to economic globalization, it is allied with neoconservatives who combine neoliberalism with liberal interventionism in foreign

---

[107] Gollwitzer, *Die kapitalistische Revolution*, 51-2.
[108] Ibid., 62. Footnote 1.
[109] Ibid., 42.

policy, which reflect American neocolonial interest in the regime of free trade (established at Bretton Woods).[110]

In fact, the modern welfare state is constituted in a synthesis of Taylorism in the organization of labor with Fordism in the wage regime through Keynesianism in its macroeconomic regulation of the state. However, Neoliberals underestimate in the international arena "the possibilities of legally regulating global markets and politically managing world economic processes."[111] Nation-state is the primary regime of the reproduction of capitalism, while it transforms its role in creating supranational institutions by facilitating and managing economic globalization to serve the national ruling class.

Seen in this perspective, economic globalization in the neoliberal regime creates interdependence fused into world systems according to core, semi-periphery, and periphery in the sense of imperialist metropolis or satellite colonialism. The First World or core zones such as imperialist metropolis can be compared to a great archipelago, which is found everywhere on our planet.

This archipelago still lies in the metropolis, but the relationship in the neocolonial reality of archipelago can no longer be comprehended by way of Global North-South relationship. It can be designated, however, in terms of stratification, inequality, class/status struggle, and exclusion. In the globalized world market, there is still a periphery in the midst of the centers. The state works as a proponent of globalization, in other words, "the political representative of the total market"[112] by facilitating the free flow of goods and capitals. This perspective finds significance in Gollwizter's approach to neocolonial structure of division

---

[110] McCarthy, *Race, Empire, and the Idea of Human Development*, 196.
[111] Ibid., 200.
[112] Duchrow and Hinkelammert, *Property for People, not for Profit*, 146.

of labor, exploitation, and infiltration occurring within the neoliberal regime of world system.

Biopolitics and Neoliberal Governance

In the discussion of globalization and empire, it is important to deal with Hardt and Negri, who focus on discipline and control of human body in the development of capitalism. They are concerned with the analysis of the subjugation of the bodies in various disciplines (universities, schools, army barracks, and workshops) and the control of population.[113]

Along with the increase of the biopolitical sovereignty, modern society runs through society in regulation and management of commodities and population. Civil society is integrated into disciplinary society and its institutions such as the school, the family, the hospital, the factory and occupation. The society of control arises in networks, while civil society withers away and disciplinary society declines.[114]

Social commands are constructed in a diffuse network of apparatuses in producing and regulating customs, habits, and productive practices in disciplinary institutions (the prison, the factory, the asylum, the hospital, the university, the school). What remains crucial is to relocate articulation between society of fetishism (commodities) and disciplinary body within the diffuse network of information and social control.

However, as we have noticed, civil society is born in transactional regimes at the social, cultural, and political spheres in taking issue with biopolitical power and its bureaucratic apparatuses for the subjugated and from them. Global civil society (for instance, Amnesty International, Greenpeace,

---

[113] Foucault, *The History of Sexuality* I: 141.
[114] Hardt and Negri, *Empire*, 329.

and the International Labor Organization, or Civil Rights Defenders) appears to be a site of popular democratic resistance based on citizen initiative and collective decision making against biopolitical colonization of life through neoliberal capitalism.

In fact, biopolitical sociology helps to understand an aspect of capital accumulation and political technique of population in terms of discipline, docility, surveillance, and control of human bodies; the human body is commercialized and subordinated to a neoliberal logic of capital.

The capitalist state in the sense of authoritarian statism shapes public health, control of the population, and security of social body through administration and medical institutions in terms of discipline, subjugation, and rupture. Bureaucratic apparatuses are controlled by executive power with direct repression, which is exercised by police and military violence against civil liberties – authoritarian statism bound to economic exploitation, social relations in diverse apparatuses, curtailment of civil liberties and rights, and class power or domination.[115]

In the midst of biopolitical times, natural science assumes a form of religion, medical religion, which is established by the dominant discourse and its authority on the parts of physicians, doctors, and bureaucrats. The government assumes executive power suspending civil liberties and human rights in the name of protecting biological existence.

Racial injustice becomes a barrier to trusting the public health system and vaccines. This marks a new regime of racism inscribed in the public health system, in which subgroups in ethnicity and race are underrepresented in clinical trials.

The biopolitical regulation of population correlates with the new knowledge of science and technology. It refers to the intersection between power relations (political, economic,

---

[115] Poulantzas, *State, Power, Socialism*, 203-17.

judicial, etc.), social discourse, and the bodily autonomy of the individual. This power of regularization and its regulatory technology "consists in making live and letting die."[116]

A neoliberal arrangement of medical resource and vaccination would reinforce the intellectual property rights to pharmaceutical companies, such that national or international governments would prolong the pandemic because they are caught into pathology of power mechanism: private property, sale monopoly of companies for profit, and laws of international trade and world market.

Biopolitics in the exceptional stage of fascism finds its sharpened point in the totalitarian racial politics through the ideological interpellation. Here, the first essential step to total domination is to kill the juridical person in the human being by categorizing certain people outside the protection of the law. Then, it erects the concentration camp outside the normal penal system, and certain people and inmates are selected to forced labor in concentration camps. In this murderous society biopower refers to the new mechanism of the dictatorship in which there is coincidence between discipline and regulation underlying biological-social racism as well as eliminating its own people.[117]

The biopolitical dogma in the neoliberal governance regulates political control of population and justifies social discourse of mass media. Its economic profit maximization contrasts with public health policies which aim to minimalize the mortality and optimize health of population. Against the neoliberal principle, however, common good must precede private interest in the biopolitical time of the Pandemic.

In an interview with *Le Monde* newspaper, Habermas explicates the moral and political implications of the current

---

[116] Foucault, "Society Must Be Defended," *Biopolitics*, 67.
[117] Ibid., 78.

global health crisis in the Pandemic. He resists temptation of utilitarian calculations on cost-effectiveness logic, urging the European Union to help the most affected member states. His deliberate democratic principle grounded life over benefits says: "We must strive to abolish neoliberalism."[118]

Biopolitical Sociology and Imperial Order of Things

Biopolitical sociology is concerned with analysis of ensemble of relational whole in social formation, while engaging in neocolonial condition of world systems. At the epistemological level of articulation, it focuses on the extent to which discourse (ideal ideas) would be causally adequate with material interests in historical and social context by finding elective affinity as materialized in the life of agents. Status and class are hierarchically stratified in diverse fields according to the social institutions, education, job opportunities, and judiciary legitimacy among others.

At the level of social organizations and ideological apparatuses, it is discipline as the primary order, which initiated the transformation of international politics and war, then gun powder comes as the second order, as seen historically in the Dutch army of the House of Orange imbued with sober and rational Puritan discipline. The use of war machinery presupposes discipline as its basis.

Although war discipline comes along with economic conditions, the discipline as the primary order has always affected the structure of the modern state, the economy, and even possibly the family relations. Biopolitical discipline becomes crucial in characterizing what the society is established along with its safety

---

[118] Habermas interview with *Le Monde*.

network. The military organization is based on bureaucratic regulation of coercion and its ideological apparatuses, which have their origin in discipline of the entire social body and population.[119]

At the level of infrastructure, agency and social structure come into their historical and social interaction and configuration in terms of division of labor, rationalization, differentiation, and specialization. This social organization at the infrastructure is consolidated within the political legitimacy of governance through bureaucratic rule of ideological apparatuses, while funding natural scientific progress and biomedical industry.

At the ideological level of political legitimacy, discourse formation and practice in the social cultural formation entail ideological primacy and interpellation, coming into network of power relations and information industry. Insofar as sociological theory of discipline of the army gives birth to all other discipline, it finds its second great agency in the large-scale economic organization through military expenditure and formation of military-complex industry.

This epistemic position can be obviously seen in situations of war in terms of bureaucratic regulations of coercion and military discipline in connection with military-industrial complex in shipments of lethal weapons for supply and profit to warring states. Insofar as elective affinity is further seen in correlation between commodity fetishism and the disciplinary-docile body, civil society is organized and reified around such correlation with legitimacy of ideological apparatuses.

Bureaucratic administration is reinforced, and phenomenon of reification prevails, such that status/class struggle (or citizen in solidarity with the subaltern) takes place around diverse forms of capital and goods (material, social, cultural, symbolic,

---

[119] Weber, "The Meaning of Discipline," *From Max Weber*, 257.

etc.) against state power in alliance with capitalist oligarchy. Furthermore, biopolitical sociology gains in prominence in analyzing the reality of structural violence in the capitalist world economy through discipline and control in transnational institutions, organizations, and neoliberal apparatuses. Euro-American mode of representation and hegemony disseminates and establishes itself as the dominant system of discourse and legitimacy in dealing with the bilateral agreement in the free trade through global institutions and agencies.

According to Thomas McCarthy, neoliberals (based on Friedrich von Hayek and Milton Friedman) continued to carry out the previous model of modernization and American national myths in terms of liberal order of internationalism, while including security institutions such as the North Atlantic Treaty Organization (NATO) and the Nuclear Non-Proliferation Treaty (NPT). They reinforce international institutions and agencies (the World Bank, IMF, the North American Free Trade Agreement, and others) to adopt market-oriented politics through the strategies: "deregulation, privatization, reduction of state expenditure, fiscal discipline, tax reform, trade liberalization, removal of barriers to foreign investment."[120]

The New Deal and the Marshall Plan give impulses to developmental theorists in supporting Keynesian economics as the key to intervening in and managing economic growth (underwritten in the Bretton Woods Conference of 1944 in connection with World Bank and IMF). Such vision of modernization in the periphery continued and developmental aid was made in ideological struggle for global hegemony with the Soviet Union. The economic geography has been reorganized

---

[120] McCarthy, *Race, Empire, and the Idea of Human Development*, 209.

into metropolis and periphery in which the former develops according to the underdevelopment of the latter.[121]

After the collapse of the Soviet Union the neoliberal paradigm has defeated a global Keynesianism and come in a new phase in promoting deregulation, privatization, and curtailment of state expenditure for globalization against the liberal modernization.[122]

In a postmodern framework, Hardt and Negri reemploy biopolitical theory in conceptualizing a notion of empire in terms of imperial, global sovereignty. The technological revolution of informational accumulation features a phase of capitalism in a new social mode of production. A theory of empire seeks to relocate the problem of imperialism within the crisis of modern sovereignty. A Gramscian perspective is wielded to clarify neocolonial reality within the context of the empire; herein, the "constitution of Empire [becomes] the site of analysis and conflict."[123]

In the postmodern theory of empire, power is exercised in communication systems and information networks in connection with the depth of consciousness and bodies of population. The normalizing apparatuses of the discipline internally animate our common and daily practices across the entirety of social relations. It regulates social life from its interior and achieves an effective command over the entire life of population and their desire in the production and reproduction.[124]

The concept of the society under ideological apparatuses, bureaucratic control, and in network of biopower relations remains crucial in describing central aspects of the reality of the empire in dealing with the globalization.[125] It seeks to explicate

---

[121] Ibid., 197-8.
[122] Ibid., 209.
[123] Hardt and Negri, *Empire*, 237.
[124] Ibid., 24.
[125] Ibid., 28.

a rupture of the systemic cycle of accumulation in the long century; a transition from geographical terrain (imperialism) to empire (under the political regulation of the global market).

As they write, "*We have to recognize where in the transnational networks of production, the circuits of the work market, and the global structure of capitalist rule there is the potential for rupture and the motor for a future that is not simply doomed to repeat the past cycles of capitalism.*"[126]

U.N. organizations (along with the IMF, the World Bank, the GATT among others) are seen as the supranational juridical constitutions, which are framed within the dynamic of the biopolitical production of world order.[127]

In this imperial order of things in the world, multinational and transnational financial corporations substantially have come to transform the new reality of capitalism. Nation-states are made merely instruments to the power of the multinational and transnational corporation and to record and set into motion 'the flows of commodities, monies, and population' in 'the new biopolitical structuring of the world.'[128]

In the biopolitical structuring of the world order, neoliberal principle comes into focus of critical analysis. It is worth considering the way in which nation-states function as the political regulator or agents of the wars in the phase of late capitalism, while involved in the systemic cycle of accumulation. The neoliberal unipolar world order (based on a liberal democracy) has faced the emerging multipolar world, coming into competition with China and Russia with regard to military power, political system, and economic realms.

---

[126] Ibid., 239.
[127] Ibid., 31.
[128] Ibid., 31-2.

In the liberal international order, we also see that nation-states with different cultures and religions (especially Islam) retain their own function, nationalism, and legitimacy, having inter-imperialist rivalry, competition among them, and regional war; they are not merely puppets of the empire within unipolar liberal international order.

War and Territory Empire

The sociological articulation materializes elective affinity in dealing with ideological interpellation to the war, material (or national) interests in the role of agency, and power relations, while explicating combination between military discipline and bureaucratic governance as the primary order in preparation for war policy in the belligerent statism; the war of statism is seen in the massive invasion of 'authoritarian' Russia into 'a liberal democratic' Ukraine.

Such full-scale invasion would be historically seen in connection with American support of the Orange Revolution (Feb. 2014) to replace the Ukrainian government (of Victor Yanukovych) and subsequent Russian annexation of the Crimean Peninsula.

Although this historical background remains crucial in the full-scale invasion (Feb. 2022), there are also several causal adequacies in social political context for consideration; it was undertaken in the creation of a *casus belli* (justification for war) for the sake of the prestige of the great power. It is drafted with ideological interpellation or propaganda of the same race (with no recognition of Ukraine as an independent state). Several pretexts for war are made as the political legitimacy in the name of protection of the citizens or self-claimed proto-states in the occupied territory.

Political military expansion of Western powers (NATO) is seen as an existential threat for the reason of Russian invasion, because of its enlargement into Russia's backyard or spheres of influence in the post-cold war arrangements.[129] Thus, the regional war attains geopolitical significance within capitalist world system under Western powers. They respond to the war by economic and financial sanctions on and unprecedented isolation of Russia, military support or arms sale, ideological information of mass media, and humanitarian aid to refugees.

The neo-liberally allied Empire, which is led by the US, faces up with an authoritarian politics of Russia for the power prestige in the sense of a new Iron Curtain (a new axis of authoritarian regimes); an imperial order of Russia in the neocolonial condition is based on violence, conquest, and super-stratification at the expense of democratic value, human liberty and civilian life on the dominated state; yet such imperial order has no intention to decouple its territorial empire from global economy.

The ideological rhetoric on the part of UN is addressed in its critique of anachronistic restoration of Russian Empire, though it sounds artificial. In reality, arms manufactures in military-industrial complex are in competition with one another among different capitalist powers within a global capitalist economy, leaning toward nuclear annihilation.

Given this ideological war, it is impossible that all states can maximize their relative powers at the same time with each other in the relentless security competition and military capacity for the balance of power. It leads to an anarchic state of international politics, an aspect of world systems (US, EU, Russia, and China) in late capitalism. States are in imperfect information about each other's intentions regarding the balance of power, such that intentions are in constant flux—becoming uncertain rather

---

[129] Eleiba, "Analysis: Failure of post-Cold War arrangements in Ukraine."

than status quo politics.[130] It is an aspect of structural violence of neocolonialism.

Here, I undertake a sociological description of war policy in dealing with system of abstract law of justification (legal-bureaucratic authority in the network of knowledge and power). It focuses on bureaucracy over military discipline, defending will of the attacked people (universal structure of culture and civil state in Rousseau's sense of people's general will), and centrifugal ideological apparatuses through interpellation, mobilization, and propaganda. A cultural aspect of people's will in the sense of civil nationalism remains an undercurrent in fighting for life-world against the metropolis' invasion and its rhetoric of liberator.

In fact, biopolitics and cultural identity (civil society and life-world) become central in the sociological discussion of the state, armament expenditure, financial support of domestic capitalists (oligarchy), and international politics, which is beset by competition, anarchy, and war in late capitalism.

In the case of authoritative statism, civil society is subsumed into coercive reality of the military fascism, and its war politics is reinforced in cumulative bureaucratic regulations of coercion, disciplinary practice, and military-industry complex. If all discipline originates in the military sphere, biopolitical discipline of human body in political, social-economic, and cultural realms and its control of population. This governing mechanism requires political legitimacy through coercion and consent, and the state biopower and its war machine are operative and reproductive through ideological apparatuses and propaganda. It monopolizes its physical forces, mobilizing the citizens to warfare, and multiplying mass deaths in its rights to kill them in war, as well as perpetrating civilian mass slaughtering in the attacked periphery.

---

[130] Mearsheimer, *The Tragedy of Great Power Politics*, 29.

Social bureaucratization of coercion and discipline through state apparatuses infiltrates into the entirety of social body along with political legitimacy of exercise of military power and ideology in utilizing the collective representations and disseminating ideological narrative in the network of information in civil society.

"Most ideological discourses invoke superior knowledge claims, advanced ethical norms and collective interests, and often rely on popular affects with a view of justifying actual or potential social action. Ideology is a complex process whereby ideas and practices come together in the course of legitimizing or contesting power relations."[131]

This sociology of war problematizes the one-sided way of seeing direct causal linkage between capitalism, militarism, and nationalism (aspired in the rising middle class for economic unity, cultural freedom, and internal unification) for the reason of the war.

Rather, it proposes an articulation of multiple relations between political legitimacy, bureaucratic mechanism of coercion, national prestige, cultural authenticity, and military discipline of social body in terms of mass ideological interpellation; in this sociological description cultural or nationalist struggle is mobilized in civil society (Ukraine) for survival, prestige, honor, and democratic value; these are seen as critical factor against mass ideologization and bureaucratic ruling in the perpetrating metropolis (Russia) for conquest.

In the domestic sphere civil society is combined with nationalism, which has the deep-seated roots in the strata of people or citizens in their sentiment of patriotism during the formative period of modern society. Depletion of civil society and nationalism (with cultural prestige) has an important factor

---

[131] Malešević, *The Sociology of War and Violence*, 9.

in the period of imperialist war, calling for solidarity of global civil society by challenging the power of despotic state.

This clarification redefines imperialism within a structural relationship of dominance and violence in dealing with multidimensional phenomena (political, economic, military, cultural, ideological, and communication). It features ideological and geopolitical reasons within the world system in the neocolonial condition and focuses on the particularistic system of thought in the phase of the late capitalism; this violent power mechanism is inscribed to the metropolis' hegemony, colonial dominion, and national supremacy, which are propelled in the process of centrifugal formation of political legitimacy, mass ideology, bureaucratic machinery of war, and military politics.

This political position critically complements a structural theory of offensive realism, in which a regional war would take place in anarchic structure of international politics. In the case of war outbreak there is no government of governments, or no central authority, which is capable of controlling the war, enforcing rules by punishing perpetrators. The states have purpose rationality, while choosing the strategy to maximize their basic aim of survival and political, military hegemony as their purpose.[132]

In fact, this realist-militarist approach needs to be described and critically renewed in terms of biopolitical bureaucracy, ideological apparatuses, and system of oligarchy in military-industry complex for imperial conquest, while including cultural aspect of civil society as resistance for survival.

The state power favors monopolists (steel and shipbuilding necessary to production of armaments) in the military industry enterprise for lucrative outlets, profitable investment of capital, and accumulation of capital. The imperialist expansion

---

[132] Mearsheimer, *The Tragedy of Great Power Politics*, 30.

produces a strong increase in arms expenditure with a growing of militarism to defend the state against rivals as well as invasion of the periphery.[133]

This clarification helps us to understand Gollwitzer's existential and socio-critical position against the Nazi regime, because he was drafted to serve as an ambulance corps in the German armed forces; this draft would prevent him from being sent to concentration camps.

For Barth, the normal task of the state is to fashion true peace among nations rather than to wage war, except for the case of extreme urgency. Christian ethics has little to do with rearmament or disarmament, but with "restoration of an order of life, which is meaningful and just."[134]

Indeed, whenever state power in centralized and well-organized structure does not serve justice, resistance to war or armament belongs to Christian responsibility. It is important to challenge the traditional war theology in face of the modern nature of nuclear weapons. Even in a limited war there remains a choice between capitulation and suicide, because a deterrent is no longer calculable, but suicidal to mass destruction.

Insofar as every Christian listens to the Word of God, it is out of question to take part in the nuclear war. Such war contradicts the meaning of the Gospel, which addresses itself as the point of decision for the whole of Christian stance to the war.

As Gollwitzer contends, "Today we cannot believe in and proclaim God's reconciliation with humanity on the cross of Golgotha without characterizing the nuclear threat itself as rebellion against the reality of reconciliation. Today we can still

---

[133] Mandel, *Late Capitalism*, 481.
[134] CD III/4: 459.

have only both Yes to the Gospel and No to the war—otherwise, one can be lost to the other."[135]

In his analysis of Vietnam War, Gollwitzer unveils the way anti-democratic character of Euro-American capitalism is embedded with its imperialism, in which an oligarchy of wealth and organized violence governs behind ideological façade of formal democracy while exploiting the periphery world. "One cannot be a Christian and remain silent about the murder in Vietnam."[136]

The military-industrial complex would turn upon the American people, when coming in alliance with underground agents with the former Nazi background. Thus, "the brutalization of American foreign policy, if not finally stopped, will lead to the brutalization of American domestic policy."[137]

In the enormous military expenditure, it is important to see that social average rate of surplus value increases in war industry and in domestic and foreign policy through the technological innovation. But its market in the arms traffic in global trade has no demand or supply but depends on the biopolitical strategy of the state military decision.

The political factor is decisive in the fusion of arms companies, military commanders, and politicians in the development of the military industrial complex. The permanent arms economy represents a mechanism for a higher level of employment, but its crisis in the fall of average rate of profit leads to an explosion in the form of war.[138]

Commodity fetishism turns its attraction into terror and destruction of necropolitics toward fetishism of death weapon.

---

[135] "Krieg und Christsein in unserer Generation," Gollwitzer, ...*Dass Gerechtigkeit und Friede sich küssen* 2: 142.
[136] McMaken, *Our God Loves Justice*, 129.
[137] Ibid.
[138] Mandel, *Late Capitalism*, 308.

A geopolitical imperialism becomes obvious in the fact that the sovereignty of periphery lacking nuclear weapons should be subordinated to the metropolis with nuclear armament.

This reality does not legitimize the traditional theory of just war. In late capitalism arms economy produces profit and monopoly capital through technological development and strengthens imperialist policy of militarism, as driven by neocolonial logic of splitting, exploitation, and infiltration.

Against the military as a secular idol, Gollwitzer argues that the commitment to peace should extend to the point of sacrificing interests of nation-states against military program of mass destruction. We die not only in war but already in the armament. "The word the madness of armament is no pictorial expression, but it is a clinically exact designation for the pathological attitude of the government and also people."[139]

5. A Biopolitical State, Racism, and Theology

A postcolonial condition can be characterized in terms of structural system of violence (global division of labor in vertical-horizontal manner, splitting for rule, exploitation, infiltration, militarism, and ecological devastation). Racism and imperialism can be seen as basic features underlying the modern world. The colonial regime was usually racially organized, such that racist beliefs and practices are justified and sanctioned in the colonial context.

The imperial order of things in the sense of global sovereignty is embedded with structural violence of the late capitalism and

---

[139] "Ohne Waffen Leben," in Gollwitzer, ...*Dass Gerechtigkeit und Friede sich küssen*, 277.

its legitimacy in its neocolonial phase. The domination and exploitation between the metropolis and the periphery appear to be obvious and legitimate in the issue of racism, according to the neocolonial type of empire. However, it is required to repair and heal the harmful effects of past injustice against the structural violence and legitimacy of late capitalism.[140]

A capitalist system can be adequately comprehended by the continual process of accumulating capital and expanding world market under the dominance of the political State with its imperialistic logic. The dominant role of political sovereignty remains autonomous as the top layer in guiding and integrating the middle layer of market with the low layers of material life (economics).[141]

"The state... makes its presence felt, disturbs and affects relationships whether it seeks to or not, and often plays a very forceful role in those architectural structures that can be classified into a typology of world socio-economic systems."[142]

This perspective concerns a global reality of late capitalism, which implies that social developments involve contradictions or crises in the advanced stage of the accumulation process (the rise of national and multinational corporations). It refers to the legitimacy of state-regulated capitalism in maintaining capital investment in the international market, technological administration, economic monopoly, social anonymity of class domination, and ideological function of mass media.

In fact, racism developed with colonization, and such a connection implies a colonizing genocide in which the political technology of body turns into necropolitics. Population of the colonized and their savage bare life turn into *homo sacer*,

---

[140] McCarthy, *Race, Empire, and the Idea of Human Development*, 4.
[141] Arrighi, *The Long Twentieth Century*, 24.
[142] Braudel, *Civilization and Capitalism*, 561.

while appealing evolutionary theory of race to justifying racial genocide.[143]

A biopolitical concept of racism and social discrimination takes place in the break between what (or who) must live and what (or who) must die. "Once the state functions in the biopower mode, racism alone can justify the murderous function of the state."[144]

This biopolitical turn occurs in the postcolonial study of the characteristic privileges of sovereign power with the right to decide life and death together with racism and discrimination. The death of the other, the bad race, or "the inferior race (or the degenerate, or the abnormal) is something that will make life in general healthier: healthier and purer."[145]

In the political power over body, however, racism becomes the precondition for exercising the right to kill. The power of a state is "obliged to use race, the elimination of races and the purification of the race, to exercise its sovereign power."[146] A racist state is a murderous state, and it turns into an absolutely suicidal state. Totalitarian solutions may well survive with us, as their form continues to perpetrate in Apartheid and Palestine. Colonial exploitation is tied to neoracism, in which race is not purely apprehended in biological sense; racist beliefs and practices are embedded with power relations and would outlive in racial stratification in the postcolonial society.

---

[143] Foucault, "Society Must be Defended," in *Biopolitics*, 76.
[144] Ibid., 75.
[145] Ibid.
[146] Ibid., 77.

Theology and Racism

Gollwitzer takes seriously the claim of James Cone's thesis—there is no Black appearing in the white theology.[147] The colonialism and slave trade were undertaken in the European Christian context, and racism was bound with colonialism and Christian mission.

In Cone's argument, American white theology defines Christianity as compatible with white racism (in the conservative southern circle) or independent of Black suffering in the liberal northern circle. When liberals speak of inevitable progress in Western culture, their discourse is undertaken at the cost of Black people enslaved and colonized for safeguarding the progress.[148]

Against this, Cone argues, "if God is not for us and against white people, then he is a murderer, and we had better kill him."[149] A Black theology of liberation refers to the most distinctive contribution to racial justice. "I was black before I was Christian."[150] James Cone presents a prophetic, radical side of public theology in actualizing the symbolic meaning of the cross in connection with people crucified in lynching tree.

However, an excessive argument remains questionable: "Black theology believes that [Black-skinned people] are the *only* key that can open the door to divine revelation."[151] This reductionist argument can be comprehended in phenomenological sense, in which the true meaning of divine revelation is grounded on Jesus Christ as the partisan of those victimized.

In the scientific theory of social cultural stratification, it is worth taking into account the way in which gender differences or

---

[147] Gollwitzer," Why Black Theology," 43.
[148] Cone, *A Black Theology of Liberation*, 22. 47.
[149] Ibid., 60.
[150] Cone, *The Cross and the Lynching Tree*, xvii.
[151] Ibid., 32.

inequality would be conceptualized as a central feature of a social-cultural system of masculine dominion in relation to woman. Black women have a different but distinguished experience of Black patriarchy from white middle-class women in relation to white middle-class men. An intersectional analysis of the system of oppression and violence can be undertaken with respect to Black women's experience in comparison with experience of white middle-class women.[152]

Gollwitzer sees Black theology against white racism in terms of the Pauline text, which contradicts the Eurocentric standpoint: "There is no longer Jew or Greek, there is no longer slave or free, there is no longer male and female; for all of you are one in Christ Jesus" (Gal 3:28).

For instance, Las Casas remains the prophetic voice in which God takes sides with the Indians, the subjugated indigenous for liberation and revolution against corrupt Christian church in Spain. Reformation and its Protestant churches were not ready for fully embracing racial justice.[153]

Gollwitzer defines the capitalist revolution as the revolution of the white Protestant people (the English and the Dutch), which won worldwide victory and led the initiate in a new age of slavery in the neocolonial form of exploitation and domination up today. Karl Marx is right in describing the situation of colonialism as the 'Christian character of primitive accumulation' (chapter 24 of the first volume of *Capital*), which every theologian must read.[154]

A theory of race can be developed in social scientific framework, in which race and ethnicity are to be seen in the social, cultural disposition. Social Darwinism has been built

---

[152] Collins, *Black Feminist Thought*, viii.
[153] Gollwitzer, "Why Black Theology," *Union Seminary Quarterly Review*, 38-41.
[154] Ibid., 41.

in colonial theory of white supremacy with its racialist feeing of white man's burden. Furthermore, racial theory of social Darwinism takes an inroad to anti-Semitism in the Third Reich as well as state socialism in the ex-Soviet Union. Unlike Marx, 'race' is an irreducible dimension in social, cultural, and political relations within social stratification as well as in the global relation between the metropolis and the periphery.

An imperial racist theory becomes a strong foundation for social separation and difference within society in terms of the strategy of differential inclusion; racial difference is subordinated according to degrees of deviation from whiteness. This differential racism orchestrates those differences in a social system of control and hierarchy, which is distinguished from modern racist theory of supremacy and subordination.

An imperial strategy of differential inclusion results in racial exclusion and inequality in public sphere. Thus, "black segregation is not comparable to the limited and transient segregation experienced by other racial and ethnic groups, now or in the past. No group in the history of the United States has ever experienced the sustained high level of residential segregation that has been imposed on blacks in large American cities."[155]

Jim Crow laws and the apartheid in South Africa become the modern paradigm of racial supremacy, segregation, and hatred. A color line underlays the reality of racial injustice and crisis, which is perpetuated in the U.S., while cultural racism is obvious in ethnic conflicts in Palestine or else. Classical racial ideology (biology) branded with cultural neoracism is still influential in shaping everyday life.

Imperialism or neocolonialism is inseparably bound to white racism. James Cone's argument—"the Black does not appear

---

[155] Massey and Denton, *American Apartheid*, 2.

in white theology"[156]— must be taken seriously. Theology and church can be vulnerable to racial injustice and religious violence in sanctioning alliance between the gospel, colonialism, and racism. Against this, the core of the Gospel implies that the great multitude from every nation, all tribes and tongues (Rev. 7:9) are united in the one Church of Jesus Christ (Gal. 3:28).

Concluding Reflection

Gollwitzer facilitates public theology in investigating the extent to which the public sphere in the metropolis would be involved in promoting a 'Christian' character of capital accumulation and expansion in the neocolonial context. Christian religion can be misused to justify the political, philosophical, legal, and ideological system in upholding Euro-American discourse of neocolonial representation, the hegemonic system, and structural violence of imperialism in a religious garment.

In examining the neocolonial reality of late capitalism, Gollwitzer provides a conceptual framework in dealing with postcolonial problematic in terms of the synthesis of exploitation, splitting strategy, and infiltration along with international division of labor in vertical and horizontal sense. It causes ecological crisis and neoracism. Body is exploited, commercialized, disciplined, and regulated for political governance, economic efficiency, and racial injustice.

This biopolitical sociology helps to reinterpret and renew Gollwitzer's thesis of capitalist revolution and its neocolonial condition in the phase of late capitalism. At the same time, the biopolitical sociology focuses on elective affinity of discourse and legal-bureaucratic governance along with ideological apparatuses.

---

[156] Gollwitzer," Why Black Theology," 43.

This sociological articulation facilitates public theology in tackling postcolonial civil society in dealing with diverse public spheres in the social cultural stratification. The latter has each field imprinted with class/status struggle, which reacts against dominion from above. Global issues are saturated with public spheres (immigration problems, multicultural diversity, racism, ethnicity, and multi-religious conflicts). Thus, public theology is premised in postcolonial condition, in which civil society must be safeguarded and developed according to the sovereignty of the people and citizen initiative for the sake of emancipation to solidarity.

Gollwitzer takes into account the line and orientation of the Gospel for public ethical commitment, which is formulated in Barth's review of Eberhard Bethge's biography of Bonhoeffer. In Barth's account, Bonhoeffer embodied in his theology and practice the following direction and orientation: "ethics—co-humanity—serving church [in prophetic diakonia]—discipleship—democratic socialism—peace movement—and all in all just political engagement."[157]

Gollwitzer represents his public theology and ethics of life-world in a concrete, universal sense, while engaging in social scientific approach to neocolonial reality in late capitalism.

---

[157] "Andreas Pangritz's Introduction" in Gollwitzer,*dass Gerechtigkeit und Friede sich küssen*, 8.

Chapter 6.

Public Ethics, Biopolitics, and Biomedical Justice

In the midst of COVID-19, we experience how deeply public health is connected with the political agenda and the economic system. Political power over biological life and health care becomes a challenging issue for public theology to critically engage in the complicated relation between human dignity and commodification of medicine.

Biomedical ethics is a way of providing a moral framework in times which the protection of life is on debate, such as whether deliberate killing may be allowed or prohibited if physicians may be legitimated to hasten the death of patients.[1] A biomedical argument from beneficence and progress challenges public theology and its moral reasoning to take seriously human dignity in social, political, and cultural context.

This chapter is a study of public theology and biomedical reasoning in dealing with life-preservation, shared responsibility, and dignity of human life. It is important to take on the moral significance of genes and ethics under the slogan of playing God, while dealing with gene editing technique, genetic engineering, artificial gametes, and stem cell debate.

Then, I explore the extent to which biopolitical control of public health would be embedded with commerce of medicine

---

[1] Beauchamp and Childress, *Principles of Biomedical Ethics*, 5.

in the neoliberal context. It aims at cutting across pathologies of power, which become operative in the biomedical enterprise, political governmentality, and bureaucratic administration.

Finally, public theology is cast upon in a constructive endeavor in examining debates about evolutionary theory, genetic determinism, and human cloning. Original sin/gay gene assumption comes into critical focus. A discourse of created co-creator is set up within the framework of God's created collaborator.

1. Theological Deliberation of Biomedical Field

In the discussion of life-protection and shared responsibility, public theology appreciates the biomedical appeal to non-maleficence and beneficence, since these two bioethical principles have gained prominence and loyalty in medical research settings and public health care programs.

The concept of non-maleficence can be seen together with a duty of beneficence in the Hippocratic Oath: "I will use treatment to help the sick according to my ability and judgment, but I will never use it to injure or wrong them."[2]

A principle of non-maleficence or beneficence is regarded as the foundation of social morality, which is the essential part of human dignity and responsibility. Especially in biomedical ethics non-maleficence (no inflicting evil or harm) is distinguished from beneficence, which includes preventing and removing evil or harm and promoting good.[3]

---

[2] Cited in ibid., 120.
[3] Ibid., 123.

Gustafson develops moral reasoning in line with utilitarian theory, which justifies forms of self-sacrifice for the increase of good consequences. Forms of suicide like martyrdom or an act of self-sacrifice relieving from pain and suffering would be permitted on consequentialist or utilitarian grounds. "The universal wrongness of suicide is at any rate not self-evident."[4]

Of special significance in the theocentric framework is that God is no longer sovereign over human life in deepest despair. Grace of justification and forgiveness does not involve renewal of life, even leading to moral failures.

Against this theocentric utilitarianism, however, it is necessary to comprehend divine forgiveness in terms of God's initiative love in Christ. The grace of forgiveness comes to us by faith, while including God's righteousness in restoring human broken life to the new creature for the common good.

Douglas John Hall states: It "embraces our freedom to manifest something life a new nonchalance about self and a new attention to the other."[5] Discipleship is the gift and command of the crucified Christ, who is present in the world of brokenness, encouraging us to live with a trust and a restorative, a non-retributive justice.

Freedom and the Right to Suicide and Abortion

In the public discussion of death with dignity we read that physician-assisted suicide would occur in some patients, who are in the extreme situation of terminal, painful, and unrecoverable illness. It is legal in nine US states and the District of Columbia.

---

[4] Cited in Gustafson, *Ethics* II: 195.
[5] Hall, *The Cross in Our Context*, 41.

Though understandable, such practice becomes questionable in view of the role of the physician as healer.[6]

Remarkably, suicide in the biblical context appears to be regarded as the consequence of extremely grave sin in the case of the traitor of Ahithophel and Judas. Nowhere in the Scripture is the suicide expressly forbidden. But in no way does it sanction suicide. In the midst of despair, human freedom is the actual originator of suicide, performing the human supreme act of self-justification. Even in the deepest despair there is a living God; suicide is wrongful as a sin of lack of faith in contrast to God's grace of justification.[7]

The right to suicide contrasts with the faith in the living God. In hours of trial, despair, shame, and failure, God can again give a meaning and a right even to a ruined life. God's merciful summons to faith, deliverance, and conversion defeats the lack of faith, which is the ultimate ground for the self-destruction. In such hours, help can come only from the comfort of grace and from the power of brotherly prayer, because God embraces and sustain human despair and failure by resistance to the hardest of all temptations.[8]

In dealing with the issue of abortion, Gustafson takes into account a conflict between the rights of the fetus and those of the mother. He maintains that the fetus does not fully have the abilities for purpose-fulfillment. He concurs with the position that "there are good reasons under a variety of circumstances to induce abortion."[9] However, he finds the antiabortion argument to be equally rational; "The fetus is a person. To take

---

[6] Physician-assisted Suicide.
[7] Bonhoeffer, *Ethics*, 166.
[8] Ibid., 170-1.
[9] Gustafson, *Ethics* II: 21.

the life of a human being, except when it is an unjust aggressor, is murder."[10]

Gustafson characterizes his ethical position in view of St. Paul: "Let no one seek his own good, but the good of his neighbor." (1 Cor 10: 24) "Let each of you look not only to his own interests, but also to the interests of others." (Phil. 2:4) The cross, and the way of the cross, are revealing symbols of what is enabled and required of persons who seek to serve and glorify God."[11]

However, a theocentric understanding of the cross in utilitarian terms becomes questionable, because it cannot become a necessary principle in dealing with the issue of supererogation. Rather the issue of abortion requires more ethical reasoning of responsibility in interdisciplinary fields.

According to Rendtorff, the legal question about the regulation and law of the practice of abortion requires medical questions about the doctor's decision concerning the danger of the mother or unborn baby. The concern of the pregnancy may result in extensive damage to the health of the mother or the baby, or even leading to death. The questions of ethical norms deal with the probation of killing (You shall not kill) in relation to abortion. They include the relationship between the wife and the husband. A sociological question concerns the social conditions, in terms of unmarried woman or financial difficulty of family situation, or in the extreme case of rape.[12] The principle of the 'preservation of life' has to be seen and discussed in multilayered questions (legal, medical, ethical, sociological) and such debate requires a new definition of shared responsibility in the affirmation of life in conflict.[13]

---

[10] Ibid., 20.
[11] Ibid., 22.
[12] Rendtorff, *Ethics*, II: 161-64.
[13] Ibid., 165-6.

God of Life, Medical Killing, and Suicide

Practices such as medical killing, or euthanasia are illegal in US whereas the physician-assisted suicide is legalized in several states. Laws in the United States make distinction between passive and active euthanasia. Active euthanasia is prohibited, however, at the request of a patient or the patient's authorized representative, physicians should not be legally punished if they withdraw a life-sustaining treatment.[14]

Barth discusses abortion and suicide under the heading of protection of life. His basic statement: "Life is a loan from God entrusted to man for His service."[15] Barth construes the moral questions about killing on the basis of this basic statement. He takes issue with the Roman Catholic position in which deliberate abortion is absolutely forbidden on any grounds. For instance, when the Russians invaded Germany in 1945, Roman Catholic nuns were raped. But they were not allowed for freedom from this consequence. Barth considers this Catholic position as "too forbidding and sterile to promise any effective help."[16]

According to the Catholic principle of double effect, an act of killing the innocent is wrong in itself. Human life begins at conception. Personhood with a right to life is established at fertilization, when a new genome is established: "The human being is to be respected and treated as a person from the moment of conception; and therefore, from that same moment his rights as a person must be recognized, among which in the first place is the inviolable right of every innocent human being to life."[17]

Despite the prohibition of abortion, the death of the fetus in the case of cancerous uterus and ectopic pregnancy of the

---

[14] Peters, Euthanasia Laws.
[15] Barth, CD III/4: 402.
[16] CD III/4: 417.
[17] Cited in Peters, "Cells, Souls, and Dignity," 11.

woman is held to be an unintended effect of morally legitimate medical procedure. However, if killing the fetus is intended as the means to the good end of saving the mother's life, this procedure is disqualified by the principle of double effect.[18]

However, Barth's position is driven first by the sovereignty of the living God over human life, thus an unequivocal No to any act of killing (abortion, suicide, euthanasia, and persons such as the socially unfit, the cripple, the incurably infirm, the insane, and imbeciles). The annihilation of the 'useless' can be regarded only as murder, which implies "a wicked usurpation of God's sovereign right over life and death."[19]

This normative position contradicts National Socialist eugenics, which seeks to eliminate life that is unworthy of being lived. On the decision on bare life in the state of exception, Nazi biopolitics turns into thanatopolitics in its governmentality of human bodies.[20] A slippery slope with small beginnings was driven by racial ideology, and it was expanded to implement the general principle of unworthy life, the severely and chronically sick through medical killing. It is "camouflaged mass murder."[21] The end justifies the means. Barth's basic stance for life is clearly seen in his critique of euthanasia, which is regarded as "a gentile, painless and almost beautiful death," set "in a condition of euphory."[22]

Against this request, Barth affirms that dying can be a blessing no less than living, from God. Euthanasia is a form of self-destruction. If the direct suicide is wrong, euthanasia as the

---

[18] Beauchamp and Childress, *Principles of Biomedical Ethics*, 128-9.
[19] CD III/4: 417.
[20] Agamben, "The Politicization of Life," in *Biopolitics*, 147-8.
[21] Beauchamp and Childress, *Principles of Biomedical Ethics*, 142. Alexander, "Medical Science under Dictatorship," *New England Journal of Medicine*, 39-47.
[22] CD III/4: 423-4.

indirect one is wrong, though undertaken in the highest form of love, or well-meaning humanitarianism of underlying motive.[23]

Barth's theological ethics concerning suicide is of dialectical character. Insofar as life is a loan from God, God is sovereign over human life. Human being is defined as the steward put in the service of God, not as the judge with self-sovereignty over life. God's gracious command is "Thou mayest live." But human being is free in self-determination in which the possibility of suicide might come. The judgmental attitude is not recommended.[24]

I sense that Barth's position is not so much different from the Catholic teaching of euthanasia, though unintended. We read in the Roman Catholic Declaration on Euthanasia in Sacred Congregation for the Doctrine of the Faith. "The Council therefore condemned crimes against life "such as any type of murder, genocide, abortion, euthanasia, or willful suicide" (Pastoral Constitution *Gaudium et Spes*, no. 27). The pleas of gravely ill people who sometimes ask for death are not to be understood as implying a true desire for euthanasia; in fact, it is almost always a case of an anguished plea for help and love. What a sick person needs, besides medical care, is love, the human and supernatural warmth with which the sick person can and ought to be surrounded by all those close to him or her, parents and children, doctors and nurses."[25]

Other than Barth and the Catholic position, I keep in view that the ethical debate of positive euthanasia (killing) and passivity (letting die or allowing to die) distinguishes the medical ethical development. According to the American Medical Association House of Delegates (AMA) in 1973, the cessation of treatment is morally justified when the patient or the patient's immediate

---

[23] Ibid., 426.
[24] Ibid., 427.
[25] Sacred Congregation for the Doctrine of the Faith.

family, based on the advice and judgment of the physician, decides to withdraw "extraordinary means to prolong the life of the body when there is irrefutable evidence that biological death is imminent."[26]

The AMA statement maintains that 'mercy killing' in medicine is unjustified on any grounds, but 'letting die' is not always wrong. In the religious context, placing patients in God's hands does not necessarily mean usurping God's sovereignty. No basis is given to form a judgment and a condemnation is impossible. Equating every form of self-killing with murder would be short-sighted.[27] "Without freedom to sacrifice one's life in death, there can be no freedom towards God, there can be no human life."[28] Human freedom for suicide brings it before the forum of God.

2. Biomedical Science and Ethical Interpretation

Theological reasoning of human dignity and shared responsibility is more complicated and sharpened, when it comes to biomedical regime and its scientific technology. For instance, a technology for modifying DNA (known as CRISPR gene editing) was undertaken by Chinese scientist He Jiankui, who made the first genome-edited human babies in 2018. The He Jiankui affair led to legal and ethical controversies. Genome editing or gene editing refers to a type of genetic engineering. Pioneered in 1990s, it randomly inserts genetic material to site

---

[26] This 1973 statement is reprinted in Rachels, *The End of Life*, 192-93.
[27] Bonhoeffer, *Ethics*, 168-9.
[28] Ibid., 165.

specific locations in a host genome, while deleting, modifying or replacing the DNA.

Ethical debates over the nature of biotechnology require a meticulous interpretation of the achievement of biotechnology and its technological application. Such interpretation can be taken from the standpoint of appropriateness and common good. The obligation to benefit others comes from social interaction through reciprocity. As recipient of the benefits of society, human beings ought to promote the interests of the society.[29] The reciprocity between society and human beings becomes crucial in biomedical ethics, dealing with health care, therapeutic research, and social policy. The principles of biomedical ethics are characterized by respect for autonomy, non-maleficence, benefice (including utility), and social justice.[30]

For the public discussion of medical issues of life and death, the primary question centers around what is the real issue of the event, and it requires a contextual analysis of the situation in terms of appropriateness, reciprocity, and common good. A question—why Christians should support stem cell research—weighs a diversity of ethical problems related to the dignity of a human person, while taking into account the prospect of increased health and wellbeing. "Regenerative medicine could lead to much more abundant life for many among us." This position is operative "primarily within the future wholeness framework."[31]

This future wholeness position, which is of eschatological orientation, is sharply formulated against a pro-embryo protection framework in the following question: "Is it moral for religious advocacy groups to shut down research that could lead

---

[29] Gorovitz, et al., *Moral Problems in Medicine*, 386.
[30] Beauchamp and Childress, *Principles of Biomedical Ethics*.
[31] Peters, et al. *Sacred Cells?* xi.

to relieving the suffering of millions if not billions of persons in the future?"³²

Such a position becomes decisive in the ethical interpretation, as it comes to undertake contextual analysis of stem cell research and its regime in terms of appropriateness, reciprocity, responsibility, and beneficence.

Gene-ethics and Public Theology

In the popular press we read: are our scientists playing God? The scientific progress such as genetic engineering challenges a traditional notion of Christian anthropology and reinforces theologians to reconstruct an ethics of new life forms, in other words, gen-ethics.

The Human Genome Project (HGP), sometimes known as the Human Genome Initiative (HGI), has been funded by the U.S since the late 1980s, and was completed in 2003. Its goal was to learn the structure of the genome and sequence of all three billion bases (nucleotides) in the DNA of the human genome in complete detail; it was to locate reference points to all the genes for advancing new strategies of diagnosis and treatment of genetic disease.³³

James Watson, together with Francis Crick, is famed for the discovery of DNA (deoxyribonucleic acid), which is arranged in two long strands forming a spiral staircase called a double helix, somewhat like a twisted ladder. Most DNA is located in the cell nucleus and the genes, made of DNA, are the individual units of heredity. They are written in the language of DNA which uses a four-letter alphabet: A (adenine), C (cytosine), G (guanine) and T (thymine).

---

[32] Ibid., X.
[33] Cole, "The Genome and the Human Genome Project," in *Genetics*, ed. Peters, 55.

In the process of DNA replication, a mutation, a mistake in copying DNA, occurs. Genetic mutation causes defective or loss of protein function, leading to disease. Like events with quantum unpredictability, mutation acts upon a direct effect on the sequences of bases in DNA and produces variations. The DNA molecule is structured in a way that makes individual atoms and even electrons significant.[34]

Back to HGP, Watson served as the head of the Office of Human Genome Research at the National Institute of Health (NIH). Moral controversy already broke out concerning patenting DNA between him and the former NIH director Bernadine Healey. Genetics is supposed to come to terms with ethics, and such espousal is called *gene-ethics*.[35]

In a Time/CNN poll a substantial majority (fifty-eight percent) showed that altering human genes is against the will of God. This is hubris or human pride; it requires a new commandment. "Thou shall not play God?"[36]

Ted Peters, one of the most distinguished prolepsis theologians and bioethical scholars, seeks to clear out the wrong assumption about DNA, because DNA's capacity should not be elevated to a higher metaphysical or moral level. Although DNA replication and sexual reproduction are crucial in biology, they are hardly the stuff of sanctity, even the essence of life. Likewise, Cole-Turner argues that "it is hard to imagine a scientific or philosophical argument that would successfully support the metaphysical or moral uniqueness of DNA."[37]

For Peters our ethical gaze is directed toward the contribution that scientific research can make on behalf of improving

---

[34] Miller, *Finding Darwin's God*, 207.
[35] Peters, "Genes, Theology, and Social Ethics," in *Genetics*, 2, 140.
[36] Ibid., 156.
[37] Cole-Turner, *The New Genesis*, 45.

human health, well-being, and flowering.[38] Peters' constructive contribution to public theology can be seen primarily in his full incorporation of a theology of nature. In fact, a theology of nature, unlike the traditional form of natural theology, is informed by natural science and its achievements. But it relies upon special revelation of God in Jesus Christ (incarnation), God's promise and grace of reconciliation in the Easter resurrection of Jesus Christ, and God's coming eschatology.

According to Peters, public theology as a theology of nature engages in global public discussion in matters pertaining to environmental crisis, climate change, bioethics, and public policy, while employing empirical research and scientific data.[39]

In dealing with genetic ethics and playing God, Peters challenges an assumption that the genetic research is supposed to lead to algeny. Algeny means 'the upgrading of existing organisms and the design of wholly new ones with the intent of "perfecting" their performance.'[40] However, from a scientific point of view, a notion of algeny is accused of being "a cleverly constructed tract of anti-intellectual propaganda masquerading as scholarship."[41]

Ethical Framework: Stem Cell Research

Ethical debates arise in the consequences of biotechnology, when it comes to the social implications of equity and justice in access to genetic service. As with the genetic technique, other topics such as in vitro fertilization, germline intervention, cloning, and artificial gametes occupy an important place in moral deliberations.[42]

---

[38] Peters, *Science, Technology, and Ethics*, 11.
[39] Ibid., 167.
[40] Rifkin, *Algeny*, 17.
[41] Gould, *An Urchin in the Storm*, 230.
[42] Cole-Turner, *The New Genesis*, 16.

An ethical problem occurs between the interests of researchers in obtaining eggs and the interests of donors. In debacle surrounding the work of Woo Suk Hwang in South Korea, Hwang was reported to have used 242 donor eggs in his attempts to create a single stem cell line. Eggs had been obtained from female employees for Hwang's research, in which female employees were treated as a part of their contractual obligations; it challenges standard ethical guidelines.[43]

The current debate over stem cells centers around: (1) the embryo protection framework (against abortion) (2) the nature protection framework (against scientist manipulation of the genetic nature of human being embedded with the playing God); it is done in post-human technoscience and ecology. (3) the medical benefit framework (for relief human suffering and enhancement of human flowering). All Jewish and most Christian theologians may share with the principle of beneficence for human embryonic stem cell research.[44]

I add another ethical criterion regarding the artificial gametes, in which the family integrity framework becomes central. The term 'synthetic gametes' or 'artificial gametes' are commonly used, but the gametes in question are created by manipulating already existing cells. The term 'stem cell-derived gametes' is used.[45] I use the term artificial gametes (shortened to AGs).

It is possible that sperm may also be made from adult cells (induced pluripotent stem cells known as iPS). A coming technological breakthrough to AGs will herald a revolution

---

[43] Hwang WS et al. "Evidence of a pluripotent human embryonic stem cell line derived from a cloned blastocyst," *Science* 2004; 303, 5664: 1669-1674.
[44] Peters, *The Stem Cell Debate*, x, 27.
[45] *The Journal of Medical Ethics*, November 2014 - Volume 40 -11.

that will "dismantle completely the reproductive structure of heterosexuality."⁴⁶

In vitro fertilization paves the way for the understanding of the complex process of human gametogenesis, which would provide human gametes for the study of infertility. Artificial gametes are mature germ cells (sperm and eggs) generated *in vitro* by specification and maturation. Sperm or eggs could be derived from embryonic stem cell lines to create artificial gametes.

This prospect would enable same sex couples to have children that are the offspring of both partners. Nonetheless, it can be argued that AGs could facilitate genetic modification of gametes and its transmission that would be inherited by future generations. It might transmit serious genetic abnormalities, and children conceived with AGs might suffer serious genetic anomalies. Proliferation of AGs would exacerbate the commodification of embryos.⁴⁷

The effects of family confusion on offspring become a worrying prospect that AGs raises regarding the relationship between parents and a child. If AGs are derived from her own somatic cells to fertilize her natural eggs, it poses threats to the integrity of the family, because AGs would encourage people to pursue reproductive aspirations without the family form. AG solo parenthood is particularly risky in creating psychological harm to the identity of a child. It would run more so than a single parent.

Where more embryos can be created, choosing between many healthy embryos becomes more feasible on the basis of parental preferences. Genetic nihilism, which is likened to Frankenstein,

---

⁴⁶ Darnovsky, Bioengineered Gametes: Techno-Liberation or Techno-Trap? *Biopolitical Times* (08.26.2020).
⁴⁷ "Nuffield Council on Bioethics Background Paper."

would disseminate the impression that the child becomes more like a 'product' that satisfies the parents' specifications.

Scientists are currently exploring derivation of AGs from embryonic stem cells, from germ-line stem cells, and from induced pluripotent stem cells. This research does not avoid the ethical problem in creating an egg (or sperm) from my male (female) skin cell in regard to the representation of the whole person. Would a male's created 'egg' represent his whole person?

Stem cells are the body's raw materials, which can perform self-renewal and differentiation (specialized cells), dividing to form more cells (called daughter cells). From the stem cells all other cells are generated with a more specific function (blood cells, brain cells, heart muscle cells or bone cells).

Among many types of stem cells, there are totipotent (totally potent) stem cells within the early embryo (until roughly the sixteen-cell stage), self-replicating and differentiating. A zygote as the first, totipotent cell is capable of forming any type of cell in the human body as well as the umbilical cord and placenta. Each totipotent cell has the potential for becoming an embryo and human being through replication and differentiation.

Technically, the zygote at a fertilization event divides many times (mitosis) until it is sixteen cells of the morula. Then differentiation occurs producing the blastocyst, which consists of the inner cell mass (embryonic stem cells) and the extra-embryonic tissue (the placenta). Totipotent cells can access to a placenta by making them available for implantation.

The inner cell mass becomes pluripotent, except for in the umbilical cord and placenta. The pluripotent stem cells are capable of dividing into more stem cells and becoming any type of the cell in the body; this versatile capacity is to regenerate or repair diseased tissue and organs.

Human embryonic stem cells (hES) are taken from inside the blastocyst, a very early-stage embryo (about 3 to 5 days old). The blastocyst is a ball of about 150 cells and it is not yet implanted in the womb. An embryonic stem cell is removed from the inner cell mass of blastocyst and continues to multiply itself over and over again in a lab in a petri dish, forming stem cell line.

Human embryonic stem cells (hES) promise regenerative medicine for organ renewal which would bring an almost revolutionary change in biomedical science. They develop into cells and tissues of three primary germ layers: endoderm, mesoderm, and ectoderm. In addition, human embryonic germ cells, taken from an aborted fetus, have capacity resembling the pluripotent stem cells in nearly all respects. The self-renewing line of the pluripotent cells is referred to as "characterized," even "immortal" previously.[48]

In the National Institutes of Health Guidelines for Human Stem Cell Research (1999), we read: "'Human embryonic stem cells (hESCs)' are cells that are derived from the inner cell mass of blastocyst stage human embryos, are capable of dividing without differentiating for a prolonged period in culture, and are known to develop into cells and tissues of the three primary germ layers. Although hESCs are derived from embryos, such stem cells are not themselves human embryos."[49]

The embryos come from (donated) eggs which are fertilized with sperm at an in vitro fertilization clinic. If hESCs are not regarded as human embryos, a question is raised about the status of the blastocyst. The blastocyst is different from other pre-embryo in each developmental stage in the preimplantation period of human embryo (zygote in cell divisions or morula). The embryo is formed when the blastocyst is implanted in the

---

[48] Peters, *The Stem Cell Debate*, 3.
[49] NIH Stem Cell Information.

uterine wall. The unborn child exists in the mother's womb (*in vivo*) with the potential of a healthy birth and a normal life, while the extra-utero blastocyst (*ex vivo*) in stem cell research has no potential for birth.

A blastocyst is destroyed during the extraction in the stem cell research process. The ethical concern is expressed against a technique using embryonic stem cells, which destroys a human blastocyst in the sense of abortion. However, in in vitro fertilization, the remaining blastocyst may be donated (with informed consent not to be involved in making profit) for medical research.

In the Roman Catholic stance, we read that there is dignity of the zygote in which the genome is set. If the genome is comprehended as the part of the body, the body is formed by the soul. This connection between the genome and the soul stands in the way to stem cell research. "*Is it morally licit to produce and/or use human embryos for the preparation of ES cells? The answer is negative.*"[50]

In discussing the moral status of the embryo outside a mother's body (*ex vivo*), it might be arguable, even not compelling if the embryo at the blastocyst stage in the laboratory should be treated as a person with dignity. It is difficult to concur with Catholic association of a divine soul with each and every zygote, because mortality or loss of natural human embryo is high during the first week after fertilization until reaching the state of pregnancy. "Nature seems quite content to eliminate the vast majority of fertilized ova and retain only a few to bring to birth." Furthermore, "if the mother's body by nature eliminates the majority of ensouled embryos, then theologically it would

---

[50] Pontifical Academy for Life, Declaration on the Production and the Scientific and Therapeutic Use of Human Embryonic Stem Cells (2000).

be difficult to see God's intentions as carried out by natural processes."[51]

Genetic Enhancement and Social Problem

Ethical warning is given to human germ-line modification. Germ-line modification intentionally alters the DNA that an individual inherits and transmits to future generations. The somatic therapy seeks to cure a disease in the body cell of a patient by adding or altering a specific gene. Such therapy will make it possible to correct genetic defects in the specific tissues that the disease affects. Somatic cell gene therapy is considered ethical in terms of the fundamental moral principle of beneficence.

In contrast, germ-line cells in the reproductive process are the body cells such as gametes, sperm, and egg cells that contain only twenty-three chromosomes. Intervention into the germ-line cells would influence and alter hereditable characteristics passing on the next generation indefinitely. It would help to eliminate the inheritance of some genetically based disease at the earliest stage of pregnancy. It would be medically necessary to prevent genetic disorders because somatic therapy would be too late.[52]

Recent advances in genetic technologies such as the new oligonucleotide approach monitoring system are promising in expressing a safe standard for germ line modification applied to future human applications. "In these cases," Kenneth Culver holds, "the moral status of the embryo can be protected and valued by correcting the mutation at that stage [in the treatment

---

[51] Peters, "Cells, Souls, and Dignity," 15.
[52] Champman, "Religious Perspective on Human Germ Line Modifications," in *Beyond Cloning*, ed. Cole-Turner, 65. For the germ line intervention, see Lee Silver, *Remaking Eden*.

of nonviable embryos] to allow for a healthy child, where no child would have otherwise resulted."[53]

However, genetic enhancement, beyond therapeutic purpose, intends to undertake genetic alterations to improve already existing normal genes. Such technology is the germ-line gene-editing for human reproduction (known Crisp-Cas9), which creates genetically modified human babies, twin girls, altering their embryos and DNA in the laboratory to give resistance to HIV infection.[54]

In the work of a multinational Commission organized by the U.S. National Academies of Sciences and Medicine and the U.K. Royal Society, we read the basic position: "Heritable Genome Editing Not Yet Ready to Be Tried Safely and Effectively in Humans; Initial Clinical Uses, If Permitted, Should Be Limited to Serious Single-Gene Diseases."[55]

Genetic technology would reshape and alter human being and society, becoming a social, political, and ethical matter. Social ethical reasoning of genetic enhancement focuses on explicating the extent to which genetic science would influence and determine social stratification of human life through power relations underlying a genetic system of knowledge.

---

[53] Culver, M.D, "A Christian Physician at the Crossroads of New Genetic Technologies and the Needs of Patients," in *Beyond Cloning*, 30.

[54] Hasson and Darnovsky, "Gene-edited babies: no one has the moral warrant to go it alone."

[55] *Heritable Human Genome Editing.*

3. Biopolitical Time, Human Dignity, and Practical Solidarity

In the new biotechnological environment, scientific revolution runs beyond good and evil, to the extent that biology threatens to replace morality. We live in a biopolitical era, in which power over the human body and public health risks violating human dignity by increasing inequality in access to biomedical achievements and benefits.

The power of biomedicine and biotechnology is constantly re-produced, disseminated, and established as the dominant discourse. It produces the cultural and material authority over human bodies and selves, which are vulnerable to human dignity, yet "more dynamic, more elusive, and more powerful than that [vulnerability]."[56]

Medical Technology and Public Health

According to Foucault, "medicine becomes a political intervention-technique with specific power-effects. Medicine is a power-knowledge that can be applied to both the body and the population, both the organism and biological processes, and it will therefore have both disciplinary effects and regulatory effects."[57]

The prospect of longevity in stem cell research disrupts the basic idea that life is a gift, in which generational exchange and contract with one's own offspring is "a basic element of the idea of justice."[58] It becomes questionable, even ethically controversial in comparison of the life expectancy between the rich and the

---

[56] Haraway, "The Biopolitics of Postmodern Bodies Constitutions of Self in Immune system Discourse," in *Biopolitics*, 275.
[57] Foucault, "Society Must Be Defended," ibid., 72.
[58] Turner, *The Body and Society*, 241.

poor. It should be kept in view that marginalized groups should be protected from the chameleon-like reincarnation of a eugenic resurgence.

Public ethics of shared responsibility can be seen in underpinning pragmatic solidarity among physicians, which remains decisive in the discussion of public health, healing, and social justice. This medical solidarity takes issue with the medical system of bureaucracy and its biopolitical control. A medical ethics of pragmatic solidarity undertakes a structural analysis of a global dominating system invalidating the rights of the poor in the periphery countries.[59]

Public Theology, Human Dignity, and Medicine Justice

Given the relation between vulnerability of human dignity and power relations, Benett Gaymon conceptualizes the meaning and horizon of human dignity in terms of spiritual politics and power; he draws attention to the vulnerability of human dignity as threatened by the distinctly modern form of power relations.[60]

He wields Foucault's concept of biopolitics to elaborate the strategy and political direction of human dignity, in which it governs the dimension of human vitality and body. Technology of biopolitics is interlaced with discipline and control as operative through the mechanism of normalization; it contrasts with the logic of human dignity in its intrinsic sense.[61]

In the biopolitical framework, public theology is concerned with social policies and common good in dealing with achievement and consequences of biotechnology, which is aligned

---

[59] Farmer, *Pathologies of Power*, 142.
[60] Bennett, *Technicians of Human Dignity*, X.
[61] Ibid., xi.

with commercial biology, political support, and institutional legitimacy. It focuses on genetic justice, while advocating the human rights of the socially disadvantaged and the impoverished in its evaluations of technological innovations and challenges.[62]

To the degree that health is a fundamental human right, the social reality of commodified medicine makes the poor or disadvantaged difficult in accesses to a desirable outcome of biomedical achievement. The slogan "the health care for all" in the American context needs to redefine in qualitative sense what it means by all. The politics of medical encounters between doctors and patients is embedded with problems of social justice and privilege of beneficence.[63]

4. Theological Construction, Evolution, and Biomedical Science

Developments in evolutionary biology raise a profound question about God's creative justice and reality of evil. Did God create the world as a field of suffering and death by using dynamics of natural selection and regeneration?[64]

A theological view of a broken creation and its value relevance for redemption does not necessary concur with evolutionary position on natural world through value neutrality. The evolutionary stance claims for naturalist realism with no teleos, which is characterized by competition, struggle for existence, and survival of the fittest through a logic of natural selection.

Meanwhile, the gay gene is discovered to be genetic in the summer of 1993 by Dean H. Hamer and his research team.

---

[62] Center for Genetics and Society.
[63] Waitzkin, *The Politics of Medical Encounter*.
[64] Bennett, et al. *The Evolution of Evil*, 8.

The possible gay gene is inherited maternally. As Hamer states, "We have now produced evidence that one form of male homosexuality is preferentially transmitted through the maternal side and is genetically linked to chromosome region Xq28."[65]

Human Sexuality and Original Sin

This scientific discovery relocates the gene myth or determinism and free will within a theological context. It brings human sexuality and original sin as the significant problematic to theological, ethical reasoning. Since the discovery of gay gene, it has been argued that there is evidence of a link between genetic inheritance and homosexuality. If the scientific fact itself does not determine the ethical interpretation of life, scientific discovery helps theologians to develop a critical reflection of Christian teaching of original sin.

Paul has no theory of a biologically inherited original sin, however, theological anthropology is exegetically mistaken to elaborate the hereditary sin on the basis of Paul in Rom. 5:21. However, Augustine takes a step further in incorporating the biologically inherited sin into his notion of original sin in terms of the typology between Adam and Christ (1 Cor 15: 22; Rom. 5:12-16). If the Augustinian notion of original sin is applied to the gay gene, Peters holds, it is suggested that the homosexual disposition and the homophobic disposition would constitute signs of a fallen human nature.[66] In Peters' basic statement: "The scientific fact still does not itself determine the direction of the ethical interpretation of that fact."[67]

In fact, the current scientific worldview in evolutionary framework does not separate nature from history, because

---

[65] Cited in *Genetics*, ed., Peters, 150.
[66] Peters, *Science, Theology, and Ethics*, 152.
[67] Ibid., 153.

nature is subject to contingency and change. This evolutionary perspective makes the Augustinian bifurcation of nature (good) from history (fallen) suspicious and unacceptable.

For Augustine, however, Adam and Eve seek disorder in their disobedience, and their punishment even affects our genetic defects through biological propagation. Augustine's theory helps to construct a theological anthropology in dealing with problem of homosexuality, because it is naturally unnecessary, but only historically inevitable through propagation. Of special significance is Augustine's connection between concupiscence and immoderate self-love (pride) in the general framework of desire, in which concupiscence is seen in relation to the perverted desire as hatred of God.[68]

Freedom, Genetic Explanation, and Reconciliation

To discuss the problem of human freedom and original sin, I take a step further in reinterpreting Reinhold Niebuhr, who draws attention to the Augustinian theory of original sin. Human sin is inevitable, but the human person is to be held accountable for sinful actions as an ineluctable fate or inevitable defect (Rom. 5:12).

In Niebuhr's breakthrough, original sin is an inherited corruption by definition, thus inevitable. The disposition toward sin is not necessary by nature but is historically inevitable. Sin is not outside the realm of human responsibility and freedom rather it belongs to human essential nature. The sin proceeds from a defect of free will in terms of accident rather than necessity of human essential nature.[69]

---

[68] Pannenberg, *Systematic Theology*, 2: 244-5.
[69] R. Niebuhr, *The Nature and Destiny of Man*, I: 241-2.

Despite his idea of inheritance of Adam's sin through propagation, Augustine keeps in view an integration between the sinfulness of sexual desire (concupiscence) and responsibility for free decision of the will. An immoderate desire is the basic form of human sin, and it flows from the responsible decision of the will. Concupiscence is generally equated with sin, while not merely conflated with sexuality. Sexual desire can be taken as an example of unveiling the perverted nature of concupiscence, which implies a structural deformation of will.[70]

It is certain that the Pauline statement points to a connection between Adam and the entire race, however it does not speak of inheriting the sin of Adam through propagation or genetic inheritance of primordial disorder. In Paul's theology of creation an eschatological hope is expressed in its eager longing for the revealing of the children of God; "the creation itself will be set free from its bondage to decay and will obtain the freedom of the glory of the children of God." (Rom. 8: 21)

The biblical notion of original sin should be seen in connection with the reality of latent sin dwelling with the individual (Rom. 7: 20), which implies a comprehensive and total sin of human beings in human flesh. In this imprisonment they become the heir of Adam, but God reveals God's self as the Liberator in Jesus Christ breaking into this imprisonment. It has little to do with the hereditary sin as disease, or genetic defect, which is naturalistic, deterministic, and fatalistic.

This said, the gay gene cannot be leveled down to a disease as a genetically hereditary sin in the naturalist and deterministic fashion. Responsibility in an Augustinian-Niebuhrian sense affirms that genetic 'defect' does not belong to a necessity of human nature, because the sin resides in free will rather than in the gay gene.

---

[70] Pannenberg, *Systematic Theology* 2: 242.

Theologically speaking, homosexual predisposition is not classified as an original sin, but the original sin is thwarted by God's reconciling love through Jesus Christ. Jesus Christ was predestined as the true *imago Dei*, taking up all humanity into unity with God. A person with the gay gene belongs to the true *imago Dei*, Jesus Christ. The natural after the Fall is directed towards the coming of Christ, who eliminates the sin, and the penultimate sin is in preparing the way (scientific contribution) for the coming of grace.[71]

Genetic Determinism and Epigenetic Networking

The theory of evolution comes to the fore as a weapon against religion, and one of Darwin's achievements is seen in enabling 'an intellectually fulfilled atheist.'[72] Richard Dawkins argues that in the universe led by materialist evolution "there is, at bottom, no design, no purpose, no evil and no good, nothing but blind, pitiless indifference."[73]

In Edward Wilson's definition, sociobiology is 'the systematic study of the biological basis of all social behavior.'[74] "The genes hold culture on a leash. The leash is very long, but inevitably values will be constrained in accordance with their effects on the human gene pool."[75]

Sociobiology attempts to describe and prescribe human behavior on the basis of certain genetic principles by legitimating a genetic basis for culture, tradition, language, and religion. Sociobiology with its scientific naturalism means the death knell

---

[71] Bonhoeffer, *Ethics*, 136, 143.
[72] Dawkins, *Blind Watchmaker*, 6
[73] Dawkins, *River Out of Eden*, 133.
[74] Wilson, *Sociobiology: The New Synthesis*, 4.
[75] Wilson, *On Human Nature*, 175.

for religious belief and impulses under the principle of natural selection, which acts on "the genetically evolving material structure of the human brain." "Theology is not likely to survive as an independent intellectual discipline."[76]

In a central dogma of molecular biology, a linear causal chain is formulated from DNA through RNA to proteins and finally to biological traits. The causal line of DNA-RNA-protein is grounded in a one-way flow of information from the genes to the proteins.

In the replication of making itself, DNA is also copied in RNA, and genomic information is passed from DNA to RNA (transcription). RNA has a type of messenger of DNA entailing information of DNA (mRNA—transcription) together with transfer (t RNA) and ribosomal (r RNA) types, travelling outside the nucleus. The ribosome, which synthesizes protein, is located outside the nucleus, and RNA binds to a ribosome and transfers the genetic code to it (translation). This refers to the protein-synthesizing procedure.[77]

In this one-way procedure of information, the gene is elevated to the driver's seat, which determines human behavior and activity. This notion of genetic determinism becomes crucial in genetic engineering, and it regards the living organism merely as a collection of genes, which is subject to random mutations and selective forces.

Is it all in the gene? Is this gene apotheosis valid? Is evolution driven by the survival impulse of DNA, which genetically determines us? Kenneth Miller sees "a hubris in which all social

---

[76] Ibid., 192.
[77] Cole-Turner, "The Genome and the Human Genome Project," in *Genetics,* ed., Peters, 52.

behaviors are therefore presumed to be the results of natural selection."[78]

In self-sustaining metabolic loops, however, DNA associates with histone proteins (DNA-binding and regulating), forming chromatin (a mixture of DNA and proteins) located in the nucleus of our cells. This condenses to form thread-like structures, called chromosomes (46 pairs). The chromatins are intertwined with the DNA strands, in which histones facilitate organization of DNA into structures called nucleosomes—the basic building blocks of chromatin fiber; this consists of a DNA sequence of about 150 base pairs wrapped around a set of eight histones, producing a chromatin fiber. Since DNA in the chromatin is packaged around histone proteins (nucleosomes), chromatin structure and gene accessibility are regulated by modifications of both DNA and histone tails in the process of transcription of DNA into RNA.

Many enzymes (enzyme complex) are involved in DNA replication beginning at specific locations within the chromosome. With the enzyme helicase (unzipping), the double helix is opened, and many enzymes slide along the DNA and copies it. The pattern of histone arrangement is perturbed, allowing progression of DNA polymerases. In the dynamic cell-cycle a complex activity of histone modifications regulates DNA replication, involving transcriptional activation, chromosome packaging, and DNA damage/repair; this epigenetic complexity makes change in gene expression without mutations.

In fact, the chromatin plays a critical role in constituting the genome's most immediate environment, altering gene expression patterns in terms of epigenetic modification (tags) and its inheritance in the cell-cycle dynamics of the histone post-translational modifications.

---

[78] Miller, *Finding Darwin's God*, 183.

This perspective reacts against an idea that inheritance happens only through the DNA. The gene can no longer be seen as set above and apart from the processes specifying cellular and intercellular organization.[79] The cellular network, highly nonlinear, contains multiple feedbacks and interactions, regulating the biological process, in which the genome is embedded with DNA. Any network goes in all directions in nonlinear relationships, correcting mistakes by regulating and organizing itself. The gene as part and parcel of processes is "brought into existence by the action of a complex self-regulating dynamical system."[80]

DNA is not the sole causal agent of biological forms and functions, but it is an essential component of the epigenetic network, in which it provides an indispensable raw material. In fact, it depends on the genetic context, on the chromosomal structure that is embedded and subject to its developmental regulation, this is the complex network of the living cell.[81] Natural selection operates on the self-organization and complexity of the organism's pattern rather than individual selfish genes.

This perspective contrasts with a unilateral interpretation of the phenomenon of life through the molecular structure of the gene. Rather the ways are to be explored in which genes communicate and cooperate in the development of an organism. The driving force of evolution is to be found in life's inherent tendency to create novelty in the emergence of complexity and order. The alphabet of the genetic code is not the sufficient condition for a truly universal language of life, but it is to be seen in a network capable of self-organization.

---

[79] Keller, *The Century of the Gene*, 71.
[80] Ibid.
[81] Ibid., 72.

This challenges the random mutation of genes, the central doctrine of neo-Darwinian theory. In the unfolding of life as a process biologists recognize that symbiosis and cooperation play a vital importance in the evolutionary process. Life did not take over the globe by combat and only competition in nature, but by symbiotic alliance and networking through continual cooperation and interdependence in the evolutionary process.[82]

This perspective finds a consonance with a theological idea of God's ongoing creation. In fact, God is more than nature and gene myth. The evolutionary process, seen in the sense of continual creation, has undergone and continues to follow its course and freedom in trials, errors, and transformation. God's goodness of creation is still given to us in such process, and God involves the broken world through immanent working of the life-giving Spirit, reconciliation, healing, and new creation.

Theological Debate and Cloning

At the Roslin Institute near Edinburgh, part of the University of Edinburgh, Scotland, embryologist Ian Wilmut and biologist Keith Kempbell produced a live adult lamb (5 July 1996). Three mothers (ewes) were involved: one egg donor, another nucleus donor, and a third surrogate mother.

The scientists took the nucleus (containing DNA) out of a normal cell from a sheep. They put that nucleus into an egg cell with no nucleus. They then had a new cell. An electric shock is given to make the new cell start to divide, grow, and develop into an embryo. At a very early stage, when the embryo is called a blastocyst, it was implanted into the womb of another surrogate

---

[82] Margulis and Sagan, *Microcosmos*, 15.

sheep, so that it could grow into a lamb and be born. In 1996 Dolly was the only lamb that survived from 277 attempts.[83]

Cloning—sometimes called somatic cell nuclear transfer, sometimes nuclear transfer or replacement—involves the transfer of the DNA nucleus from a cell to egg. The birth of Dolly made people wonder if scientists were on the threshold of "playing God."

Should we clone the human being? Ian Wilmut maintains "that the prospect of human cloning causes us grave misgivings. It is physically too risky, it could have untoward effects on the psychology of the cloned child, and in the end we see no medical justification for it."[84]

The possibility of human cloning raises profound challenges to theology and ethical concern. In June 1997, the National Bioethics Advisory Commission issued *Cloning Human Beings* in which a provisional or temporary ban is expressed concerning cloning technology. A period of time as a moratorium is imposed in which "no attempt is made to create a child using somatic cell nuclear transfer."[85]

Lisa Cahill seeks to evaluate cloning as a social sin in terms of R. Niebuhr's position of Christian realism and the Catholic liberation commitment to the poor. Placing the problem of cloning in a broader social context, she takes issue with scientific rationality as a moral methodology.[86] Several instances of cloning would be deployed in cases such as an infertility therapy or a reproductive tool for same-sex couples or dead or dying loved ones. No wonder that negative sides can be seen in enhancing

---

[83] Southgate, et al. *God, Humanity, and the Cosmos*, 358-9.
[84] Wilmut et al. *The Second Creation*, 5.
[85] "Appendix I: Recommendations of the National Bioethics Advisory Commission," in *Human Cloning*: Religious Responses, ed., Cole-Turner, 133.
[86] Cahill, "Cloning and Sin" in *Beyond Cloning*, ed. Cole-Turner, 98.

profitability through cloning as an exportable commodity. She judges cloning to be a form of social sin or collective egotism underlying cloning as the profit-making business.[87]

However, Karen Lebacqz sees a paradox in justifying the cloning technology for gay and especially lesbian couples in the light of the principle of justice. Granted that cloning is encompassed under the right of procreative liberty, reproductive technology does not provide advantages for women, the poor, or children. It will only recreate unjust patterns and practices in a heterosexist world. Her principle of social justice challenges the right of procreative liberty and argues against beneficence, which privileges heterosexual couples in a heterosexist society while discriminating against gay and lesbian couples.[88]

However, in Peters' account, no distinctively theological legitimacy would make cloning humans immoral, rather it might be unwise. A temporary moratorium against human cloning is placed rather than an absolute ban. His theological anthropology evinces that the human soul is not formed from DNA, but it is apprehended in relationship with God. It is determined by God's grace, not by DNA. In the word of Karen Lebacqz: "In such an understanding, 'soul' is not an individual possession but a statement about relationship. Soul has to do with our standing before God."[89]

In so doing, it is important to establish society's moral obligation, which treats cloned persons with dignity as individuals as any of the rest of us, because God's love has little to do with discriminating our genetic makeup.[90] In theological debate about human cloning the term 'soul' leaves itself open

---

[87] Ibid., 109-10.
[88] Lebacqz, "Genes, Justice, and Clones," in *Human Cloning*, ed. Cole-Turner, 54-6.
[89] Cited in Peters, "Cloning Shock" ibid.,18.
[90] *Genetics*, ed., Peter, 15.

to debate, becoming such problematic that we could create it in human reproductive cloning.

Image of God and Soul

In the creation story God formed a human being from the dust of the ground, breathing into his nostrils the breath of life. Then a human being became alive, a living being (*nephesh*) (Gen. 2: 7). The spirit of human beings enters them through the divine breath of life (Yahweh's *ruach*), which makes them alive. They are dust to which they shall return (Gen. 3:19). After death this spirit returns to God: Into thy hands I commit my spirit (Ps. 32, 5; Luke 23.46).

In this relationship with God human beings are created in the image of God, thus this relationship cannot be destroyed even by their death. This relationship is generally used as the spirit, though occasionally called soul in the Scripture (Matt. 10:28).[91]

A human being exists because he/she has spirit, which is equipped with our freedom, dignity, transcendence, and creativity. God through the Spirit creates the soul, the animating power of human life in which we are a person. The creative Spirit is also the life-principle of the beasts as well as their host of heaven (Ps. 33:6). The Spirit is to be sought in soul and body in which human spirit is the basis and guarantees the wholeness of individual being as soul of body. The Spirit of God bears witness to our spirit, that we are children of God (Rom 8:16).

The working of the Spirit in us is not meant to be a constituent part of living creature, such that the Spirit of God cannot be seen as a part of human creatures along with the soul and body in opposition to trichotomism.[92] A human being is constituted

---

[91] Moltmann, *The Coming of God*, 72-3.
[92] Pannenberg, *Systematic Theology* 2: 190.

and maintained as soul of his/her body by the life giving Spirit of God. Not merely soul, but a human being as a living being stands in relationship with God. "Without the works of the divine Spirit in us there could be no personality in the deeper sense of the term."[93]

It implies that a body of a baby grows, engaging in the environment of the womb through relationship, interaction, influence, and even receiving education from the mother. Human dignity is the gift of God's grace upon the soul of the body, a person, which grows and is nourished in relationship with the mother through the grace of God, the source of life. God promises: "I will pour out my Spirit upon all flesh" (Acts 2:17). The divine gift of life, the human spirit is given to us, and it cannot be duplicated or cloned. This theological perspective removes the Platonic idea of the immortality of the soul, which affirms the human being as the possessor of the divine identity beyond death.[94]

Concluding Reflection: God's Created Collaborator

Philip Hefner thinks of an interaction between biological evolution and cultural development in the light of the God of theism. For him evolution is comprehended as the work of God, which allows for the emergence of that which is necessary for the fulfillment of God's intentions.[95]

A symbiosis of genes and culture constitutes our biocultural evolution, and it has bequeathed freedom to the human race which further develops on the evolutionary course. As free creatures, we

---

[93] Ibid., 198.
[94] Moltmann, *The Coming of God*, 59.
[95] Hefner, *The Human Factor*, 45.

are in a position to act creatively. With this freedom we become created co-creators. As Hefner states, "*The Freedom that marks the created co-creator and its culture is an instrumentality of God for enabling the creation (consisting of the evolutionary pas of genetic inheritance and culture, as well as the contemporary ecosystem) to participate in the intentional fulfillment of God's purpose.*"[96]

Likewise, Peters incorporates a notion of created co-creator into developing a theological anthropology for human dignity through the Kantian categorical imperative. A notion of created co-creator emphasizes the dignity of a human being as the end itself, not merely as a means to some further end. The notion of 'created co-creator' focuses on our dependency upon God, while placing human opportunity and responsibility under a high value of human dignity.[97] This perspective refutes any assumption of pride, which is the core of perverted desire wanting to be like God, or the immoderate nature of the sinful will in Augustinian sense.

Nonetheless, Cole-Turner is cautious about several difficulties of the underlying concept of co-creation or co-exploration. It is one thing to understand something through scientific knowledge, but it is quite another to claim for science to have found the purpose of the Creator. When human technology is characterized as co-creation, it implies optimistic assessment which fails to recognize the disorder of nature permeating our intellect and will. The reality of sin is not to be subsumed under the optimistic notion of co-creation. Rather we stand in need of grace and redemption.[98]

---

[96] Ibid. (Italics in original).
[97] Ibid., 158.
[98] Cole-Turner, *The New Genesis*, 102.

"Creator and Redeemer are one in identity and purpose."[99] This characterizes Cole-Turner's stance, which stands parallel with Barth's rejection of the idea of 'co-creation.' Human participation in God's activity "does not mean that [human being] becomes a co-creator, a co-savior or co-regent in God's activity. It does not mean that he becomes a kind of co-God."[100]

However, a discourse of co-creation does not necessarily express that we are the creator of the world. Rather it refers to a wider spectrum of stewardship in which we are created with responsibility to carry on, or even collaborate with God in the world. As stewardship of God's creation, we are assigned as created creator (*homo faber*) to fulfill God's purpose. Human creativity as God's gift has nothing to do with a Promethean myth.[101]

At this point, I propose the discourse of co-creator to bear on created collaborator by featuring it in a biblical sense. "For we are God's servants, working together" (1 Cor 3:9). We are stewards of God's mysteries (1 Cor. 4:1) as well as administers of God's new covenant (2 Cor. 3:6).

A biblical language of God's co-worker facilitates public theology in elucidating its meaning and horizon in wider culture, especially in discussion of natural science, ecosystem, public health, and biomedical justice. Faith seeks understanding of God's purpose and mysterious working in the creation, such that human intelligibility is expressed in creative project in theology and natural science (other social human sciences included), working as God's created collaborator for common good, responsibility, and justice in wider culture.

---

[99] Ibid.
[100] Cited in ibid., 102; CD III/4: 482.
[101] Peters, et al. "Religious Tradition and Genetic Enhancement," in *Altering Nature* 2. Ed. Lustig et al., 130.

God does not work in us without us, and we may cooperate with God, "whether his kingdom through his general omnipotence, or inside his Kingdom by the special virtue of his Spirit."[102] Freedom and self-creativity is gift from God, who creates us in divine image. St. Paul implies the telos of a human being is sharing in God's glory in Jesus Christ. A spiritual and intellectual maturity is capable of, with unveiled faces, seeing the divine glory, "as though reflected in a mirror"; All of us "are being transformed into the same image from one degree of glory to another; for this comes from the Lord, the Spirit" (2 Cor 3: 18).

Seen in the created collaborator, a theology of embodiment and healing finds it significant to make the biomedical practice into the realm of Christian discipleship. This position is formulated in Kenneth Culver's ethics of discipleship through genetic engineering. As a physician, he made history in 1990, involved in administering and implementing the first approved human gene therapy. Discipleship in compassion brings the genetic scientist to cooperate with God, who works through medical care and treatment.[103]

---

[102] Luther and Erasmus: *Free Will and Salvation*, 289.
[103] Culver, "A Christian Physician at the Crossroads of New Genetic Technologies and the Needs of Patients," in *Beyond Cloning*, ed. Cole-Turner, 15.

Conclusion

Public theology is concerned with diverse public spheres in civil society. It investigates these regimes (or systems) in social cultural formation and stratification in terms of interpretation and clarification of social discourse through the genealogy of effective history and postcolonial condition; it is enmeshed in power relations, biopolitical governance, and bureaucracy. Civil society implies an indispensable regime for public theology to express and perform its ethical stance of life-world for common good, citizen initiative, politics of recognition, and solidarity with the subaltern.

Public issues within the social stratification cannot be apprehended apart from global domination of capitalism in the neocolonial relation between the metropolis and the periphery under global sovereignty of Empire. This complex situation, called 'postcolonial condition' shapes a multicultural character of civil society, and its inside is not differentiated from the outside. The metropolis is transferred to the periphery, as conversely the periphery is incorporated into a significant component of the metropolis.

1. I conceptualize public theology and ethics in a hermeneutical frame of reference, by appropriating H.R. Niebuhr's theocentric theology. He analyzes the western tradition of moral philosophy and creates a space for Christian moral theory of response. Niebuhr's ethical type focuses on the significance of the interpretation regarding what's going on, while taking into account human responses to external events.

However, a problem is seen in his ethical passivity in accommodation to the reality of powers and principalities. He is not capable of grounding ethical reasoning of discipleship and resistance in taking on the gospel of *theologia crucis* and reconciliation in light of the resurrection of Jesus and the coming kingdom of God.

Niebuhr's moral theory of responsibility can be interrogated by Levinas' ethics of responsibility and the Other. An ethics of the Other remains crucial in public theology involving the comparative study of religious ethics and recognizing cosmopolitan condition in multicultural civil society.

Life complexities and ambiguities are not reducible to any single moral principle or type. Rather, they require meta-ethical reasoning and social scientific enquiry in interdisciplinary framework to engage with public use of reason and social, ethical guidance in the discussion of political, economic, cultural, and biomedical realms.

2. Troeltsch conceptualizes Christian social teaching within the history-of-religions. His sociological enquiry takes the initiative into constituting ethical reality of life as the apex of theological belief system. The sociological study of Christian social teaching plays a decisive role in exposing social dimensions of Christian ethics in different historical contexts. Christian public theology and its social ethic are to be reformulated and reinterpreted for a new synthesis in response to the contemporary culture. It is safeguarded from simply reiterating the biblically fixed normative codes. Public theology as ethical theology is of constructive character in terms of interpretation (based on historical criticism) and involvement of contemporary challenge.

Troeltsch is appreciated as a classic example of a public theologian in a constructive framework, in which a post-Eurocentric stance is positioned in his comparative study of religions. Trolestch's type of a human being-in-correlation is on the threshold to philosophy of life-world, which enhances the significance of historical-critical method.

His ethical theology, together with historical sociology, is renewed and reinforced in phenomenology of life-world, in which a problematic way of thinking comes to terms with a dialectical type between the master and the servitude in terms of struggle, genealogy of social discourse, and universal recognition. At this point, I am concerned with sociological theory of articulation, interpretation, and discourse clarification in a multivariate frame to advance a project of public theology and ethics of life-world; it is buttressed from the standpoint for the margins and from them.

3. In dealing with cultural issues and public justice, I call attention to the theory of life-world in Husserl and Gadamer's philosophical hermeneutics. A human being as a social, historical being is moved and influenced under the objective reality of life-world through language, history, culture, and tradition. Granted that there are many forms of life-world in Europe, America, Africa, and Asia, their truth claims or moralities are not simply relativistic, despite their differences. At the meta-ethical reasoning, theory of language can be featured as catalyst or even harbinger in constituting moral enquiry in social location and in historical effectiveness. Social political impact on language produces a hierarchy of language and its mechanism of domination and violence.

This perspective helps to articulate an aspect of a human being-in-the-discourse as effected by history as well as conditioned in social stratification, which is invested with power relations and ideological interpellation. In so doing, it is important to conceptualize the relationship between public theology and discourse ethics in terms of sociological enquiry of life-world and hermeneutical reflection of human response; this position underwrites a socio-biographical practice of life-script through genealogical examination of race, gender, and sexuality.

Given this, I set out to take up a theory of life-world in terms of the Christian symbol of reconciliation. In the institutionalized structure of reification, injustice, and violence in which we live, Christian discourse of *parrhesia* refers to a testimony to God's justice revealed in Christ's reconciliation for politics of recognition and difference. It corresponds to Jesus' solidarity with the public sinners and tax collectors (*massa perditionis*). Gospel ethic would be ineffective and abstract without *parrhesia* in concrete time and place, while *parrhesia* without God's grace would be judgmental and legalistic. God's grace of forgiveness leads to metanoia and restorative justice in light of the coming kingdom of God. This theological position of the concrete-universal comes to terms with Hegel's dialectical phenomenology, while critically renewing its presentative position of absolute knowledge in light of prolepsis of God's future.

A sociological reading of Hegel focuses on his dialectics of externalization and alienation by reinterpreting the idea of absolute knowledge in terms of mutual recognition in universal-concrete sense. A reality of social formation is driven in contradiction, negativity, mediation, freedom, and creative principle. This sociological stance critically complements historical critical method (critique, analogy, correlation, and religious apriori), in which there is a lack of struggle, negativity, and mediation. Hegel may become a forerunner of historical materialism and critical theory of social formation.

4. Postcolonial epistemology takes issue with the disguised form of neocolonial assumption after the disappearance of colonies, because such disguised reality is characterized by exploitation, division, infiltration, and racial inequality. It is significant to analyze the extent to which Euro-American

discourse would become a major arbiter in disseminating and penetrating the entirety of social relations in a network of power relations according to its own knowledge/power assumption and biopolitical control of world order under empire.

The postcolonial stance is concerned with the structure of the legitimation and hegemony under empire in late capitalism, advocating a prophetic tradition of the scriptures and other prophetic voices in religion, culture, and politics. The colonized use the cultural capital to dismantle the imperial system in dominating knowledge system and to counter neoliberal discourse. Translation, a form of interpolation, relies upon local wisdom and language, transferring power away from the center to self-reflexivity and creativity. The notion of interpolation becomes an important part of archeological hermeneutics. It takes into account effective history in order to write the vivid present in retrieving the foreclosed discourse against the marching of dominant discourse and its legitimacy. Anamnesis reasoning and effective history become an undercurrent in constituting public theology with conceptual problematic.

A postcolonial notion of re-presentation in the sense of counter discourse can be promoted to countenance the project of rewriting the history of the present (the non-identical, rupture, irregularity, and fissure), which has been subsumed or discarded by the colonialist epistemic system. Epistemic position of life-world remains central in shaping postcolonial public theology in World Christianity, especially African Christianity, which entails distinctive problematic of public sphere, civil society, and cultural integrity; the mission of God's prolepsis comes to terms with the politics of decolonization, recognition of cultural difference and distributive justice of biomedicine in struggle against HIV/AIDS and the pandemic disaster.

The Western developmental approach to World Christianity should be corrected in archeological analysis of different cultures, histories, and traditions, in which history of colonialism must be seen in resistance narrative to it. Aspects of the coalescence of diverse patterns and fusion of different life-worlds are not reduced to a Eurocentric assumption of purpose rationality and its technological domination along with dialectics of modernity and colonialism.

5. Gollwitzer elaborates public theology in a social scientific framework in dealing with history, society, and culture, and he presents a conspicuous method by which to formulate theological engagement with neocolonial condition between the metropolis and the periphery. In scrutinizing the reality of social stratification and structural violence, his prophetic public theology is actualized in his ethical commitment to live in line and direction with coming kingdom of God. It characterizes his eschatological politics based on reform and revolution, in which civil society initiative plays a significant role in guiding democratic, socialist position. It is headed toward universal recognition among equals, popular sovereignty, social movements, and ecological sustainability in contrast to the power mechanism of capitalist revolution.

Along with Gollwitzer, I incorporate archeological theory of discourse and biopolitical discipline into the neocolonial condition beset by exploitation, division, and infiltration. Racial justice is of special significance in challenging the Christian character of capital accumulation and its discourse of colonialism and slavery. James Cone should be appreciated for the postcolonial insight into theology and racial justice. He becomes a great example of Black public theology of liberation in critically involving Western classic thinkers such as Barth, Tillich, Bonhoeffer, and Reinhold Niebuhr.

Cone may share in Gollwitzer's notion of class struggle from above (power mechanism) and below (ethics of life-world), which shows parallel with Gramsci's idea of hegemony and leadership. Gramsci makes an effective distinction between political society and civil society. Culture is found as an operative within the area of civil society through the influence of ideas and consent, not through domination. The ruling class achieves domination not merely by force or coercion, but also by creating—through intellectual integrity and moral leadership—subjects who are willing to be ruled. The state comprises political society plus civil society, in which hegemony is protected by the armor of coercion. The ethical or civil aspect of the state is maintained by moral leadership and consent.

Gramsci's theory of hegemony needs to be recast in exploring social discourse in regard to power, legitimacy, and moral integrity of public intellectual. A critical theory of social formation improves on limitation of Gramsci's philosophy of praxis, as premised upon its commonsense framework and historic bloc (or alliances of the subaltern) for mass movement. Critical theory of social stratification can be utilized to prevent a theory of cultural hegemony from falling into an absolute historicism. In fact, there are differences, colonial subjugation, transformation, and rupture in the marching history of Western dialectics of enlightenment. Civil society in the postcolonial condition continues to be reified and stratified at the level of social-cultural relations through power mechanism, which is embedded with political governance, technological rationality, ideological interpellation, and commodity fetishism.

Without conceptual problematic, a philosophy of praxis degenerates into common sense, or natural attitudes in assimilating to ideological appellation, racial hierarchy, and masculine domination (sexuality and gender). The life-world-enhancing consensus is required to salvage the realm of civil society from the colonizing system of the political society with its ideological apparatuses.

This complex reality makes it difficult to generalize a notion of hegemony or the problematic regime of social, cultural stratification in terms of the common-sense position or Orientalist mode of binary opposition. Class/status consciousness of liberation is fragmented, disciplined, and dispositioned under phenomenon of reification, and social habitus is inscribed into human consciousness through its cultural sedimentation or ideological interpellation. In dialectical diversity and plurality, we observe the complexity of multiple realities in different power struggles for capitals in politics, culture, economics, religion, education.

In this systemic theory of multiple realities and their functional differentiations in civil society, I seek to refine a phenomenology of recognition underlying the intersubjectivity between the dominant and the dominated in relevance to biblical symbols of reconciliation, *theologia crucis*, and prolepsis of God's future, in which ethics of life-world comes to terms with practice of one's identity and cultural authenticity of life-script; it buttresses struggle for freedom, mutual recognition, and reparative justice in postcolonial civil society. This implies civil society initiatives (alliance between citizen and the subaltern) from below and across, which underlines lateral practice over against the class struggle from domination above.

Seen in critical theory of social formation (ideological interpellation, commodity fetishism, biopolitical technology and racial hierarchy), an epistemic stance is positioned in life-world practice, which problematizes a prestige struggle in a fascistic sense and its ethnocentric nationalism and racism. In this reality of social reification, the subaltern is threatened to subjection, or commercialized by a representation system of ideological apparatuses.

In the civil society the subaltern retains its broader spectrum and significance in political economic realm and cultural justice. When it comes to the poor, the subaltern reality includes cultural problems such as racial injustice, gender discrimination, or sexual hierarchy. The subaltern should be given more space for speaking of themselves as innocent victims as well as active agents. The subaltern cannot be simply found in the context of technology of productive forces, but stratified in diverse social fields and controlled by power mechanism.

6. Said defines Orientalism as a Western style for dominating, restructuring, and having authority over the Orient as the Other. Unlike Said's generalizing mode of binary opposition, I am concerned with micro-analytical genealogy of discourse clarification and power relations by critically synthesizing Foucault's archeology and biopolitical technology with phenomenological, dialectical significance; it is elaborated by way of problematization, justice struggle, and mutual recognition. Thus, I conceptualize a theory of effective history in terms of rationality of anamnesis (Benjamin) and scientific analysis of social formation to undertake thick description.

Without this conceptual problematic and thick description, history is no longer vividly present, but it is manipulated into binary opposition to underpin ethnic hegemony, privilege, and prestige for power struggle. Finally, the subaltern in history and society are represented and commercialized in the hands of those in power privilege and daily network of totalitarian culture.

Foucault's archeological clarification is not far removed from sociological articulation of critical dialectics and life-world between Hegel and Husserl. With this combined position in mind, I emphasize the ethical significance of liberating discourse in the Christian tradition of *parrhesia*. It appears in the biblical texts as the courage to tell the truth on the part of those who are pure and noble in spirit. It involves human confidence in the overflowing love of God and the belief that God will answer the prayers of the Christian.

7. A way of 'thinking problematically' is a critical reflection by establishing a certain distance from and suspense of existing forms of acting, understanding, and ideological representation. Clarifying these forms as the problem, it seeks to reform and remediate them in a constructive manner.

In the discussion of decolonization, biopolitical theory does not dispense with an archeological theory, which focuses on social episteme in multiple realities or fields (political, economic, cultural, textual, religious, and erotic, and biomedical). Sociological theory of articulation focuses on scrutinizing an aspect of technological rationality operative in maintaining a 'colonialist' type of hegemony and racism; a dominant discourse inscribes into and subjugates human body to its ideological apparatuses and commodity fetishism.

To problematize is to think differently, as dialectically conceptualized in commitment to the narrative of the dominated. An epistemic stance of problematic dialectics strives to scrutinize the governmentality, social process of normalization, or judicial legitimacy as involved in establishing a certain discourse or episteme as the dominant one. Such procedure entails a therapeutic or political significance for postcolonial society.

8. Public theology is concerned with cultural issues and justice in terms of social scientific inquiry into race, sexuality, and gender. Racial justice becomes a major component in the public sphere, together with gender and sexual division of labor in the mechanism of production and reproduction. A phenomenology of the human body and its reification take place in the social

cultural totality. It disseminates and imprints its legitimate discourse upon human consciousness and social disposition through rationalization, specialization, and differentiation. Social discourse and power relations over the human body are built in the masculine system of domination and symbolic violence. A social scientific analysis of masculine episteme and domination helps to take into account cultural diversity and its construct of sexuality.

9. Biomedical ethics implies a pressing issue together with biotechnology, challenging Christian social ethics. Biotechnology and such achievements are discussed and developed in the biomedical principles: respect for autonomy, non-maleficence, beneficence (including utility), and justice. I relocate these principles with the confine of interpretation for responsibility, recognition of the disadvantaged and social solidarity. This stance challenges social Darwinism and the laissez-faire position, which are instilled with biotechnological rationality in its instrumental character. A neoliberal policy of public health and medicine perpetuates pathologies of power in terms of its principle of cost-effectiveness and more profit.

Furthermore, it is important to take on several issues such as protection of life (suicide, euthanasia, and sexuality), stem cell research, germ-line intervention, cloning, genetic enhancement, and artificial gametes. When these issues risk violating human dignity, family integrity, and social institutions, they would be a slippery slope to social discrimination, a resurgence of eugenics while justifying the social stratification built on power, privilege, and domination.

10. A theology of prolepsis dethrones a place of social Darwinism and underpins a theology of God's collaboration. We are created in the image of God as collaborator with God's work of reconciliation. We create, but we cannot redeem what

has been created in technological development. Rather, the reality of impersonal forces has brought technological rationality and social formation into iron cage of commodity fetishism reproducing ideological value of money representation more than its exchange value.

Social systems driven by technological capitalist revolution administers social-economic systems, commercializing the environment and threatening ecological networking. A reality of commodity fetishism deflects human life through reification in the field of political system, economic relation, and networking of communication, and biomedical industry. The representable economic value is inscribed into entirety of social body, its systems, and human consciousness collectively controlled under bureaucratic administration, mass media, and biopolitical governance. This refers to political economic logic, which brings democratic participation, cultural religious integrity, principle of recognition, and moral solidarity down to an iron cage of totalitarian homogenization.

Against the iron cage, public theology summons the church to be faithful to the Gospel about the kingdom of God in terms of ethical discipleship, *metanoia*, and *parrhesia* in preferential option for Jesus Christ, a partisan of the poor (Karl Barth). His Gospel of forgiveness, reconciliation, and restorative justice has come into our midst in its prolepsis of the coming kingdom of God.

Afterword: Genealogy of Jeju 4.3 Massacre and Biopolitics

Historical Background

In the Russian-Ukrainian war the Russian killing of civilians in the town of Bucha (the bodies of nearly 300 civilians were buried in a mass grave) shocked the world. Horrendous war crimes and genocide continue to occur down the road. This reality reinforces research on an effective history of Jeju's uprising (1948) under American occupation authority in comparison with the Philippine-American war (1899-1902). There is a historical bridge connecting these two political events through the Taft-Katsura Memorandum of 1905. American colonial rule of the Philippines was formalized by imperial Japan, while the US agreed to the Japanese treaty (the Eulsa) with Korea.

The Philippine-American War (1899-1902) remains obscure, arguably least-known to the United States, but it cannot be dissociated from colonial torture and racism in the bellicose interests. American war and subsequent colonialism were ideologically buttressed by a famous novel laureate Rudyard Kipling in "White Man's Burden." Kipling's poem was first published in the London Times on February 4, 1899, shortly after fighting erupted between the United States and the Philippines. The poem appears to promote Western colonization and domination in the name of civilizing mission.

During the Second World War, the United States and the Soviet Union became allies, and the Soviets were spoken of by the American President with such warm regard as the "gallant Red Amy."[1] The friendly relationship came to an end shortly, and this changed international order became crucial in comprehending the Cold War division of Korea by the U.S. and Soviet Union. The American colonial power continued to find hegemony in fighting against Japan during the Pacific War and involved rivalry with the Soviet Union in matters pertaining to the future of Korea in liberation from imperial Japan.

Just after Japanese surrender (August 14, 1945), Korea was divided through the 38th Parallel, by U.S. Army colonels Charles Bonesteel and Dean Rusk, who drew a line on a map of the Korean Peninsula. Such design aimed to facilitate Korea's transition from the former colonial system to national independence. General John R. Hodge was the commander of the XXIV Corps in Okinawa, and the State Department pressed him to collaborate with the Soviets.

Hodge's political strategy was to establish a coalition of moderate left and moderate right, while excluding extremes of both the right (Syngman Rhee) and left (Pak Hon-yong). It came to no avail. The United States Army Military Government had established the administration in Korea (USAMGIK) in occupation of the southern area of Korea, which includes Jeju Island.

When the American military government arrived on Jeju (November 1945), the Jeju People's Committee (PC) was functioning well with popular support. It was in collaboration with the USAMGIK, which sponsored the PC plan of commemoration on March 1, 1946 for the 1919 movement of independence.

The March First Movement was inspired by Woodrow Wilson's famous principle of fourteen points (January 8, 1918),

---

[1] Lee et al. *Korea Old and New*, 333.

especially with respect to humanism, self-determination of the peoples, and international cooperation for peace. It was a truly nationwide resistance movement to Japanese colonial occupation (since 1910). "The end of World War I and the Versailles Peace Conference inspired hopes for colonial peoples throughout the world. In part, this was sparked by the peace settlement and in particular by President Wilson of the United States."[2]

Meanwhile, the Worker's Party of South Korea was established in November 1946 and was reinforced with socialist politics through the leadership of Pak Hun-yong, who escaped to the north in October the same year. The Communist leader Pak after his visits to North Korea (April to July, 1946) began to seriously challenge the alliance committee between moderate socialists and moderate nationalists, which was led by Yo Un-hyong.

Pak's 'New Tactics' was declared (July 26, 1946) and meant direct confrontation with American military authority, while attacking on Yo's effort of collaboration between the rightists and the leftists through the allied Democratic National Front for temporary democratic government. The 'New Tactics' was to strengthen the Communist forces only by rejecting the alliance committee. The Communists viewed the American strategy as more colonial power, while challenging the UN-supervised elections (May 10, 1948) as a sham and not a true representation of the interest of the whole country.

Given this conflict, it is not surprising that the American military government prohibited any meetings (including the commemoration of March 1) in the year of 1947, because it was worried about the Jeju PC call for independence and unification, which reacted against the plan of general elections under UN supervision (May, 1948).

---

[2] Seth, *A Concise History of Modern Korea*, 47.

Jeju 4.3 Event as Effective History

People on Jeju Island in 1947 were to commemorate the March 1, 1919 nationwide movement against Japanese colonialism. A rally was held, attracting around 30,000 people. When the Jeju police were ordered to break them up, a child was injured by the horseshoe of a mounted police officer. When the officer ignored the injured child, the crowd was enraged, confronting the police with stone-throwing. The police forces misjudged their action as attacking the station and fired indiscriminate warning shots above their heads. Six civilians were killed as innocent bystanders, while eight people were injured.

This clash fired villager's protests. The police responded to them with indiscriminate arrests and discriminatory treatment. Such a measure led finally to an armed uprising against police oppression (April 3, 1948). The armed uprisings and the counterinsurgent strategy resulted in a prolonged confrontation with guerrilla warfare in the rugged and precipitous region of Mountain Halla until 1954. The counterinsurgent operation was extremely brutal, and countless lives were lost due to the punitive measures and shootings.[3]

The "Jeju 4.3 Massacre" belongs to a dark side of modern Korean history. "During decades of right-wing rule in South Korea, even casual mention of the 4·3 incident was taboo. There were times when even mentioning the uprising risked running afoul of the country's draconian National Security Law…The silence was finally broken by the 4·3 law of January 2000. This was followed by President Roh Moo-hyun's formal apology to the people of Jeju in October 2003"[4]

---

[3] *Jeju 4.3 at a Glance*, 10-11.

[4] Merrill, "Reflections on the Jeju 4.3 Incident," in *The JEJU 4.3 Mass Killing Atrocity, Justice, And Reconciliation*, 332-3.

The secrecy veiling this tragic event has been gradually lifted by a series of official reports and in extensive media coverage of its 70th anniversary. It is explored in dealing with the transitional justice by focusing on how human rights are abused and destroyed during political transition from colonialism to postcolonial society. To discuss this dark history, it is helpful to utilize a critical notion of effective history, which is concerned with a genealogical analysis of political discourse, material interests, and power relations by retrieving previously supposed insignificant truths and subjugated knowledge.

Here, a concept of liberty and liberation is unveiled as a metaphysical invention of the dominant class as imposed upon the burden of the subjugated. A notion of effective history takes issue with the marching history of progress, violence, and hegemony, by problematizing the knowledge-power interplay as inscribed into the history of the dominant. It elaborates counter memory of those buried as innocent victims by transforming history into an ensemble of social relations in difference, violence, and rupture. This epistemic stance reinforces the notion of transitional justice in undertaking a thick description of history and civil society in the process of decolonization and political legitimacy in international order of the Cold War.

Postwar Colonial Politics and Korea Division

The United States made a formal diplomatic treaty with Korea in 1882 as the first Western nation, and its first foreign embassy had to leave in November 1905 after the Japanese forced a protectorate treaty. In the Taft-Katsura Memorandum William Howard Taft, the United States Secretary of War, expressed that US President Theodore Roosevelt would concur in this view.

However, the Taft-Katsura agreement violated the Korean-American Treaty of Amity and Commerce (signed at Incheon on May 22, 1882), which included a mutual defense treaty against foreign invasion or oppression.

The Japanese colonial regime (1910 to 1945) established the Government-General of Korea, the power of which was centralized in the hands of the authoritarian figure of governor-general. All governors-general were appointed from military high ranks, and they possessed the military power to mobilize and command the troops (this included the right of appointment of all important local officials and control of the police system).

Its governmentality is likened to a military administration in a theater of war, which was beset by its authoritarian, top-down centralized rule, its mass mobilization campaigns, and its intensive, forced assimilation; it shook and disturbed the lives of Korea in remarkably challenging, or traumatizing ways. At last, it would result in ushering to the ideological divisions after the course of history after 1945.[5]

The United States had hostile relations with the Russian Communists. They sent 9,000 troops between 1918 and 1920 to Siberia to crush the Russian Revolution. During the Second World War, however, the United States and the Soviet Union became allies. General John R. Hodge was pressed by the State Department to collaborate with the soviets.

Despite his personal dislike, Hodge chose Rhee, who was in the process of founding the Representative Democratic Council. Meanwhile, the political climate underwent a major change, because President Franklin D. Roosevelt's (1933-1945) democratic international order was in transition to Truman's (1945-1953) policy of containment and cold war, along with the

---

[5] Seth, *A Concise History of Modern Korea*, 43.

Truman Doctrine (1947), which was expressed in a speech to Congress on March 12, 1947.

It implies the open declaration of Cold War according to which the US should support countries or people when threatened by the Soviet Union or Communist insurrection. The US was successful in forming a United Nations Temporary Commission on Korea (UNTCOK, November 1947), which was to supervise general elections for an independent, united Korean government. However, such a proposal was rejected by the Soviet Union, because the American proposal would contradict the Moscow Conference (December 1945), which reached an agreement of a four-power Trusteeship (the Soviet Union, the United States, the United Kingdom, and China) for a period of up to five years. This decision was responded to with fierce opposition from all Koreans.

But the Joint Soviet-American Commission in Seoul (1946) continued to carry out the Soviet Union's trusteeship in the northern part of Korea. The Korean Communist Party in Seoul changed its earlier opposition through the order of Soviets and became the only political group to support the Moscow decision.

In fact, Stalin was interested in maintaining balance of power and competing interests through the artificial division of peninsula, pursuing a more complicated strategy in Korea. This is the reason why Soviet occupation authority in the northern part did not agree with the UN's proposal of general elections for an independent united Korea. Stalin's strategy of cautious expansionism was reluctant to involve the American zone, while putting a damper on the illegal activities of the communist party in South Korea.[6]

---

[6] Weathersby, *Soviet Aims in Korea and The Origins of the Korean War, 1945-1950*, 16.

The American plan of general elections in the southern part became one of the major targets for nationalist leftists and their organizations to revolt, especially in the case of the Jeju 4.3 uprising. However, the U.N. General Assembly (December 12) accepted the UNTCOK report according to which the elections were "a valid expression of the free will of the electorate" of the country in southern part where the elections were monitored. The ROK was declared a "lawful" government as well as "the only such government in Korea."[7]

On August 15, 1948, the Republic of Korea was established in the south, the first president was Syngman Rhee. On September 9, 1948, the Democratic People's Republic of Korea was established in the north, with Kim Il Sung as premier. This division set the stage for a three-year civil war (1950), as an inevitable outcome of this ideological confrontation.

Jeju Resistance and Civilian Movement

The Jeju 4.3 event is not only of great importance within modern Korean history, but also holds international significance. During the imperial Japanese rule, there were frequent ferries for transportation between Jeju and Osaka. In Osaka, one of the most important industrial cities, many Jeju people sought to find jobs, better education and were active in labor organizations. Those experienced and educated among them returned after Japan's surrender and played an initiative in the emerging self-governmental structures on Jeju, the People's Committee.

In the transfer of power, the Japanese Government-General in Seoul headquarters made an agreement with Yo Un-hyong, who was highly respected as a leftist nationalist and popular as political leader (with a Christian background). He formed a Committee

---

[7] Seth, *A Concise History of Modern Korea*, 95.

for the Preparation for Korean Independence (CPKI), with the headquarters in Seoul, and local committees (PCs) began to understand themselves as branches of the CPKI. The Seoul headquarters convened a representative assembly (September 6) with several hundred delegates forming the Korean People's Republic (KPR).

However, General John R. Hodge refused to recognize any Korean government, and he had revived the discredited structure of the former colonial administration in which almost all the higher positions were filled in the provincial office and police organizations with officials in former collaboration with imperial Japan. Hodge favored the Korean Democratic Party (KDP), which was founded in a group of wealthy landlords and businessmen (September 16), and some of the Korean personnel in the American military government were affiliated with this party.

However, when the socialist or nationalist party had come to realize the American strategy as a reiteration of colonial power, it began to reject American military governance and its plan of elections, because the elections would lead to permanent division of the south from the north.

It is not surprising that the American military government prohibited any meetings (including the commemoration of the March 1) for the year of 1947, but it had to allow the Jeju PC and its Democratic National Front to plan on the commemoration.

In fact, Jeju PC grew out of preparing the Committee for Rehabilitation led by Yo for collaboration between moderate nationalists and moderate leftists just after liberation from Japan. In the confidentiality report about the Jeju political situation (December 4-6, 1946), based on the common opinion among police, American personnel, and the general public; the report states that Jeju PC has a mild leftist or oppositional leaning, but nothing to do with the communist party nor any uprising scheme.

During the civilian resistance, many people were arrested under interrogation and even maltreated, and this ignited mass demonstration over the island; it occurred even in the sense of general strike against the U.S. military government (March 10), with some 40,000 participants. Most of the participants were civilians concerned with independence and unification, having nothing to do with the communism-inspired insurrection.

In response, however, the U.S. military government repressed the locals, with racial prejudice and ideological distrust through Cho Pyung-ok, who was the chief of the National Department of Police Agency under the U.S. military authority. More police officers were dispatched from the government in the mainland, together with an extreme right-wing paramilitary group (known as the Northwest Youth League), which was excessively ruthless running on borderline terroristic in hunting 'communists.'[8]

Insurgency and American Intervention

The increased reinforcement led to a strong suppression of civilians and caused the Jeju PC to mobilize their resistance. Around 2,500 people were arrested, tortured, and imprisoned from the March shooting event (1947) to April 3, 1948. However, 350 people decided to arm themselves and began to attack 12 police stations, right-wing youth, and their families on April 3, 1948. The armed people were members and sympathizers in the branch of the Worker's Party on Jeju Island, but their rebellion occurred as voluntary resistance against the bloody treatment and atrocities on the part of the police and an extreme right-wing paramilitary group against civilians. It was not originally targeted

---

[8] *Jeju 4.3 at a Glance*, 13.

at the Korean constabulary army or the U.S. military. An all-out guerrilla extermination campaign came to an effective end in June, 1949.

Colonel Rothwell H. Brown, the commander of the 6th Infantry Division's 20th Regiment, was sent to Jeju as supreme military commander in May 1948. He was placed in charge of military operations of all Korean National Guard forces on the Island. His military carrier already was characterized by the Silver Star, awarded for conspicuous gallantry and intrepidity in connection with military operations fighting in the China-Burma-India Theater during World War II. Nationalist Chinese Unity was commanded by Colonel Rothwell Brown.

When Brown was dispatched to the Jeju uprising, he said in a press conference: "I believe the situation will be subjugated in about two weeks if things go as I planned."[9] His mission was to quell only the uprising. His mission of 'quick repression' takes a hardliner stance in the subjugation of rebellion in about two weeks, which was to be carried out by Park Jin-kyeong for reckless arrests (amounted to over 5,000 people from May 22 to May 30).

"Direct American involvement in suppressing the rebellion included the daily training of counterinsurgent forces, interrogation of prisoners, and the use of American spotter planes to ferret out guerrillas."[10] It nullified a peaceful negotiation in a meeting (April 28) between Lieutenant Colonel Kim Ik-ryeol, the commander of constabulary forces on the island and the armed leader Kim Dal-sam, a pro-Communist leader; they came to reach an armistice.

In fact, in the memoir of the Colonel, the reason for the rebellion was primarily caused by police and right-wing groups

---

[9] Ibid., 23.
[10] Cumings, *The Korean War*, 305.

in their punitive measures and plundering of villagers; it has nothing to do with the communist class struggle.

However, on May 1 the ultra-rightist youth razed fire to a village, the Ora-ri arson attack (known as *May Day on Jeju Island*, officially filmed by the US). In this propaganda documentary film, it was falsely accused that the rebels committed this crime, derailing the peace negotiation. The American military authority dismissed the Colonel and was charged to order a scorched earth policy against the guerrilla forces. On May 22, 1948, Col. Brown sought to "break up" the revolt: "police were assigned definite missions to protect all coastal villages [from guerrillas]; to arrest rioters carrying arms, and to stop killing and terrorizing innocent citizens."[11] He anticipated a long-range program "to offer positive proof of the evils of Communism," and to "show that the American way offers positive hope"[12] for the people on Jeju Island.

Carrying out Brown's operation, however, Park's brutal atrocity resulted in his assassination by his subordinate, shocking everybody. This circumstance crippled Brown's quick and indiscriminate repression through which he sought to have re-election of June 23 by validating a failed election in May 10.

After this tragedy, Brigadier-General William Lynn Roberts in his memorandum to Col. Brown (June 21, 1948) states that "Today, we sent Lt Col Chai to be Regimental Commander of the 11th and Major Song [Yo-Chan] to be the Exec…I understand that Song is a strong man and has a record of being ruthless. Song is the best we have and you can use him as such."[13]

---

[11] Ibid., 306.
[12] Ibid.
[13] From National Archives & Records Administration, in American Document 4, 22.

Furthermore, Colonel Brown submitted a report, entitled "Report of Activities on Cheju-Do from 22 May 48 to 30 June 1948" on July 1, 1948, to the commander of the USAMGIK. It entails useful information about the Jeju 4.3 uprising, with reference to the Worker's Party of South Korea. The mountain Halla is an extinct volcanic crater and at 6,000 feet the highest peak features itself as a symbol of Jeju Island. Those who escaped to the mountain were shot, because they were condemned to be sympathizers with the armed group. Witnesses of the survivals were recorded about such barbarism, but in official weekly summary reports, victims were falsified as communist raiders.

It is unfortunate to see that Brown fabricates a politically charged discourse of communist rebellion as the major reason for the Jeju 4.3 uprising. He maneuvered such ideologically tainted discourse in terms of material interest justifying his punitive operations and power relations in regards to general elections and anti-communism.

A genealogical analysis of the dominant discourse focuses on the extent to which it is embedded within the network of power relations and consolidates political legitimacy in rationalizing death politics (necropolitics) against the resistant and the civilians. Isn't the American military government entitled with such biopolitical power that is normally given only to the sovereignty of a nation-state just in the case of exception? American military intervention reinforced the autocratic regime, thus crippled down the significance of transitional justice underlying stable democratic institutions and improving civil society.

Starting from November 1948, President Rhee declared martial law (deemed to be illegal), and the suppression forces carried out through a hardliner, Korean Col. Song Yo-Chan, who was in charge of the 9th Regiment of the Korea National Guard stationed in Jeju (December, 1948). He undertook the scorched-earth operation as a program of mass slaughter and made a collective massacre of all villagers and their home located near Halla mountain.

Ideological Interpellation and Innocent Victim

Entangled in the ideological interpellation, crimes against humanity on Jeju Island in 1948-49 have been buried through mass media, the punishing system of surviving family members, and disseminating anticommunist discourse. According to John Merrill, "the Jeju 4.3 uprising is a testament to the failure of the American occupation to develop viable policies and to create the foundations of democracy in Korea. Violent opposition on this scale to a postwar American occupation occurred nowhere else in Asia or Europe…The American crackdown on the left spread to Jeju after the U.S. military unit on the island and the local People's Committee had a falling out."[14]

1992 brought the discovery of eleven bones of women and children in Darangshi Cave, who were revealed as victims (December, 1948). The cave discovery is the symbol of the effective history of innocent victims through the narrative of those buried. John Eperjesi at Kyunghee University, Seoul, is right in his rhetoric "caves as storied matter" in dealing with the Jeju massacre under U.S. Imperialism.[15]

Such a story requires genealogy in unveiling state-enforced silence as displacing the atrocities and justifying the killing of the innocent villagers in a counterinsurgent campaign. It symbolizes the Jeju massacre under U.S. imperialism, featuring the storied matter of Darangshi cave as a regime of effective history. "[It]

---

[14] Merrill, "Reflections on the Jeju 4.3 Incident," 335.
[15] Eperjesi, "Caves as Storied Matter."

was a powerful threat to stability and order on Jeju in the present because it contributed to the production of a narrative that destabilized the official state-sanctioned memory of the past which held that the Jeju uprising was a communist revolution, and the people executed in the mountains were communist guerillas."[16]

Can absolute innocent victims speak? By no means. However, their buried voice is present in our life-world, calling for our *parrhesia* (speaking the truth audaciously) from and for them.

Colonial War and Effective History in the Philippines

The Jeju 4.3 uprising has "similar ones in Taiwan, Vietnam and elsewhere found themselves almost immediately caught up in the maelstrom of the Cold War—and often at loggerheads with the United States. The results were predictably tragic."[17]

To develop a conceptual clarity of effective history and transitional justice, I find it critical to undertake a comparative study of the Jeju massacre and the Philippines for reparations, creation of memorials, and educational importance. When the U.S. came to occupy Korea under military authority, it was close to ending its colonial rule in the Philippines (1946).

As noted at the beginning of the chapter, Taft-Katsura Agreement (1905) has an international significance in affirming Japanese-American collaboration in which Japan disavows any aggressive designs on the Philippines. In fact, William Howard Taft was the first civilian governor of the Philippines, and expressed his patronizing attitude in conversation with President McKinley; "our little brown brothers would need fifty

---

[16] Ibid., 141.
[17] Merrill, "Reflections on the Jeju 4.3 Incident," 334.

or one hundred years of close supervision to develop anything resembling Anglo-Saxon political principles and skills."[18]

After the victory in the Spanish-American War (1898), however, the United States ignored Filipino representatives (declared by Emilio Aguinaldo to be independent from Spain on June 1898). It began a war of conquest, while sending 70,000 troops and involving three years of brutal fighting against the Filipinos.

President McKinley assured in his 1898 proclamation to the Filipino people that America's mission was one of "benevolent assimilation substituting the mild sway of justice and right for arbitrary rule."[19] The 1893 depression strengthened colonialist policy developing for overseas markets within the political and financial elite for American goods, while uniting the government and people into American exceptionalism or Manifest Destiny.[20]

Aguinaldo was captured and took an oath of allegiance to the U.S. government (April 1901). But the Philippine War lasted from 1899 through 1913, and it resulted from the imperialist policy within the Republican Party of President William McKinley (1843-1901), who sought to civilize and Christianize the Filipinos. It refers to "the first Vietnam," since the death of 1.4 million Filipinos has been usually accounted for as victims of insurrection. In the study of American imperialism in the Philippines, attention takes on "the nature of America's policy of aggression, the depth of popular mass resistance to the American forces and the duration of the struggle in what became, ultimately, suicidal refusal to capitulate to imperialism."[21]

---

[18] Miller, *Benevolent Assimilation*, 134.
[19] The American Presidency Project, McKinley's Executive Order (December 21, 1898).
[20] Horsman, *Race and Manifest Destiny*, 18.
[21] Luzviminda Francisco, "The first Vietnam," 3.

Guerrilla activity was becoming increasingly effective, continually counterattacking the Americans. Filipinos in guerilla warfare and civilians were racialized by the Americans as "savages." This racial ideology characterizes the significance of the biopolitical strategy of defining the enemy as the inferior and backward; it continues to be dominant in shaping the articulation of race and empire in Philippine-American colonial history as well as American military authority in Korea. An American mission of benevolent assimilation was embedded with a racial ideology of social Darwinism, which appears to be central in political rule over the Philippines as well as versed in military terms.

Colonial Racism and Biopolitics

In late 1899, Filipino forces shifted to guerrilla tactics in response to America's superior might. Americans downplayed this resistance to be a type of "savage" warfare. Torture of Filipinos was undertaken with the infamous method of "water cure," in which the victim's mouth was forced open to pour gallons of water down the throat.

General Shafter was not averse to killing half of the island population in the name of the *mission civilisatrice*. In January 1900 he disclosed: "My plan would be to disarm the natives of the Philippine Islands, even if we have to kill half of them to do it."[22]

War brutality in the Philippines continues to be seen in the Korean army and police force under the directive of the American military government in the earlier phase of suppression.

Nonetheless, Americans had a clear human rights standard to follow in their democratic traditions and constitution, but this standard was not extended to Filipinos nor Jeju Island. Filipino

---

[22] Ibid., 6.

nationalists, like Korean nationalists, were inspired by Wilson's principle, but they were treated as lower races incapable of self-determination and as backward in need of benevolent hegemon.

In the period from 1899 to 1905 Americans carried out scorched-earth tactics and its brutal operation against guerilla skirmishes. A strategy of "reconcentration" was to quarantine the populace from the guerillas; this anti-guerilla strategy resulted in widespread torture, disease, and mass starvation, which afflicted the civilians, women and children. Likewise, this strategy also occurred in filthy refugee camps along the coast of Jeju Island, in which evacuated villagers were treated like pigs.

The most notorious example in the Philippines was the orders for indiscriminate attacks on the island of Samar, which were issued by Colonel Jacob H. Smith in retaliation for the Balangiga Conflict. It was the notorious Samar Campaign of 1902 in his reprisals against the entire population of the island of Samar, in which more than forty U.S. soldiers were killed by Filipino guerrillas.

All persons capable of bearing arms (over ten years of age) against the United States should be killed. "Kill Everyone over Ten" (New York Journal cartoon, May 5, 1902). Around 2,500 people were killed, and the island was burned, turning into devastation. The Balangiga massacre took place two months after the transfer of the government from the US military to its civilian authorities as headed by future President William H. Taft. The American Governor of Abra Province in the first Philippines commission (1899) undertook the depopulation campaign: "Whole villages had been burned, storehouses and crops had been destroyed and the entire province was as devoid of food products as was the valley of Shenandoah after Sheridan's raid during the Civil War."[23]

---

[23] Cited in ibid., 7.

Masculine white supremacy has bearings upon a bellicose spirit. This ideological interpellation has come into play in the interests of national struggle and survival of the fittest in the international political arena. Acts of 'Benevolent Assimilation' are done in the white masculine supremacy and carries out the benign tutelage of South Korea and the Philippines. Ideology of benevolent hegemon was used to justify a colonial war, or occupation military authority, while dehumanizing the Filipino as savage, or Jeju villagers as commies; such hegemony rationalizes atrocities and discards alternative interpretations of events. Bare life and racial hierarchy are integrated into the political-discretionary realm through the totalitarian authority of the state.

When biopolitical sociology articulates an aspect of political technique of population in terms of discipline, surveillance, torture, and killing, bureaucratic apparatuses are exercised by police and military violence against civil liberties -such authoritarian statism can be seen in the American military government in its approach to the Jeju 4.3 massacre through ideological interpellation of 'communist' rebellion. Biopolitics in the exceptional stage of colonialism finds its turning point in totalitarian death politics through ideological interpellation and genocide. A biopolitical clarification promotes and sharpens transitional justice approach to address indigenous oppression, racial justice, and ideological discourse in the network of power relations.

As Howard Zinn argues, "there is not a country in world history in which racism has been more important, for so long a time, as the United States."[24] Here, the first essential step to total domination is to kill the juridical person in the human being by categorizing certain people outside the protection of the law.

---

[24] Zinn, *A People's History of the United States*, 23.

This takes place in the Jeju 4.3 massacre in the carrying out of the indiscriminate killing of juridical civilians. To justify such barbarism, American military authority branded Jeju as "the island of the Reds," and remained an undercurrent in conducting ruthless scorch-earth operations.

Then, it erects a punishing system of surviving family members (law of complicity, or the guilt-by-association system) by locating them outside the normal penal system for deploying mechanisms of scapegoat, which is characterized by restriction of their human rights in every corner of life. They have been degraded to being the pariah people in the caste system of this murderous society.

Epilogue

Biopolitical strategy has failed the history of the bereaved family members surviving the Jeju massacre, but the lives of the victims continue to be remembered and kept alive over the years. The guilt-by-association system, or law of complicity, has done grave damage to the surviving family members.

The family members and relatives of victims become prey to mechanisms of scapegoating, while unfair treatment was done in employment, promotions, social engagement, isolation, and even travel. Past violence can haunt the present and be reiterated and reproduced in different forms of human rights violations. Global efforts for transition justice and civil society seek to overcome past violence, which can haunt the present and be reiterated in different forms of human rights violations.

In Walter Benjamin's seventh thesis of philosophy of history we read: "There is no document of civilization which is not at the same time a document of barbarism. And *just* as such a document is not free of barbarism, barbarism taints also the manner in which it was transmitted from one owner to another." [25]

The historical document of barbarism belongs to the regime of the genealogy of effective history and transitional justice, which require to be rewritten for vivid present in healing haunting history; it should be undertaken through anamnestic reasoning, counter memory, and common good against the marching history of barbarism and hegemony.

---

[25] Benjamin, *Illumination*, 256.

I hear forgiveness and reconciliation as transitional justice in a post-apartheid South Africa in the 1990s, especially from the Kairos Document (1985): "The fact that the State is tyrannical and an enemy of God is no excuse for hatred. As Christians we are called upon to love our enemies (Matt. 5:44)...But then we must also remember that the most loving thing we can do for both the oppressed and for our enemies who are oppressors is to eliminate the oppression, remove the tyrants from power and establish a just government for the common good of all the people."

Bibliography

Abu-Lughod, Janet. *Before European Hegemony. The World System A.D. 1250-1350.* New York: Oxford University Press, 1989.

Agamben, Giorgio. *Homo Sacer: Sovereign Power and Bare Life,* trans. Daniel Heller-Roazen Stanford: Stanford University Press, 1998.

Agang, Sunday B. et al. *African Public Theology.* Carlisle: Hippo Books, 2020.

Alexander, Leo. "Medical Science under Dictatorship," *New England Journal of Medicine* 241 (1949): 39-47.

Althusser, L. *On the Reproduction of Capitalism: Ideology and Ideological State Apparatuses.* London and New York: Verso, 2014.

Althusser, Louis and Etienne Balibar, *Reading Capital,* trans. Ben Brewster. London: Verso, 1979.

Amin, Samir. *Eurocentrism: Modernity, Religion, and Democracy,* trans. Russel Moore and James Membrez. New York: Monthly Review Press, 2009.

Arendt, Hannah. *The Human Condition,* 2nd ed. Chicago and London. The University of Chicago Press, 1998.

Arghiri, Emmanuel. *Unequal Exchange: A Study of the Imperialism of Trade,* trans. Brian Pearce. New York: Monthly Review, 1972.

Aristotle, *A New Aristotle Reader,* ed. J. L. Ackrill. Princeton, New Jersey: Princeton University Press, 1987.

Arrighi, Giovanni. *The Long Twentieth Century: Money, Power, and the Origin of Our Times.* London, New York: Verso, 1994.

Baehr, Peter. Ed. *The Portable Hannah Arendt.* New York: Penguin, 2000.

Baran, Paul A. and Paul Sweezy, *Monopoly Capital: An Essay on the American Economic Social Order*. New York and London: Monthly Review, 1966.

Barth, Karl. *Church Dogmatics*, Geoffrey Bromiley and Thomas F. Torrance. Trans. G.T. Thomson. 5 vols. in 14 parts. London and New York: T. & T. Clark, 2004.

_____. *Epistle to the Romans*, trans. Edwyn Hoskyns. London: Oxford University Press, 1933.

Beauchamp, Tom L. and James F. Childress. *Principles of Biomedical Ethics*, 3rd ed. New York, Oxford: Oxford University Press, 1989.

Bellah, Robert N. *Religion in Human Evolution: From the Paleolithic to the Axial Age*. London, England. Cambridge, Mass.: The Belknap Press of Harvard University Press, 2011.

_____. *Beyond Belief: Essays on Religion in a Post-Traditionalist World*. Berkeley, Los Angeles, Oxford: University of California Press, 1991.

Benedict, Ruth. *Patterns of Culture*. New York: Houghton Mifflin, 2005.

Benjamin, Walter. *Illuminations*, trans. Harry Zohn. New York: Schocken Books, 2007.

Bennett, Gaymon. *Technicians of Human Dignity: Bodies, Souls, and the Making of Intrinsic Worth*. New York: Fordham University Press, 2015.

Bennett, Gaymon, et al. (ed.), *The Evolution of Evil*. Goettingen: Vandenhoeck & Ruprecht, 2008.

Bernauer, James and Jeremy Carrette, eds. *Michel Foucault and Theology: The Politics of Religious Experience*. London: Ashgate, 2004.

Bhabha. Homi (1984), "Of Mimicry and Man," in *Discipleship: A Special Issue on Psychoanalysis*, 125-133.

Boff, Clodovis. *Theologie und Praxis: Die erkenntnistheoretischen Grundlagen der Theologie der Befreiung.* Munich: Kaiser. Grunewald, 1986.

Boff, L. and C. Boff, *Introducing Liberation* Theology. Maryknoll, N.Y.: Orbis, 1987.

Bonhoeffer, Dietrich. *Ethics,* trans. Neville H. Smith. New York: Simon & Schuster, 1995.

Bourdieu. P. and L.J.D. Wacquant, *An Invitation to Reflexive Sociology.* Chicago and London: University of Chicago Press, 1992.

Bourdieu, P. *Masculine Domination.* New York: Polity Press, 2001.

Braudel, Fernand. *The Mediterranean and the Mediterranean World in the Age of Philip II,* trans. Siân Reynolds, 2 vols. London and New York, 1972-73.

_____. *Civilization and Capitalism 15th - 18th Century* I and II. New York: Harper & Row, 1982.

Campbell, Timothy and Adam Sitze, eds. *Biopolitics: A Reader.* Durham and London: Duke University Press, 2013.

Carr, E.H. *The Bolshevik Revolution 2: 1917-1923.* New York: Penguin, 1986.

Chung, Paul S. *Critical Theory and Political Theology: The Aftermath of the Enlightenment.* Cham: Palgrave Macmillan, 2019.

Cole-Turner, Ronald. *The New Genesis: Theology and Genetic Revolution.* Louisville, Kentucky: Westminster/John Knox Press, 1993.

_____. Ed. *Human Cloning: Religious Responses.* Louisville, Kentucky: Westminster John Knox Press, 1996.

_____. *Beyond Cloning: Religion and the Remaking of Humanity.* Harrisburg, Pennsylvania: Trinity Press, 2001.

Colletti, Lucio. *From Rousseau to Lenin: Studies in Ideology and Society*. Trans. John Merrington and Judith White. New York: Monthly Review Press, 1972.

Collins, Patricia H. *Black Feminist Thought: Knowledge, Consciousness, and the Politics of Empowerment*, 2nd ed. New York: Routledge, 2009.

Cone, James H. *A Black Theology of Liberation*. Philadelphia and New York: J.B. Lippincott Company, 1970.

_____. *The Cross and the Lynching Tree*. Maryknoll, NY: Orbis, 2011.

Conrad, Joseph. *Heart of Darkness*. London: Blackwood's Magazine, 1902.

Cooper, M. *Surplus Life: Biotechnics and the Transformations of Capital*. Seattle: Washington University Press, 2007.

Cumings, Bruce. *The Korean War: A History*. New York: Modern Library, 2010.

Dawkins, R. *River Out of Eden*. New York: HarperCollins, 1995.

Derrida, J. "Violence and Metaphysics," in *Writing and Difference*, trans. Alan Bass. Chicago and London: The University of Chicago Press, 1978. Pp. 79-153.

Du Bois, W.E.B. *Black Reconstruction in America, 1860-1880*, rep. in 1992. New York: Atheneum, 1935.

Duchrow, Ulrich and Franz J. Hinkelammert, *Property for People, not for Profit: Alternatives to the Global Tyranny of Capital*. London: Zed, 2004.

Durkheim, Emile. *The Elementary Forms of Religious Life*, trans. Karen E. Fields. New York: The Free Press, 1995.

Dussel, E. *The Invention of the Americas, Eclipse of the Other and the Myth of Modernity*, trans. Michel D. Barber. New York: Continuum, 1995.

Eperjesi, John. "Caves as Storied Matter: The Jeju April 3 Events and U.S. Imperialism," *Journal of American Studies* 51. 2 (2019): 129-54.

Fanon, F. *Black Skin White Masks* 2nd ed. and rev. trans. Richard Philcox. New York: Grove, 2008.

Farmer, Paul. *Pathologies of Power: Health, Human Rights, and the New War on the Poor*. Berkeley and Los Angeles: University of California Press, 2005.

Ferrarello, Susi. *Husserl's Ethics and Practical Intentionality*. London and New York: Bloomsbury Academic, 2016.

Fetscher, Iring. *Rousseaus politische Philosophie: Zur Geschichte des demokratischen Freiheitsbegriffs*. Suhrkamp: Frankfurt am Main, 1968.

Figes, Orlando. *A People's Tragedy: The Russian Revolution 1891-1924*. New York: Penguin, 1996.

Foucault, M. *The History of sexuality: An Introduction* I and 2, trans. Robert Hurley. New York: Vintage, 1990.

_____. *The Archaeology of Knowledge and the Discourse on Language*, trans. A. M. Sheridan Smith. New York: Pantheon, 1972.

_____. *Discipline and Punish: The Birth of the Prison*, trans. Alan Sheridan. New York: Vintage, 1995.

_____. *Power/Knowledge: Selected Interviews and Other Writings, 1972- 1977*, ed. Colin Gordon. New York: Pantheon Books, 1980.

Frank, Andre G. *Capitalism and Underdevelopment in Latin America: Historical Studies of Chile and Brazil*, rev. ed. New York: Monthly Review, 1968.

Gadamer, Hans. G. *Truth and Method*, 2nd. Rev. ed. Joel Weinscheimer and Donald G. Marshall. New York: Continuum, 2004.

Garner, Richard T. and Bernard Rosen. *Moral Philosophy: A Systematic Introduction to Normative Ethics and Meta-Ethics*. New York: Macmillan. 1967.

Gayhart, Bryce A. *The Ethics of Ernst Troeltsch: a Commitment to Relevancy*. Lewiston: E. Mellen Press, 1990.

Geertz, Clifford. *The Interpretation of Cultures*. New York: Basic, 1973.

Gollwitzer, Helmut. *Krummes Holz-aufrechter Gang: Zur Frage nach dem Sinn des Lebens*. Munich: Chr. Kaiser. 1985.

_____. *Auch das Denken darf dienen: Aufsätze zu Theologie und Geistesgeschichte* I. Ed. F. W. Marquardt. Munich: Chr. Kaiser, 1988.

_____. *Umkehr und Revolution: Aufsätze zu christlichen Glauben und Marxismus* 1. Ed. Christian Keller. Munich: Chr. Kaiser, 1988.

_____. *...dass Gerechtigkeit und Friede sich küssen: Aufsätze zur politischen Ethik* 1.II. Ed. Andreas Pangritz. Munich: Chr. Kaiser, 1988.

_____. *Die kapitalistische Revolution*. Tubingen: TVT Medienverlag, 1998.

_____ (1975). "Why Black Theology," *Union Seminary Quarterly Review* 31. no. 1. Pp. 38-58.

Gorovitz, Samuel, et al. *Moral Problems in Medicine*. Englewood Cliffs, N. J.: Prentice-Hall, 1976.

Gould, Stephen J. *An Urchin in the Storm: Essays about Books and Ideas*. New York: Penguin Books, 1987.

_____. *The Mismeasure of Man*. New York: W.W. Norton, 1996.

Gramsci, *Selections from the Prison Notebooks*. London: Lawrence and Wishart, 1971.

Gustafson, James M. *Ethics from a Theocentric Perspective, I: Theology and Ethics*. Chicago: The University of Chicago Press, 1981.

_____. *Ethics from a Theocentric Perspective II: Ethics and Theology.* Chicago and London: The University of Chicago Press, 1984.

Gutierrez, Gustavo. *A Theology of Liberation.* Maryknoll: Orbis, 1999.

Habermas, J. *Between Facts and Norms: Contributions to a Discourse Theory of Law and Democracy,* trans. W. Rehg. Cambridge, Mass,: MIT Press, 1996.

_____. *The Theory of Communicative Action, 1: Reason and the Rationalization of Society,* trans. Thomas McCarthy. Boston: Beacon Press, 1984.

_____. *The Structural Transformation of the Public Sphere: An Inquiry into a Category of Bourgeois Society,* trans. Thomas Burger, Cambridge: Polity, 1989.

_____. *Theory and Practice,* trans. John Viertel. Boston: Beacon Press, 1974.

_____. *Legitimation Crisis,* trans. Thomas McCarthy. Boston: Beacon, 1973.

Hall, Douglas J. *The Cross in Our Context: Jesus and the Suffering World.* Minneapolis: Fortress, 2003.

Hamilton-Paterson, James. *America's Boy: A Century of Colonialism in the Philippines.* New York: Henry Holt, 1999.

Hardt, Michael and Antonio Negri. *Empire.* London and Cambridge: Harvard University Press, 2000.

Hefner, Philip. *The Human Factor: Evolution, Culture, and Religion.* Minneapolis: Fortress, 1993.

Hegel, G.F.W. *The Philosophy of History,* trans. J. Sibree. Kitchener: Batache Books, 2001.

_____. *The Science of Logic,* trans. and ed. George di Giovanni. Cambridge: Cambridge University Press, 2010.

_____. *The Phenomenology of Mind,* trans. J. B. Baillie. New York: Mineola, 2003.

_____. *Hegel's Philosophy of Right*, trans. T. M. Knox. Oxford: Oxford University Press, 1949.

Hinkelammert, Franz J. *The Ideological Weapons of Death: A Theological Critique of Capitalism.* Maryknoll, N.Y: Orbis, 1986.

Hoganson, Kristin L. *Fighting for American Manhood: How Gender Politics Provoked the Spanish-American and Philippine American Wars.* New Haven: Yale University Press, 1998.

Holmes, Mary. *What is Gender? Sociological Approaches.* London: Sage Publications, 2007.

Honneth, Alex. *The I in We: Studies in the Theory of Recognition,* trans. Joseph Ganahl. Cambridge and Malden: Polity, 2012.

Horkheimer, Max. *Critical Theory: Selected Essays Max Horkheimer*, trans. Matthew J. O'Connell and others. New York: The Seabury Press, 1972.

Horsman, Reginald. *Race and Manifest Destiny: The Origins of American Racial Anglo-Saxonism.* Cambridge: Harvard University Press, 1981.

Hubbard, Thomas K. Ed. *Homosexuality in Greece and Rome: A Sourcebook of Basic Documents.* Berkeley: University of California Press, 2003.

Huppert, George. *After the Black Death: A Social History of Early Modern Europe*, 2nd ed., Interdisciplinary Studies in History. Bloomington: Indiana University Press, 1998.

Husserl, Edmund. *The Essential Husserl: Basic Writings in Transcendental Phenomenology*, ed. Donn Welton. Bloomington, Indianapolis: Indiana University Press, 1999.

Hyppolite, J. *Logic and Existence*, trans. Leonard Lawlor and Amit Sen. Albany: SUNY, 1997.

Jeju 4.3 Peace Foundation, Jeju 4.3 at a Glance: Handbook for the Jeju 4.3 Peace Memorial Hall. South Korea: Jeju 4.3 Peace Foundation, 2021.

Jennings, W. J. *The Christian Imagination: Theology and the Origins of Race*. New Haven and London: Yale University Press, 2010.

Jessop, Bob. *The Capitalist State: Marxist Theories and Methods*. Oxford: Martin Robertson, 1982.

_____. *State Theory: Putting the Capitalist State in its Place*. Pennsylvania: Penn State University Press, 1990.

Kahn, Paul. *Political Theology: Four New Chapters on the Concept of Sovereignty*. New York: Columbia University Press, 2011.

Keller, Everlyn F. *The Century of the Gene*. Mass., Cambridge: Harvard University Press, 2000.

Kellner, Douglas, ed. *Baudrillard: A Critical Reader*. Oxford and Cambridge: Blackwell, 1994.

Kojeve, A. *Introduction to the Reading of Hegel: Lectures on the Phenomenology of Spirit*, ed. Allan Bloom. Ithaca: Cornell University Press, 1980.

Kramer, Paul A. *The Blood of Government: Race, Empire, the United States, and the Philippines*. Chapel Hill: University of North Carolina Press, 2006.

Lee, Ki-baik et al. *Korea Old and New*. Mass. and Seoul: Harvard University Press and Ilchokak, 1990.

Lehmann, Paul. *Ethics in a Christian Context*. New York and Evanston: Harper & Row, 1963.

Lenin, I. *Lenin Collected Works 38*. Moscow: Progress Publishers, 1976.

Levinas, Emmanuel. *Ethics and Infinity: Conversations with Philippe Nemo*, trans. Richard A. Cohen. Pittsburgh: Duquesne University Press, 1985.

____. Emmanuel *Levinas Basic Philosophical Wrings*, eds. Adrian T. Peperzak, et al. Bloomington and Indianapolis: Indiana University Press, 1996.

Lopez, Robert S. *The Commercial Revolution of the Middle Ages 930-1350*. Cambridge: Cambridge University Press, 1971.

Lukacs, Georg. *The Young Hegel: Studies in the Relations between Dialectics and Economics*, trans. Rodney Livingstone. Massachusetts: MIT Press, 1976.

____. *Tactics and Ethics, 1919-1929: The Questions of Parliamentarianism and Other Essays*. London and New York: Verso, 2014.

Luther, Martin and Desiderius Erasmus: *Free Will and Salvation*, trans. and eds. E. Gordon Rupp and Philip S. Watson. Philadelphia: The Westminster Press, 1969.

Luxemburg, Rosa. *The Accumulation of Capital*, ed. Kenneth J. Tarbuck, and trans. Rudolf Wichmann. New York and London: Monthly Review Press, 1972.

Machiavelli, N. *The Prince*, ed. Philip Smith. Mineola, New York: Dover Publications, 1992.

MacIntyre, Alasdair. *After Virtues*, 2nd ed. Notre Dame, Indiana: University of Notre Dame Press, 1984.

Mahan, Alfred. *The Influence of Sea Power Upon History, 1660-1763*. Boston: Little, Brown and Co.: 1890.

Malešević, Siniša. *The Sociology of War and Violence*. Cambridge: Cambridge University Press, 2010.

Mandel, Ernest. *The Formation of the Economic Thought of Karl Marx, 1843 to Capital*, trans. Brian Pearce. New York and London: Monthly Review Press, 1971.

____. *Late Capitalism*, trans. Joris De Bres. London, New York: Verso, 1975.

Mar, Tracey Banivanua and Penelope Edmonds, eds. *Making Settler Colonial Space: Perspectives on Race, Place and Identity*. New York: Palgrave Macmillan, 2010.

Marcuse, *Reason and Revolution: Hegel and the Rise of Social Theory*. Boston: Beacon, 1960.

Margulis, Lynn and Dorion Sagan. *Microcosmos*. New York: Summit, 1986.

Marquardt, F.W. *Eia, warn wir da–eine theologische Utopie*. Gutersloh: Chr. Kaiser/Gutersloher Verlagshaus, 1997.

Marx, K. *Capital, I and III: A Critique of Political Economy*, trans. Ben Fowkes. London: Penguin, 1990.

Massey, Douglas S. and Nancy A. Denton. *American Apartheid: Segregation and the Making of the Underclass*. Cambridge, M.A: Harvard University Press, 1993.

McCarthy, Thomas. *Race, Empire, and the Idea of Human Development*. Cambridge: Cambridge University Press, 2010.

McMaken, W. Travis. *Our God Loves Justice: An Introduction to Helmut Gollwitzer*. Minneapolis: Fortress, 2017.

Meade, E. Grant. *American Military Government In Korea*. New York: Kings Crown Press, 1951.

Mearsheimer, John J. *The Tragedy of Great Power Politics*. New York: Norton, 2001.

Mendieta, Eduardo. Ed. *The Frankfurt School on Religion: Key Writings by the Major Thinkers*. New York and London: Routledge, 2005.

Merrill, John. "Reflections on the Jeju 4.3 Incident: Korea's "Dark History" and its Implications for Current Policy," in *The JEJU 4.3 Mass Killing Atrocity, Justice, And Reconciliation*. Seoul: Yunsei University Press, 2018. Pp. 331-355.

Miller, Kenneth R. *Finding Darwin's God: A Scientist's Search for Common Ground between God and Evolution*. New York: Harper Perennial, 1999.

Miller, Stuart C. *Benevolent Assimilation: The American Conquest of the Philippines*. New Haven: Yale University Press, 1982.

Moghaddam, Mahsa H. and Ali Zare (2017). "Responsibilities of Multinational Corporations on Environmental Issues," *Journal of Politics and Law*, Vol.10 Nr. 5. Pp. 78-84.

Moltmann, J. *The Coming of God: Christian Eschatology*. Minneapolis: Fortress, 1998.

National Academy of Medicine, U.S. National Academy of Sciences and the U.K.'s Royal Society.

Heritable Human Genome Editing. Washington, DC: The National Academies Press, 2021.

Nessan, Craig L. *Orthopraxis or Heresy: The North American Theological Response to Latin American Liberation Theology*. Atlanta, Georgia: Scholars Press, 1989.

_____. *The Vitality of Liberation Theology*. Eugene, OR: Pickwick, 2012.

Niebuhr, H.R. *The Responsible Self: An Essay in Christian Moral Philosophy*. Louisville, Kentucky: Westminster John Knox Press, 1999.

_____. *Radical Monotheism and Western Culture with Supplementary Essays*. Louisville, Kentucky: Westminster/ John Knox Press, 1969.

_____. *Christ and Culture*. New York: Harper: Harper & Row, 1951.

Niebuhr, R. *The Nature and Destiny of Man, vol. I: Human Nature*. New York: Charles Scribner's Sons, 1964.

Ott, Michael R. *Max Horkheimer's Critical Theory of Religion: The Meaning of Religion in the Struggle for Human Emancipation*. Lanham: University Press of America, 2001.

Pangritz, Andreas. *Der ganz andere Gott will eine ganz andere Gesellschaft: Das Lebenswerk Helmut Gollwitzers (1908-1993)*. Stuttgart: Verlag W. Kohlhammer, 2018.

Pannenberg, Wolfhart. *Systematic Theology* 2. Trans. Goeffrey W. Bromiley. Edinburgh: T & T Clark, Grand Rapids, Mich.: Eerdmans, 1994.

Peters, Ted, et al. "Religious Tradition and Genetic Enhancement," in *Altering Nature: vol. 2. Religion, Biotechnology, and Public Policy*, ed. B. Andrew Lustig et al. Heidelberg, Springer Science, 2008. 109-59.

Peters, Ted. *Science, Technology, and Ethics*. Aldershot and Burlington: Ashgate, 2003.

———. Ed. *Genetics: Issues of Social Justice*, Cleveland: The Pilgrim Press, 1988.

———. Karen Lebacqz, and Gaymon Bennett, *Sacred Cells?: Why Christians Should Support Stem Cell Research*. Plymouth: Rowman & Littlefield, 2008.

———. *The Stem Cell Debate*. Minneapolis: Fortress, 2007.

Pocock, J.G.A. *The Machiavellian Movement: Florentine Political Thought and the Atlantic Republican Tradition*. Princeton: Princeton University Press, 1975.

Pomeroy, William J. *The Philippines: Colonialism, Collaboration, and Resistance*. New York: International Publishers, 1992.

Poulantzas, Nicos. *State, Power and Socialism*, trans. Patrick Camiller. London and New York: Verso, 2000.

Rachels, James. *The End of Life: Euthanasia and Morality*. Oxford: Oxford University Press, 1986. Reinhard, Bendix. *Max Weber: An Intellectual Portrait*. Berkeley, Los Angeles, and London: University of California Press, 1977.

Rendtorff, Trutz. *Ethics I: Basic Elements and Methodology in an Ethical Theology*, trans. Keith Crim. Philadelphia: Fortress Press, 1986.

Rousseau, J.J. *On the Social Contract*, ed. Roger D. Masters and trans. Judith R. Masters. New York: St. Martin's Press, 1978.

Said, W. *The Edward Said Reader*, eds. Moustafa Bayoumi and Andrew Rubin. New York: Vintage, 2000.

Sassoon S. Anne. *Gramsci's Politics*, 2nd ed. Minneapolis: University of Minnesota Press, 1987.

Scalapino, Robert and Chong-sik Lee, *Communism in Korea, Part I: The Movement*. Berkeley: University of California Press, 1972.

Schmitt, Carl. *Political Theology*, trans. George Schwab. Chicago: University of Chicago Press, 1922.

Schulkind, Eugene. Ed. *The Paris Commune of 1871: The View from the Left*. New York: Grove Press, 1974.

Seth, Michael J. *A Concise History of Modern Korea: From the Late Nineteenth Century to the Present*. Lanham, Maryland: Rowman & Littlefield, 2010.

Silver, Lee. *Remaking Eden: How Genetic Engineering and Cloning Will Transform the American Family*. New York: Avon Books, 1998.

Skocpol, Theda. *Social Revolutions in the Modern World*. New York: Cambridge University Press, 1994.

Southgate, Christopher. Et al. *God, Humanity, and the Cosmos: A Text Book in Science and Religion*. Edinburgh: T & T Clark, 1999.

Sweezy, Paul M. *The Theory of Capitalist Development: Principles of Marxian Political Economy*. New York and London: Monthly Review Press, 1942.

Taylor, Charles. *Hegel*. Cambridge: Cambridge University Press, 1995.

———, et al. *Multiculturalism: Examining the Politics of Recognition*, ed. Amy Gutmann. Princeton. New Jersey: Princeton University Press, 1994.

Tharoor, Shashi, *The Looting of India*: Inglorious Empire: What the British Did to India. UK, London: C. Hurst & Co., 2017.

Tombs, Robert. *The Paris Commune, 1871*. London: Pearson Education, 1999.

Troeltsch, E. *The Social Teaching of the Christian Churches* I, trans. Olive Wyon. Louisville: Westminster John Knox, 1992.

———. *The Christian Faith*, ed. Gertrud von le Fort, and trans. Garrett E. Paul. Minneapolis: Fortress, 1991.

Turk, Richard W. *The Ambiguous Relationship: Theodore Roosevelt and Alfred Thayer Mahan*. New York: Greenwood, 1987.

Turner, Bryan S. *The Body and Society*, 3rd ed. London: Sage, 2008.

Vansina, Jan. *Being Colonized: The Kuba Experience in Rural Congo, 1880-1960*. Madison: University of Wisconsin Press, 2010.

Waitzkin, Howard. *The Politics of Medical Encounter: How Patients and Doctors Deal with Social Problems*. New Haven: Yale University Press, 1991.

Waitzkin, H. and C. Iriart (2001), "How the United States Exports Managed Care to Developing Countries." *International Journal of Health Services* 31 (3). Pp. 495-505.

Wallerstein, Immanuel. *The Modern World-System I: Capitalist Agriculture and the Origins of the European World-Economy in the Sixteenth Century*. San Diego, CA: Academy Press, 1974.

———. *The Essential Wallerstein*. New York: The New Press, 2000.

———. *The Capitalist World-Economy: Essays by Immanuel Wallerstein*. Cambridge: Cambridge University Press, 1979.

Weathersby, Kathryn. *Soviet Aims in Korea and The Origins of the Korean War, 1945-1950: New Evidence from Russian Archives*, Florida State University Working Paper No. 8 (November 1993).

Weber, Max. *The Protestant Ethic and the Spirit of Capitalism*, trans. Talcott Parsons. Mineola, New York: Dover, 2003.

_____. *From Max Weber: Essays in Sociology*, eds. H.H. Geerth and C. Wright Mills. New York: Oxford University Press, 1958.

West, Cornel. *Race Matters*. New York: Vintage Books, 1994.

Wilmut, Ian. Et al. *The Second Creation: Dolly and the Age of Biological Control*. New York: Farrar, Straus and Giroux, 200.

Wilson, Edward O. *Sociobiology: The New Synthesis*. Cambridge: Harvard University Press, 1975.

_____. *On Human Nature*. New York: Bantam, 1978.

Wogman, J. Philip. *Christian Ethics: A Historical Introduction*. Louisville. Westminster/John Knox Press, 1993.

Zinn, Howard. *The People's History of the United States*. New York: Harper & Row, 1980.

Zizek, Slavoj *The Sublime Object of Ideology*. London , New York: Verso, 1989.

Journal

The Journal of Medical Ethics, November 2014 - Volume 40 -11

Internet Resources

Azétsop, Jacquineau and Michael Ochieng, "The right to health, health systems development and public health policy challenges in Chad," https://www.ncbi.nlm.nih.gov/pmc/articles/PMC4336701/

Center for Genetics and Society, available at https://www.geneticsandsociety.org/topics/ biopolitics

Coman, Julian. "Vive la Commune?" available at https://www.theguardian.com/world/2021/mar/07/vive-la-commune-the-working-class-insurrection-that-shook-the-world

Darnovsky, Marcy, Bioengineered Gametes: Techno-Liberation or Techno-Trap? *Biopolitical Times* (08.26.2020), available at https://www.geneticsandsociety.org/biopolitical-times/bioengineered-gametes-techno-liberation-or-techno-trap

Eleiba, Ahmed. Analysis: Failure of post-Cold War arrangements in Ukraine available at https://english.ahram.org.eg/NewsContent/50/1203/462088/AlAhram-Weekly/World/Analysis-Failure-of-postCold-War-arrangements-in-U.aspx

English Citation from https://www.marxists.org/ history/etol/newspape/ni/vol01/no03/engels.htm

Francisco, Luzviminda. "The first Vietnam: The U.S.-Philippine war of 1899," available at https:// www.tandfonline.com/doi/pdf/10.1080/14672715.1973.10406345

Habermas interview with *Le Monde* available at https://www.tellerreport.com/news/2020-04-15-corona--from-a-philosophical-perspective-----habermas-sees-a-global-behavior-that-shows-an-outright-ignorance. B1evlNyHdU.html

Hasson, Katie and Marcy Darnovsky, "Gene-edited babies: no one has the moral warrant to go it alone." available at https://www.theguardian.com/science/2018/nov/27/gene-edited-babies-no-one-has-moral-warrant-go-it-alone

Hwang WS et al. "Evidence of a pluripotent human embryonic stem cell line derived from a cloned blastocyst," *Science* 2004; 303, 5664: 1669-1674.

Jeju 4.3 Peace Foundation, From National Archives & Records Administration, in American Document 4, 22.

Maya Jasanoff, "How Joseph Conrad foresaw the dark heart of Brexit Britain," available at https://www.theguardian.com/books/2017/oct/28/how-joseph-conrad-foresaw-the-dark-heart-of-brexit-britain

NIH Stem Cell Information available at https://stemcells.nih.gov/policy/2009-guidelines.htm

"Nuffield Council on Bioethics Background Paper," available at http://nuffieldbioethics.org/project/ briefing-notes/ experimental-treatments.

Peters, J. Euthanasia Laws available at https://lawi.us/euthanasia-laws/

Peters, Ted. (2006) "Cells, Souls, and Dignity: A Theological Assessment," available at *file:///C:/Users/hj/ Downloads/2008DignityBostonLawPeters%20(2).pdf*. Pp. 1-21

Physician-assisted Suicide, available at https://www.ama-assn.org/delivering-care/ethics/physician-assisted-suicide

Pontifical Academy for Life, Declaration on the Production and the Scientific and Therapeutic Use of Human Embryonic Stem Cells (2000), available at http:// www.lifeissues.net/writers/ doc/doc_03 embryostemcells.html.

Reyes, Maritza Vasquez. "The Disproportional Impact of COVID-19 on African Americans" available at https://www.ncbi.nlm.nih.gov/pmc/articles/PMC7762908/

Sacred Congregation for the Doctrine of the Faith, available at http://www.vatican.va/roman_curia/ congregations/cfaith/ documents/rc_con_cfaith_doc_19800505_euthanasia_en.html

Skoda, Hannah. "How slavery thrived in Renaissance Europe," available at https://www.historyextra. com/ period/medieval / renaissance-medieval-slave-trade-human-stories-europe-africa/

The American Presidency Project, McKinley's Executive Order, December 21, 1898. http://www. presidency. ucsb.edu/ws/index. php?p), 2.id=69309&st=&st

About the author

Paul Chung specializes in theology (Basel, Switzerland) and sociology (Berkeley, California). Dr. Chung is also a Distinguished Service Professor of Public Theology at Hanshin University, South Korea. After serving as an associate professor at Luther Seminary, MN., he was nominated as a distinguished professor at LSTC. He serves as Editor-in-Chief of Historians' Debate — Public Theology and teaches at Berkeley.

Previous books by the author include Postcolonial Public Theology (Cascade, 2017) Critical Theory and Political Theology: The Aftermath of Enlightenment (Palgrave, 2019), and Public Theology and Civil Society: Constructive Formation (EBL, 2022)

Index

A

absolute historicism, 153

absolute knowledge, 132, 133, 135-137

Achebe, Chinua., 146

African Apocalypse, 107, 144

    colonial,132

Agamben, G., 140, 315

Algerian War, 108

Allende, Salvador., 197

Althusser, Louis., 171, 189, 190, 207-219, 221-224, 226

American Civil War, 149

Amin, S., 273, 274, 279

analogia fidei, 104

analogia verbi, 104

anamnesis, 85, 133-137, 213

a new Cold War, 22

anti-humanism, 216

anti-Semitism, 142, 305

apartheid, 132, 302, 305

apatheia, 73,

Aquinas, Thomas., 70, 71

archeology, 136

Arendt, Hannah., 11, 36, 139

Aristotelian law of excluded means, 143

Aristotle, 11, 12, 35, 36, 38, 70, 71, 75, 77, 78, 122, 131, 167, 168

artificial gametes, 25, 321-323

Augustine, 191, 278, 332, 333

B

Barth, Karl., 23, 34, 41-43, 172, 176, 203, 298, 314, 315, 316, 352, 358

beautiful soul, 133, 163, 190

Bellah, Robert., 46, 47

benevolent hegemon, 376

Benjamin, Walter., 107, 133, 134, 257, 379

Berlin Conference, 145-147

Bhabha, Homi., 113, 114

biomedical justice, 234, 309

biopolitical colonization, 285

   dictatorship, 155

   genocide, 147

   governance, 27, 98, 103, 143, 228, 232, 285, 347, 358

   racism, 20

   sociology, 24, 25, 230, 245, 260, 265, 282, 285, 285, 288-290, 306, 377

   sovereignty, 139, 152, 153, 268, 285, 288

Biotechnology, 313, 330, 357

Bismarck. Otto V., 223

Black Death, 274-276

Black Lives Matter, 151

Black Man's Burden, 144

Blastocyst, 325, 326, 339

Bloch, E., 174

Boff, Clodovis., 208, 209, 211, 241, 242
Bonhoeffer, D., 23, 32, 42, 57, 307, 312, 317, 335, 352
Boomerang effect, 109, 111
Braudel, F., 252, 268, 275, 276, 301
Bretton Woods, 284, 290
British Opium War, 145
Buber, M., 83

C

Caesarism, 225
casus belli, 293
city state, 160, 193
civil religion, 46
    state, 156, 160, 162, 193
civilizing mission, 142, 144-148, 263, 359
class struggle from above, 193, 198
cloning, 310, 339, 340, 341
colonial genocide, 145
    racism, 20, 139, 375
co-creation, 345
colonialism extractive, 146, 147
Collectivization, 155, 271
Columbus, Christopher., 165, 118
commercial capitalism, 252
Commercial Revolution, 274
commodity fetishism, 143-145, 147, 190, 213-215, 221, 255, 256, 262, 263, 265, 285, 289, 299, 353, 354, 358
conceptual principle, 122, 130, 136

Cone, James., 151, 302, 303, 305, 352-354

Confessing Church, 24, 172

Congo Free State, 144, 146

Conrad, Joseph., 105, 107, 146

Constellations, 135, 137, 138

correspondence of relations, 208

cosmopolitan principle, 17

created co-creator, 310, 344

Cultural Revolution, 271

Cumings, Bruce., 241, 369

D

Dasein, 127

Dawkins, Richard., 335

Death politics of terror, 144, 145

Decameron, 275

Deliberative democracy, 55

Deontology, 29, 74, 93, 94

Dependency theory, 175, 240

Descriptive method, 37, 39

deus sive natura, 133

Discourse Ethics, 56

disgrace effect, 48, 183, 188, 256

Du Bois, W.E.B. 149

Durkheim, E., 18, 27, 45- 49, 51, 164

Dussel, E., 105

E

effective history, 26, 57, 127, 133, 135-139, 145, 149, 151, 169, 210, 212, 213, 216, 362-364, 372, 373

elective affinity, 25, 136, 184, 246, 255, 256, 262, 288, 289, 293, 306, 363

empirico-transcendental doublet, 128

Encomienda, 166

Engels, F. 174, 177

English reform bill, 161

enlightened despotism, 147

Enlightenment, 104, 105, 191, 192

epigenetic networking, 335

episteme, 14, 47, 77, 128, 135, 138, 256, 356

Epistemic effect, 228

epistemic practice, 208, 210

Erasmus, 191

ethics of conviction, 50

eugenics, 315

Eurocentrism, 213, 273, 279

Euthanasia, 314-316

evil contract, 159

F

Fanon, Frantz., 107, 109-111, 113, 114

Fascism, 137, 171, 190, 193, 195-197, 204, 287

Fetscher, I., 56, 162

Feuerbach, L., 179,

Fordism, 258, 281, 284

Foucault, M., 14, 16, 19, 60, 62, 86, 107, 127-130, 150-152, 185, 211, 228, 230, 260, 285, 287, 302, 329, 330, 355

French Revolution, 142, 163, 181, 202

Friedman, Milton., 198, 290

Fusion of horizons, 48, 84

G

Gadamer, H.G., 13, 78, 349

Galtung, Johan., 246, 280, 283

gametogenesis, 323

gene editing, 317, 328

gene-ethics, 319

gene myth, 339

genealogy of discourse, 19

general will, 55, 56, 159, 295

genetic determinism, 310, 335, 336

    nihilism, 323

God's politics, 34, 35, 37

Gollwitzer, H., 22, 24, 25, 171-177, 180-197, 201, 202, 204-206, 231, 238, 245-249, 259, 278-284, 298-300, 303, 304, 306, 307, 352, 354

governmentality, 62, 152, 223, 224, 232, 235, 263, 310, 315

Gramsci, A.,108, 152-154, 157, 258, 353, 354

Gustafson, J., 23, 39, 40-42, 311-313

Gutierrez, G.,167, 206

H

Habermas, J., 15, 53-55, 90, 161, 163, 271, 272, 287, 288

Heart of Darkness, 107, 145-147

Hegel, G.W.F., 12, 18, 20, 24, 54, 107-110, 113-134, 136, 138, 139, 143, 144, 154, 156, 159-164, 176, 187, 189, 215- 218, 253, 254, 278, 350, 355

Hegel's ethical state, 160

Hippocratic Oath, 310

historic bloc, 353

historical criticism, 183, 278, 348

historical materialism, 173, 174, 178-181, 183, 184, 192, 201, 206, 207, 279, 350

Holocaust, 132,

homor sacer, 140, 166, 301

Horkheimer, Max., 187, 195, 196

Husserl, E., 51, 52, 61, 104, 105, 349, 355

Hyppolite, J., 123, 127

I

ideal type, 33, 61, 255

ideological extrapolation, 137,
    interpellation, 84, 171, 189, 190, 192, 214, 216, 223, 224, 227, 263, 265, 272, 293, 296, 349, 353, 354, 372, 377

immanent critique, 13, 46, 51, 135-137, 181, 185, 192, 256

impersonal forces, 9, 12, 22, 43, 96-98, 103, 106, 138, 185, 190, 358

innocent victim, 138, 147, 372

Inquisition, 167

Instrumental rationality, 179, 255

Interpolation, 355

invisible hand, 160

iron cage, 255, 256, 358

ISAs, 217, 221, 224

J

Jacobin, 157, 161, 164

Jasanoff, Maya., 146

Jeju 4.3 event, 359, 362

Jim Crow laws, 149, 150, 305

Just war, 168, 300

K

Kairos, 138

Kant, I., 74, 78, 83, 89, 93, 123, 124, 174

Kenosis, 132

Kipling, Rudyard., 143, 359

Kojeve, A., 110

Ku Klux Klan, 149

L

Las Casas, Bartolome de., 108, 165-169, 304

Lebenswelt, 128

Lehmann, P., 23, 34, 35

Lenin, I., 154, 159, 270, 279-281

Leviathan, 161, 201

Levinas, Emmanuel., 23, 67, 88, 89, 91-94

life-script, 9, 13, 14, 15,18. 23, 51, 60, 61,119, 147, 350

Livingstone, David., 145

Lukacs, G., 12, 115, 116, 119, 156, 176, 179, 180, 184, 257, 258, 266, 267

Luther, M., 191, 253, 254, 346

Luxemburg, Rosa., 195, 266, 267, 280

lynching tree, 150, 151, 303

M

Machiavelli, N., 156-159

Mandel, E., 198, 205, 237, 270-272, 298, 299

manifest destiny, 374

Marcuse, H., 116, 126

Marquardt. F.-W., 65

Marx, Karl., 112, 115, 116, 127, 154, 168, 173, 175-179, 181, 183-187, 191, 193, 198-201, 204, 215, 216, 221, 224, 236, 238, 241, 245-255, 258-270, 275, 278. 280, 283, 304, 305

massa perditionis, 62, 86, 350

McCarthy, Thomas,, 48, 63, 148, 231, 232, 283, 284, 290, 301

Medical apparatus, 230, 231

killing, 314

Medical-industry complex, 233-235

Messianic history, 137

    rupture, 105

mercantilism, 140, 166

Metahistory, 136

Metanarrative, 135

metanoia, 101, 137, 187, 358

Middle Passage, 142

military-complex industry, 235, 289, 295, 299

mimicry, 111, 113, 114

Moltmann, J., 172, 342, 343

Montesquieu, 119

Multiple realties, 136

N

National Socialism, 142, 143, 196

National Socialist eugenics, 315

Natural servitude, 168

Nazism, 196, 224, 298, 299

necropolitical genocide, 144

Necropolitics, 140, 299, 301, 371

Negative Dialectics, 155, 152-155

Neocolonial condition, 282, 293, 297, 306

Neoliberal governance, 285, 287

    principle, 271, 287

neoracism, 302

NEP, 155, 281

New Deal, 281, 290

Niebuhr H.R., 17, 18, 23, 40, 44, 45, 67-76, 79-81, 83, 84-88, 93-102, 347

Niebuhr, Reinhold., 333, 334, 340, 352

Nietzsche, F., 110, 127, 352

noema, 48, 52

noesis, 48, 52

no harm principle, 310, 131

non-maleficence, 310, 318, 357

O

Oikos, 35

organic solidarity, 51, 163, 164, 229

Orientalism, 57, 355

P

Pannenberg, W., 333, 334, 342

Paradigm shift, 207

Paris Commune, 198, 199

parrhesia, 56, 57, 131, 132, 139, 350, 356, 358, 373

passive revolution, 258

Peters, Ted., 9, 313, 314, 318, 320-322, 325, 327, 329, 332, 341, 344, 345

Phenomenology of Discourse, 85

phronesis, 77

pieds noirs, 108, 110, 111

Plato, 77, 122

Politics of eschatology, 193, 202

Popular Sovereignty, 156, 159, 160

Poulantzas, N., 156, 164, 194, 200, 225, 229, 286

power-knowledge relations, 228

problematic unity, 211, 214

problematic whole, 213

prolepsis, 133, 350, 357, 358

proleptic eschatology, 137

prestige struggle, 110

Protestant principle, 37, 38

Q
Quarternity, 132

R
radical monotheism, 45

recognition, 20, 22, 23, 26, 29, 51, 107, 108, 116, 129, 130, 133, 134-138, 162-164, 202, 214, 347, 354, 358
   mutual or reciprocal, 126, 154, 162, 206, 215, 350
   universal, 22, 133, 159, 163, 167, 189, 190, 215, 349

Reformation, 37, 304

reification, 12, 147, 179, 180, 221, 239, 256, 257, 259, 289, 354, 356, 358

religious construction of reality, 21

religious socialism, 24

Renaissance, 140, 141, 157, 159, 167, 168, 191, 246, 274, 276, 277

Rendtorff, T., 16, 23, 28, 67, 313

reparative justice, 22, 135, 137, 214, 358

representing value, 262

res publica, 158

Ricoeur, Paul., 208

Rousseau, J.J., 55, 56, 108, 155-164, 203, 229, 295

Roosevelt. Franklin D., 364

Roosevelt. Theodore., 363

Russian chauvinism, 186,

Russian Revolution, 364

S
Said, Edward., 14, 57, 355

Sale value, 142

Sanculottes, 199

Schmitt, Carl., 226

Semantic circle, 13, 48

Scramble for Africa, 20, 144, 145

settler colonialism, 113

sexual racism, 20, 60

Shakespeare, William.,115

Smith, Adam., 160

Social Contract, 157, 160, 224, 229

Social Darwinism, 48, 49, 113, 143, 144, 148, 304, 305, 357, 375

social stratification, 12, 22, 62, 63, 150, 179, 185, 213, 216, 222, 239, 240, 267, 280, 282, 302, 307, 328, 354, 357

Socialist principle, 173

Sociobiology, 335

Sociology of war, 246, 296

Spencer, Hebert., 48

Spinoza, 133,

Stakhanovism, 155

Stem Cell Research, 313, 318, 321, 322, 325, 326, 329, 357
    Debate, 25, 309, 322, 325

Stoic ethics, 71

structural theory of imperialism, 25, 235, 246, 259, 279, 280, 282

structural underdevelopment, 239

structural violence, 13, 22, 63, 67, 195, 201, 231, 237, 290, 295

suum cuique, 205

symptomatic reading, 211, 214

Sweezy, P., 197, 253, 264, 266, 267, 279, 281, 282

T

Taft-Katsura Memorandum, 363, 364, 373

Taylor, Charles., 123, 162

Taylorism, 229, 258, 281

Taylorist system, 270, 281

Thanatopolitics, 315

The Philippine-American War, 143, 359, 374

The Prince, 157-159

theologia crucis, 21, 22, 25, 65, 66, 97, 100, 102, 104, 106, 107, 131, 137, 138, 348, 354

theoretical practice, 208, 210, 214

thick description, 14, 355, 363

Tillich, P., 173, 181-183, 195, 352

totaliter aliter. 89, 103, 106, 132, 137, 187

Transatlantic Slave Trade, 140

transitional justice, 363, 373, 380

Trans-Modernity, 105

tributary mode of production, 273

Troeltsch, E., 23, 37-40, 53, 73, 348, 349

Truman Doctrine, 365

Totemic principle, 49

U

unequal exchange, 236, 240

unhappy consciousness, 114, 121

unmoved Mover, 131

USAMGIK, 360

V

vita activa, 11, 12

vita contemplativa, 11

vivid present, 57, 84, 114, 136-139, 214

W

Wallerstein, I., 166, 240

War of position, 258

WASP, 91

Weber, Max., 18, 27, 50, 51, 54, 76, 179, 217-228, 245, 249, 250, 252, 256, 261, 269, 270, 289

White Man's burden, 113, 143, 144, 281, 282, 305, 359

Wilson, Edward., 335

Wilson, Woodrow., 360, 361, 374, 376

www.ingramcontent.com/pod-product-compliance
Lightning Source LLC
Chambersburg PA
CBHW061228070526
44584CB00030B/4030